# THE MENTORING CONTINUUM

Also published by The Graduate School Press of Syracuse University

*Collaborative Futures*
*Critical Reflections on Publicly Active*
*Graduate Education*

*Building Community*
*Stories and Strategies for Future Learning*
*Community Faculty and Professionals*

*Pedagogy, not Policing*
*Positive Approaches to Academic*
*Integrity at the University*

*Interrupting Heteronormativity*
*Lesbian, Gay, Bisexual and Transgender Pedagogy*
*and Responsible Teaching at Syracuse University*

*Building Pedagogical Curb Cuts*
*Incorporating Disability in the University*
*Classroom and Curriculum*

*Using Writing to Teach*

# THE MENTORING CONTINUUM

## CONTINUUM

*From Graduate School through Tenure*

Edited by

Glenn Wright

**SYRACUSE UNIVERSITY**
THE GRADUATE SCHOOL PRESS

Chapter 12 originally appeared in *Change: The Magazine of Higher Learning*. Reprinted by permission of the publisher, Taylor & Francis Ltd. (http://www.informaworld.com).

**Library of Congress Cataloging-in-Publication Data**

Names: Wright, Glenn, 1968- editor of compilation.
Title: The mentoring continuum : from graduate school through tenure / edited
  by Glenn Wright.
Description: Syracuse, New York : Graduate School Press of Syracuse
  University, [2015] | Includes bibliographical references and index.
Identifiers: LCCN 2015041060 | ISBN 9780977784769 (pbk.)
Subjects: LCSH: Mentoring in education. | Graduate students--Vocational
  guidance.
Classification: LCC LB1731.4 .M455 2015 | DDC 371.102--dc23
LC record available at http://lccn.loc.gov/2015041060

This volume is published with support from the
Syracuse University Graduate Student Organization

For more information about this publication, please contact:

The Graduate School Press
220 Bowne Hall
Syracuse University
Syracuse, NY 13244

http://graduateschool.syr.edu/programs/graduate-school-press

Manufactured in the United States of America

# CONTENTS

# Figures and Tables

## Figures

## Tables

# CONTRIBUTORS

**Amanda (Manda) S. Adams** is Director of Education and Cross-Cutting Activities for the Atmospheric and Geospace Sciences Division of the National Science Foundation (NSF). Prior to her position at NSF, Manda was an assistant professor at the University of North Carolina at Charlotte. She is on the Board of Directors for the Earth Science Women's Network.

**Jan Allen** is Associate Dean for Academic and Student Affairs in the Graduate School at Cornell University in Ithaca, New York (since 2012). Previously she was Associate Dean for PhD Programs in the Graduate School of Arts and Sciences at Columbia University in New York City (2005–12), and Associate Dean in the Graduate School, Northwestern University (2002–5). She was a faculty member in human ecology at the University of Tennessee–Knoxville (1982–2002) and Assistant Dean in the Graduate School (1997–2001). She is the author of the forthcoming, *The New Faculty and Graduate Mentor* (Stylus Press). She can be contacted at Jan.Allen@cornell.edu.

**Michael Amlung** is a postdoctoral fellow in the Department of Psychological Sciences at the University of Missouri. He received a PhD in psychology from the University of Georgia, where he was involved in teaching undergraduate courses, mentoring undergraduate research, and promoting teaching-related training for graduate students. He has presented his teaching scholarship at the Lilly Conference on College Teaching and the American Psychological Association Annual Convention. In addition to his teaching-related interests, he has an active research program in the area of alcohol and drug abuse.

**Rebecca T. Barnes** is Assistant Professor in the Environmental Program at Colorado College in Colorado Springs. Her research focuses on understanding the intersection between biogeochemical cycles, water, and society. Barnes serves on the Leadership Board of the Earth Science Women's Network, a nonprofit organization dedicated to the promotion and career development of women in the geosciences.

**Beth A. Boehm** is Professor of English at the University of Louisville. She completed her PhD in 1987 at the Ohio State University, where she specialized in twentieth-century British and American literature and rhetoric and composition. Since 2009, she has been focused on graduate student professional development as an administrator in the School of Interdisciplinary and Graduate Studies, where she is currently dean. Her current research is on mentoring and graduate student engagement.

**Phyllis Bolin** is Director of Pursuit, the Quality Enhancement Plan, for Abilene Christian University (ACU). She is an associate professor of mathematics in the Department of Mathematics and served as the Director of Faculty Mentoring at ACU for 6 years. Active in the field of technology, her research interests involve use of mobile devices in teaching and learning.

**Janet Branchaw** is Director of the Wisconsin Institute for Science Education and Community Engagement (WISCIENCE) and an assistant professor of Kinesiology in the School of Education at the University of Wisconsin–Madison. Her scholarship and program development expertise are in mentee professional development, particularly preparing undergraduate STEM students for graduate education. She has created training curricula for undergraduate research mentees (*Entering Research*) and their research mentors (*Entering Mentoring*) and empirically established the positive impact and effectiveness of these curricula on research mentoring relationships and the persistence of underrepresented minority students in research.

**Susanna Calkins** directs the faculty programs at the Searle Center for Advancing Learning and Teaching and teaches in the School of Education and Social Policy at Northwestern University. She is co-author, with Greg Light, of *Learning and Teaching in Higher Education: The Reflective Professional* (Sage 2009), and has published twenty scholarly articles related to the conceptions of learning, teaching and research; mentoring; teaching and learning with technology; and the history of higher education.

**Leonard Cassuto**, a professor of English at Fordham University, writes a monthly column for *The Chronicle of Higher Education* called "The Graduate Adviser," and is the editor of a recent special cluster on graduate students in the journal *Pedagogy*. He is the author of *The Graduate School Mess: What Caused It and How We Can Fix It* (Harvard Univerity Press, 2015). The most recent of his seven other books are *The Cambridge History of the American Novel* (2011), of which he was General Editor; *The Cambridge Companion to Baseball* (2011), winner of the Best Anthology Award from the North American Society of Sports Historians; and *Hard-Boiled Sentimentality: The Secret History of American Crime Stories*, which was nominated for an Edgar Award and named one of the Ten Best Books of 2008 in the crime and mystery category by *The Los Angeles Times*. Cassuto is also an award-winning journalist who writes on subjects ranging from science to sports.

**Paula Chambers** is founder and CEO of Versatile PhD, a leading web-based career resource for PhDs seeking to transition into non-academic careers. Originally founded in 1999 specifically for humanities PhDs, Versatile PhD has broadened out over the years to include STEM disciplines and is now supported by over 80 subscribing research universities. The Versatile PhD mission is to help graduate students and new PhDs envision, prepare for, and excel in non-academic careers. Chambers earned her PhD in Rhetoric and Composition from The Ohio State University in 2000 and spent several years as a Grant Writer and Development Director for Los Angeles–area nonprofits before devoting herself completely to Versatile PhD. She now runs her socially positive business from her home office in Los Angeles, with the help of one employee based in Washington, DC.

**Mary Dankoski** is Executive Associate Dean for Faculty Affairs and Professional Development at Indiana University School of Medicine (IUSM), where she is also the Lester D. Bibler Scholar and Vice Chair for Faculty and Academic Affairs in the Department of Family Medicine. Dr. Dankoski's scholarly interests include the advancement of women, the study of faculty vitality, and organizational and faculty development in academic medicine. She holds a PhD in marriage and family therapy with a graduate minor in women's studies from Purdue University.

**Miriam Cohen Dell** served as a graduate assistant in the Office of Faculty Affairs and Professional Development for the Indiana University School of Medicine. She completed her master's degree in applied communication from Indiana University in 2013 and is currently managing U.S. franchisee communication for an international restaurant organization based in Denver, Colorado.

**Melissa Dengler** completed her undergraduate studies at Niagara University where she majored in Psychology. Her interests in infant development lead her to choose the University of Georgia for graduate school. At the University of Georgia her research interest expanded to include the development of the nervous system across the lifespan. Melissa's teaching interests include Developmental Psychology, Introductory Psychology and Sensation and Perception courses.

**Denise P. Domizi,** PhD, is Coordinator of the Scholarship of Teaching and Learning at the Center for Teaching and Learning at the University of Georgia (UGA). She works to promote and support innovation and research in teaching and learning at UGA through the design, development, and delivery of workshops, programs, graduate seminars, and one-on-one consultations.

**Mirjam S. Glessmer** is Coordinator of Teaching Innovation at the Center for Teaching and Learning at Hamburg University of Technology, Germany, where she works with professors and teaching staff on improving the teaching of university courses in STEM. She runs workshops on ocean/climate topics for various audiences, and on ocean/climate education for STEM educators. She publishes in the peer-reviewed literature on education, serves as associate editor in a journal on education, and blogs about her "adventures in oceanography and teaching" at mirjamglessmer.com.

**Meredith G. Hastings** is an assistant professor at Brown University in the Department of Earth, Environmental and Planetary Sciences. She joined the faculty at Brown in 2008, and continues to pursue her varied research interests in biogeochemistry, atmospheric chemistry and climate. She is co-founder and Vice President of the Earth Science Women's Network (ESWN; eswnonline.org), which facilitates career development for women scientists in the early stages of their careers.

**Krista Hoffmann-Longtin** is Assistant Professor of Communication Studies at Indiana University–Purdue University Indianapolis (IUPUI) and an Assistant Dean in the IU School of Medicine Office of Faculty Affairs and Professional Development. Her work focuses on faculty development, organizational/professsional identity, and strategic communication in academic health settings. Before returning to university life, Krista worked as an advertising account executive. She earned a BA in telecommunications from Ball State University in Muncie, Indiana, an MA in Communication and Creative Arts from Purdue University, and a PhD in Education Leadership and Policy Studies at Indiana University.

**Kevin Johnston** is an adjunct professor in the Hunter Division of Humanities at Southern Vermont College. Much of his academic career has focused on developing future faculty pedagogically. Presently, his research focuses on how professional development programs engender adjunct faculty loyalty.

**Ron Krabill** is Associate Professor of Interdisciplinary Arts and Sciences and Faculty Coordinator of the MA program in cultural studies at the University of Washington Bothell. He is also affiliated with the Department of Communication, the African Studies Program, and the Graduate Interdisciplinary Group on Public Scholarship at the University of Washington, Seattle. He is the author of *Starring Mandela and Cosby: Media and the End(s) of Apartheid* (University of Chicago Press, 2010).

**Greg Light** is retiring as Director of the Searle Center for Advancing Learning and Teaching at Northwestern University, where he will remain as a senior fellow. A professor in the School of Education and Social Policy at Northwestern, he has published over 50 papers and chapters in national and international peer-reviewed publications and given over 100 invited talks, workshops, and conference presentations in North and South America, Europe, Africa, and Asia. He is the author, with Susanna Calkins, of *Learning and Teaching in Higher Education: The Reflective Professional* (Sage, 2001, 2009); and, with Marina Micari, of *Making Scientists: Six Principles for Effective College Teaching* (Harvard University Press, 2013).

**Yvonna S. Lincoln** holds the Ruth Harrington Chair of Educational Leadership and is University Distinguished Professor of Higher Education at Texas A&M University. She is a former president of the American Evaluation Association, and also the former president of the Association for the Study of Higher Education (ASHE), and has been an evaluation and organizational development practitioner and consultant for over 25 years. She is the co-author of *Naturalistic Inquiry, Effective Evaluation, Fourth Generation Evaluation*; the co-editor of the first, second, third, and fourth editions of the *Handbook of Qualitative Research*; and the co-editor (with Norman K. Denzin) of the *Handbook of Critical and Indigenous Methodologies*. She has authored more than 100 chapters and journal articles on research and evaluation practice, qualitative methodologies, new paradigm inquiry, ethics in inquiry, and higher education. Her interests lie in democratic, inclusive, participative, and social justice issues in research, evaluation and public policy formulation for higher education.

**Steven Paul Lee** is the Graduate Diversity Officer for STEM (Science, Technology, Engineering, and Mathematics) disciplines at UC Davis. His work focuses on strengthening graduate education through diversity. He loves to translate research into evidence-based activities for professional development, covering topics such as mentoring, oral and written communication skills, self-assessment, and career planning. Previously, he was the assistant director of a graduate diversity program at Northwestern University, and served as faculty at Roosevelt University and Wheaton College. He earned a PhD in organic chemistry from the University of Illinois at Urbana-Champaign and BS in chemistry from Carnegie Mellon University.

**Amy J. Lueck** is a doctoral fellow in Rhetoric and Composition at the University of Louisville. Her dissertation research explores rhetorical practice and instruction in nineteenth-century high schools. In addition, she has researched and contributed to graduate student professional development and mentoring as research assistant in the University of Louisville School of Interdisciplinary and Graduate Studies, and was recognized for this work by the American Association of Colleges and Universities' (AAC&U) K. Patricia Cross Future Leaders Award in 2014. She currently represents graduate students on the Executive Council of the Conference on College Composition and Communication (CCCC).

**Richard McGee** has been mentoring biomedical scientists and designing novel research training programs for nearly 40 years. He currently is Associate Dean for Faculty Recruitment and Professional Development at Northwestern University Feinberg School of Medicine, assisting new faculty to launch their research careers through individual mentoring and group coaching. He also leads the Scientific Careers Research and Development Group, a team of 15 social and natural scientists studying the development of young scientists. They are following more than 250 biomedical PhD students with annual in-depth interviews. They are also conducting a randomized controlled trial of a novel coaching model as a new approach for increasing faculty diversity.

**Nina B. Namaste** is Associate Professor of Spanish in the World Languages and Cultures department at Elon University, North Carolina. Her disciplinary research focuses on culinary imagery as a means to express issues of identity formation in contemporary Spanish and Spanish-American fictional works. Her interdisciplinarity and dedication to the liberal arts have led her towards her new role as Arts and Humanities Director of the Elon College Fellows, an undergraduate research program. Her Scholarship of Teaching and Learning (SoTL) focus on transformative learning experiences, for students and faculty, have led her towards her other new role as co-director of a three-year research seminar on global learning sponsored by Elon's Center for Engaged Learning.

**Christine Pfund** is a researcher with the Wisconsin Center for Education Research and the Department of Medicine at the University of Wisconsin–Madison (UW). She serves as PI and Director of the Mentor Training Core of the National Research Mentoring Network and as an Associate Director with the UW Institute in Clinical and Translational Research. Dr. Pfund's work focuses on developing, implementing, documenting, and studying research mentor training interventions across science, technology, engineering, mathematics, and medicine (STEMM) and understanding specific factors in mentoring relationships that account for positive student outcomes.

**Daniel Rusyniak** is a professor of Emergency Medicine and the Vice Chair for Faculty Development in the Department of Emergency Medicine at the Indiana University School of Medicine. An active teacher and researcher, he has served as the Faculty Development

Chair for the Society of Academic Emergency Medicine.

**Jennifer W. Shewmaker**, PhD, is an associate professor of psychology and the Director of Faculty Enrichment at Abilene Christian University in Abilene, Texas. She has worked with hundreds of students and teachers in her career and is the founding developer of ACU's master teacher program.

**Elizabeth A. Simpson** is a postdoctoral fellow at the University of Parma and carries out research on early social cognitive development in infants at The Eunice Kennedy Shriver National Institute of Child Health and Human Development. She helped to develop the *Specialized Undergraduate Research Experience (SURE) Workbook*, a mentoring handbook to enrich undergraduate students' hands-on research experiences, and is interested in training new college teachers. Her teaching interests include research methods, statistics, and evolutionary psychology.

**Christine A. Stanley** is Vice President and Associate Provost for Diversity and a professor of higher education administration in the College of Education and Human Development at Texas A&M University.

**Brian Stone,** PhD, is a visiting assistant professor of psychology at Franklin and Marshall College. He co-founded the Psychology Educator Development Association at The University of Georgia. His research investigates how humans and other animals perceive, represent, and track their body and its parts, especially during tool use.

**Jane Van Slembrouck** is a postdoctoral teaching fellow in the Department of English at Fordham University. Her research interests include medicine, disability, gender, and sexuality in nineteenth-century American literature.

**Julie Welch** is Assistant Dean for Faculty Affairs and Professional Development (OFAPD) at Indiana University School of Medicine (IUSM) and Co-director of Mentoring Training for the Indiana Center for Translational Science Institute (CTSI). She works to advance mentoring initiatives across the institution for trainees and faculty. In addition, she oversees programs for the advancement of women in medicine and science. As an associate professor of clinical emergency medicine at IUSM and a board-certified physician, she practices medicine at an urban, level-one trauma center and teaching hospital. She was honored in 2014 with the EMRA (Emergency Medicine Residency Association) National Mentorship Award and the AMA (American Medical Association) Inspirational Physician Award.

**Grace Williams** earned an undergraduate degree in psychology from the University of Georgia (UGA) and a master's degree in social work from the University of Texas at Austin. While at UGA, she contributed to a large-scale study of the impact of peer mentoring on graduate student teaching assistant development. In her final graduate internship, Grace focused on using group-based therapy in individuals with severe mental illness.

**Glenn Wright** is Director of Graduate School Programs at Syracuse University. He holds a BA in English from Carleton College in Northfield, Minnesota, and an MA and PhD from the University of Michigan, Ann Arbor. He has worked in academic assessment, publishing, and administration, and has taught English at the University of Michigan and the University at Albany, SUNY.

# ACKNOWLEDGMENTS

Good mentors are sometimes born, but more often made—like this book, through collaborative effort. Discussions on the Syracuse University campus; at SU Future Professoriate Program retreats in Hamilton, New York; and within the mentoring literature have helped shape the book's concept and content. Publication was enabled by financial support from Syracuse University's Graduate Student Organization (GSO). Antonina Distefano, Laura Lisnyczyj, and Judith Ricks contributed their time, and Courtney Garvin and Dan Moseson their expertise, to the book's striking cover images. Sue Hoxie and Mike McGrath with the Syracuse University Publications Office facilitated production and provided design work. Special thanks are due to those among the volume's contributors who have been with the project from the initial call for publications (let no one speak the year). May you find your patience rewarded.

# INTRODUCTION

*Glenn Wright*

Recent years have seen a resurgence of interest in mentoring as a point of discussion in higher education, an area of particular concern being the cultivation of new faculty. This is not accidentally related to tectonic shifts taking place within the sector as to the nature and conditions of academic employment. Academic mentoring is trending now in large part because it is more difficult than it used to be, demanding a broader skill set, more reflective engagement, and more time. Of necessity, graduate students, postdocs, and junior faculty have become more discriminating consumers of mentoring, more mindful of their own needs and unafraid to request that they be met. Colleges and universities, in turn, wish to be seen as promoters of mentoring, resulting in various administrative initiatives, enhanced incentives for faculty, and added heft for mentoring in tenure and promotion review.

With increased attention has come increased recognition of some of the complexities and challenges of mentoring, and of its rewards. Even at high-powered institutions where research is understood as the meal ticket, skill at mentoring has to an extent clambered out of the category of things that less professionally fit academics pursue, and attained a certain cachet among those at all career stages who find in it an alternative way of being in academe—one that tilts away from the endemic competition of the research environment in favor of cooperation and mutual purpose. Part of mentoring's appeal lies in its ability to gesture in two directions at once: forward, as we will see, to new modalities and more egalitarian relationships, and backward, to a tradition of cross-generational support and identification as old as universities themselves, and that continues to feed the romance of the academic life in the minds of would-be faculty. This expansive view of mentoring is both celebrated and interrogated in the following chapters.

Whatever fine ideals we associate with the practice, an unsentimental look at the academic career ladder shows that tradeoffs abound where mentoring is concerned, and that knowing when and how to erect constraints around one's mentoring commitments becomes a professional imperative. The same academics who, as grad students or postdocs, found in a mentor the image of groundedness in the face of bewildering realities, ascend the tenure track to discover that mentoring is, far from a grounded experience, a moving target if ever there was one. Rapid changes in their own needs (e.g., regarding role models) occur alongside increased obligations to *provide* mentoring for undergraduates, and possibly for graduate students and postdocs. They come to know that they exist on a mentoring continuum, one that imposes obligations as surely as it dispenses benefits. While the continuum includes both emeritus professors and children only dimly aware of an academic calling, this book takes as its purview the crucial phase between graduate school and tenure, where the academy either succeeds or fails in renewing itself.

One thing to observe initially when considering this interval of the mentoring continuum is its spiral organization. That is, graduate school is in conspicuous ways analogous to assistant professorship. To begin with, these respective levels of apprenticeship are roughly equal in duration (allowing both for the current trend toward more compact doctoral programs and the ongoing reality that many students, often but not exclusively in the humanities, take far longer than projected to complete their degrees). More to the point, the tasks, tests, and markers of progress defining each career stage present a nontrivial symmetry.

| *Graduate Student* | *Assistant Professor* |
|---|---|
| early years largely devoted to coursework | early years largely devoted to developing and teaching courses |
| comprehensive/qualifying exams | third-year review (and variants) |
| dissertation proposal and writing | building record of publications, grants, and other research products |
| dissertation defense | tenure/promotion review |

For scholars in fields and institutions where the "book for tenure" rule applies, this symmetry is typically reinforced by the strong continuity of their research programs—which is to say, the necessity of revising their dissertations for publication in book form and securing a suitable publisher, within about the same time frame required to produce the original thesis. Meanwhile, those in the natural sciences are faced with what might be seen as a third discrete iteration of the cycle, in the form of serial postdocs that can easily consume as many years as graduate school or a pre-tenure faculty appointment (but not more, if a tenure-track job is forthcoming). This model is currently enjoying rapid exportation across disciplines, as various forms of visiting, fellowship, and fixed-term appointments become expected CV-builders.

The concentric spiral of graduate school and assistant professorship provides the book's structure. Part I ("Origins") deals primarily with the professional development of graduate students. The benefits of administrative collaboration with grad students are on display in chapters 1 and 2, as is the spectrum along which these efforts are arrayed, from the institution-driven to the grass-roots (i.e., with the institution providing funding and/or nominal sponsorship only). Most particularly, these chapters reflect the current heyday of peer-mentoring initiatives—especially at the graduate level, and especially with active promotion by administrative units and through the Scholarship of Teaching and Learning (SoTL).

### Doing It for Themselves

Michael Amlung and colleagues describe in chapter 1 the successful partnering of a home-grown student group with their institution's Center for Teaching and Learning (along with departmental funding) to create a formal peer-mentoring program supporting the development of TAs in the classroom. In chapter 2, Jan Allen powerfully argues the special merits of peers as mentors, and draws on her experience at multiple institutions to show how administrative units (like Graduate Schools) can harness the potential of peer mentoring through well designed and structured programs (like dissertation-writing "boot camps"). In their discussions we can see several key variables with peer-mentoring efforts: the extent to which they rely on programmatic facilitation by the institution, the level of involvement by graduate students in program development, and funding. In many situations, for peer mentoring to have traction it must take place within an institutional cocoon, such as provided by career centers, Graduate Schools, centers for teaching, faculty development and postdoctoral studies offices, academic units, and so forth. In fact, administrative support—in the form of funding and, crucially, professional-development-oriented offices, centers, and dedicated staff—is surely the second most important factor in creating the conditions for peer mentoring to thrive (departmental culture remaining firmly in pole position).

At the same time, graduate students are nothing if not an independent-minded and skeptical lot, ready to equate institutional benevolence with paternalism. This they share with those former graduate students, the faculty. To say that graduate students regard the support of administration as a Faustian bargain might push the point too far, but it is best to acknowledge that such support inevitably brings with it a set of assumptions and concerns that many graduate students do not share, and may indeed regard with some disdain. An experiment of possible advantage to program administrators, given their work environment, would be to image and record the brain patterns of graduate students and faculty when presented with a series of terms:

Accountability
Agility
Assessment
Evidence-based
Impact
Measurable
Student-centered

Results, I think, would show an uncanny correlation between the items on the administrator's performance review worksheet and the activation of pain centers in their client population's brains. All this is well within the reach of modern neuroscience.

But there is another, wholly different force animating the peer-mentoring movement: a proletarian spirit clearly born in the realities of the job market. For fields in which doctoral graduates have non-academic career options, those options generally present a more favorable employment picture. Fields where nonacademic career paths for PhDs are less readily defined endure a multigenerational struggle with the dearth of good faculty jobs. And so most graduate students pursuing faculty careers are likely to do so within depart-mental and disciplinary cultures in which the self-defeating or quixotic nature of their ambition is accepted as normal. In circumstances like these, peer mentoring can offer not only the reliable advantage of proximal (readily emulated) role models, but a reservoir of affirmation and comradeship. With a common purpose in their sails, they tack against jaundice and resignation, and even against the hard-headed wisdom their advisors are duty-bound to deal out.

Academia is simultaneously extolled and reviled in the popular imagination as a bastion of left-leaningness. Whatever the justice of this portrait, it is difficult to call to mind other economic sectors today in which employment is so rigorously stratified by class. Even those who are not attracted to graduate school initially by the expectation of a congenially progressive environment soon find that they are members of a class, and that this class is engaged in a struggle. As mostly younger people with similar inclinations, interests, and goals congregate in what is initially understood to be a battle against the odds, it is natural that a bond of kinship should evolve, and translate into mutual reinforcement in professional development. As will be seen later in the book, similar patterns of kinship emerge among junior faculty, because of the comparable pressures they face. There is a deep, perhaps a sinister secret in the efficiency with which the academy replenishes itself despite the abnegation of individual self-interest required.

Much less in evidence is the academy's skill in demonstrating the value of its doctoral degrees to nonacademic employers, and facilitating access to a range of meaningful careers for PhDs outside the STEM and professional fields. One significant difference between the graduate student and the junior faculty circuit on the upward spiral of academic professional development is the likelihood of "making the cut." That is, the chances of an assistant professor earning tenure are in most fields and institutions considerably higher than the chances of a doctoral graduate securing a tenure-track job. For this reason preparation for nonacademic or "alt-ac" careers has penetrated graduate education in a way foreign to faculty development efforts. Or rather, recognition of *the need* for such preparation has penetrated. We have now a situation in which advisement of graduate students regarding nonacademic jobs falls primarily on the shoulders of those who by dint of profession lack any experience with such jobs.

Chapters 3 and 4 attempt to fill a void for faculty nudged outside their comfort zone by the growing number of graduate students actively or even exclusively pursuing extra-academic opportunities. In chapter 3, Paula Chambers offers a crisp and actionable answer to the question, "what specific practices can I adopt that will make me a better advisor to multi-career-track graduate students?" If all graduate faculty were to take her "Career Climate Departmental Assessment" (pp. 62–64) and compare scores with their colleagues, a discussion of significant benefit to graduate students might ensue. The nonacademic domain with the greatest appeal across disciplines is surely represented by NGOs and other publicly oriented ".org" entities; in chapter 4, Ron Krabill expertly dissects the consolation-prize mentality that has adhered to these professional destinations within academe, and notes how the shedding of assumptions and fears by career academics can lead to productive relationships with graduate mentees whose working lives may unfold primarily within the public sphere, whether as researchers, change agents, or both.

As one advances along the mentoring continuum, unexpected realities and new priorities assert themselves. Whether a succession of postdocs, fellowships, or visiting positions (less often adjunct appointments or ones that combine teaching and administrative duties) or the holy grail of a tenure-track job (how soon exchanged for a new grail!), the next stage in an academic's life entails many similarities to the graduate student experience, including its probationary character; its adjustment to new demands in research, publication, sponsorship-seeking, and general professionalism; and its linear, well defined path to a conspicuous goal. There are differences as well, such as the need to navigate in a primary role the external funding regime in one's discipline (if applicable), to consider one's options regarding re-entering the job market and transferring institutions (before tenure restricts those options considerably), and to assume advisory and supervisory responsibilities. These are matters on which peer mentoring is likely to be less effective than mentoring by senior scholars.

## On the Log with Mark Hopkins

In President James Garfield's possibly apocryphal phrase, the ideal higher educational experience would be realized by his Williams College teacher and mentor Mark Hopkins "on one end of a log and a student at the other." This tips the hat not only to Hopkins' genius as a pedagogue (attested by others as well), but to the possibility and value of an intergenerational nurturing that in academic life can long outlast the "formative years." We remember Garfield's words because of his office, and both point to the special potential that can reside within mentoring relationships involving considerable separation in age and professional standing. The senior partner has an opportunity, given the skill and dedication, to perceive the interests of the junior partner with greater clarity than the latter can muster. The mentor can discern the course of most advantage to the mentee (e.g., in an academic context, the choice of research project or method, teaching style and formats, particular pockets of academe that represent a good fit), based on a sympathetic understanding of the junior colleague *as a person*. This does not need to entail deep friendship, although it may. What mentoring of this kind requires is a serious conviction of one's obligation to "pay it forward"—to give as one has received, or as one should have received. The segment of the mentoring continuum occupied by junior faculty, like the log on which Mark Hopkins is imagined to sit, points in two directions. The assistant professor must, perhaps for the first time, extend a hand behind as well as ahead.

Part II ("Transitions") examines the mentoring landscape primarily from the junior faculty point of view. In chapter 5, Susanna Calkins and Greg Light propose a fourfold typology of faculty mentors based on their self-conception in the role. The axes they use to derive their categories of Model, Shepherd, Guide, and Companion—mentor-focused vs. mentee-focused and active vs. passive—yield highly intuitive types readily populated by faculty in one's experience. Calkins and Light afford tools that will be useful in refining thinking about mentor-mentee "fit" and the continuing evolution of individual needs as relationships progress along the mentoring continuum.

Chapters 6 and 7 assert in the faculty context the same prominence of peer-based approaches and bottom-up directionality that we have seen with graduate mentoring. Mirjam Glessmer and colleagues in chapter 6 describe how they were able to "take ownership" of their mentoring through the formation and extension of the Earth Science Women's Network, a grass-roots peer-mentoring collective (defined in this case more by discipline and gender than by career stage, though skewing young). They also introduce another of the volume's important themes, mentoring as an online phenomenon, emphasizing the Internet's capacity to multiply mentoring options and to permit meaningful human bonds without regard to distance. Even more forceful advocates of mentee ownership of the mentoring process are Steven Lee and colleagues, who in chapter 7 draw on the techniques of "managing up," popularized in the corporate context by Gabarro and Kotter, to trace the contours of an academic equivalent, "mentoring up." Elsewhere in the volume, especially in the dialogues of Part III, we find mentors reflecting on the need to encourage agency in their mentees, and the difficulty of knowing in every instance what the optimal amount of agency might be.

The mentoring literature frequently asserts the benefits of a productive relationship *for the mentor*, and may even posit reciprocal professional development as definitional of true mentoring. Several contributions to the volume address this dynamic, none more directly and convincingly than Jennifer Shewmaker and Phyllis Bolin in chapter 8. One of the most challenging areas of mentoring is to prepare aspiring faculty for the virtual certitude that they will start their professorial careers in an academic environment unlike what they knew in graduate school or on their postdocs. As Shewmaker and Bolin note, the teaching-centered (or at any rate less research-intensive) schools that provide the majority of tenure-track jobs stand to gain enormously from the infusion of current research experience embodied in their recent hires, specifically from the standpoint of continued professional development for senior faculty. Meanwhile, junior colleagues in this situation feel affirmed as positive contributors and thus invest more easily in their new surroundings. These potentialities of the mentoring continuum are perhaps most likely to be realized when intentionally (i.e., administratively) cultivated, as with the New Faculty Mentoring Program at Shewmaker and Bolin's institution. Also noteworthy is the authors' engagement with an under-discussed issue, the culture shock faced by many new faculty transitioning to schools with religious affiliations and missional commitments not previously integrated with their academic lives.

In chapter 9, Julie Welch and colleagues further develop the ideas of mutuality, reciprocity, and institutional benefit as aspects of a successful academic mentoring relationship. Both as a description of the experience of constructing an online nexus for mentoring activity, and as a "how-to" blueprint easily adapted to other situations, Welch and colleagues' discussion of the Indiana University School of Medicine Faculty Mentoring Portal bears comparison to Glessmer and colleagues' account of the Earth Science Women's Network. While ESWN reaches outward, across universities and continents, the IUSM mentoring portal demonstrates how web-based initiatives can effect change locally, and can address the generally held aspiration of "building a culture of mentoring" at the college or institutional level. There will be more to say about web-facilitated mentoring shortly.

Less often discussed, though, are the *costs* of mentoring for the mentor, significant as these may be in a variety of ways. For instance, an underappreciated variable in the mentoring equation is the legitimate interest of the more advanced scholar in defending territory painstakingly carved out. Does the maxim, "a pupil rewards his master poorly who remains a pupil forever," apply in academe? Perhaps not, and for good reason. The ideal outcome of one's mentoring efforts, at least from a research standpoint, would be to populate the field with protégés whose work will advance *one's own* agenda, forming a wave whose crest one will ride. If this is consistent with the protégé's interests, how fortunate! But for many specialists, a mentoring relationship of true benefit to the senior partner would entail preservation of access to grants, publishing venues, and other tenuous arenas of professional achievement. If your former student makes the NSF cut and you don't, well, what kind of mentor were you? Answer: the kind that gets removed from the academic competition. And even if the danger of giving birth to a rival is not grave, there remains the crucial issue of time. Often in academe, career "success" is reducible to the rate at which one accumulates the recognized tokens of accomplishment (publications, grants, invited talks or visiting appointments, conference appearances, and other CV categories); by and large, those who succeed best are those who devote the most time to these activities, as opposed to service obligations or the dedicated mentoring of colleagues earlier in their careers. An unfortunate logic is at work here, such that one is least likely to get good mentoring from those whose careers one would most like to duplicate. The mentoring literature to date has not grappled much with such conflicts of interest, but ignoring them can only dampen prospects for the healthy propagation of the professoriate.

## Does Mentoring Exist?

Whatever its ongoing vitality, the Mark Hopkins model clearly no longer provides an adequate compass for what it means to mentor and be mentored in the 21st-century academy. Not only must we agree that one can be mentored by those of similar age and equal rank, but as noted above, several of the book's contributors urge us to consider that we might, in effect, be mentored by a website. Certainly the ESWN site "mentors" in large part by facilitating connections between human beings (like MentorNet and other websites noted in the Resources section) and Welch and colleagues' Faculty Mentoring Portal strives to promote fruitful interactions between flesh-and-blood mentors and mentees. At the same time, these sites provide many excellent non-human resources, and it is not in every case obvious where facilitation ends and mentoring begins. Nor is the distinction necessarily coherent, insofar as how to be a good mentor is one of the things a good mentor would mentor you on.

Is it still possible to draw meaningful boundaries around the concept of mentoring? Does any attempt to enhance the success of aspiring academics qualify? Or does there abide some unquantifiable element rooted in an authentic engagement between specific people? Part III ("Dialogues and Reflections") makes several approaches to these questions in the form of mentor-mentee dialogues and deliberate reflections on mentoring by seasoned scholars. In chapter 10, Beth Boehm and Amy Lueck return us to the territory of graduate student peer mentoring, from the perspectives of faculty/administrator and grad student mentee/mentor, respectively. By proceeding more or less chronologically, they are able to illustrate not only the process of creating a mentoring program (usefully set beside the efforts discussed in chapters 1, 2, 6, 8, and 9), but the progressive engagement with mentoring as a domain of professional development by individuals at a distance on the mentoring continuum. Chapter 10, Leonard Cassuto and Jane Van Slembrouck's discussion of family as part of the graduate education equation, points to the difference between a mentor who thinks, "my job is to advise you on how best to succeed as a graduate student in our program," and one who thinks, "my job is to help you integrate your academic pursuits with all aspects of your life, so as to maximize your human happiness." We can see here the sketch of a holistic approach to mentoring, another crucial dimension of which is explored in chapter 12, Christine Stanley and Yvonna Lincoln's dialogue on the factor of racial difference in a mentoring relationship. In a volume heavily concerned with the value of mentoring by/with one's peers (those, by definition, like oneself), Stanley and Lincoln bring into belated focus the mentoring imperative of "identification with difference"—that is, an identification of individuals achieved *despite* some categorical difference, but also the identification of both partners *with* the condition of alterity they share: "I know what you are going through. Here's how it was for me …."

Of course all mentoring relationships are criss-crossed with vectors of otherness, sometimes glaringly and uncomfortably obvious, sometimes insidious enough to go unrecognized. Much of this more opaque difference has to do with career stage. Faculty run the risk of mentoring poorly when they fail to examine the assumptions that served well in their own job search and career climb. In the case of senior scholars, these assumptions may have been formed under very different employment circumstances. Handing out the same advice to today's mentees that your students of ten or twenty years ago received puts an undue burden of interpretation on the junior partner, who may be perfectly, even painfully aware of the problem but still unsure how to discern which pronouncements can be accepted at face value, which require a particular adjustment, and which must be discarded.

When mentor and mentee are closer in age, the latter may be tempted to turn off the critical filter, smoothing the way for an equally damaging if less visible set of assumptions—those of faculty members whose own graduate institutions rested considerably higher up the academic food chain than the ones their graduate students will receive degrees from. A very high proportion of grad students at nonelite universities are being advised by faculty who were grad students at elite universities. Does the mentor have a realistic sense of the kind of placement that would represent success for the mentee? If Yes, does the mentor sufficiently appreciate the specific advantages that an elite degree and/or name-brand advisor has conferred, to be able to provide the correct adjustment when advising? Not all mentors may be confident in their answers to these questions, but a frank admission of fallibility to the mentee is infinitely preferable to avoidance of the issue.

Open channels of communication regarding blind spots and knowledge deficits can humanize the mentoring relationship and increase the odds of mentee success. Modeling such communication is Jan Allen and Kevin Johnston's dialogue in chapter 13, which like Boehm and Lueck's earlier exchange triangulates faculty, administrative, and student perspectives on mentoring. Distilling an 18-year conversation around mentoring, Allen and Johnston draw together many of the book's main preoccupations, including mentee agency and responsibility, the virtues of peer mentoring, non-academic career preparation, teaching as a critical area of focus, and the key role of administration in providing the impetus, initial frameworks, and ongoing support for mentoring efforts.

Nina Namaste's reflections on her career vis-à-vis mentoring in chapter 14 capture some of the ironies enmeshed in the mentoring continuum, such as the tension between her early desire for a "sage on the stage" mentor (in Calkins and Light's formulation, a Model) and her evolving commitment to egalitarian and cooperative ideals in all arenas of practice. Namaste's "Guided Self-mentoring Reflection" (p. 244), a kind of rough Individual Development Plan for faculty seeking satisfaction in their work, represents another terrific tool, easily adapted to all stretches of the academic career path. A sterner rebuke, surely, to the reality of mentoring comes in the final chapter, wherein Leonard Cassuto reveals how he inferred the principles of good mentoring in Lacanian style, by tracing the imprint of their absence in his own professional development as a grad student. That this should stand—let the reader judge—as the method most effective in delineating the frontiers of mentoring may give us pause.

However problematic a definition, if measured by SoTL output, mentoring not only exists but is enjoying an unaccustomed vogue. This is due in no small part to the consolidation, legitimation, and expansion of SoTL itself as an academic enterprise and research area. The sheer proliferation of SoTL studies has made apparent the consistency with which graduate students and junior faculty report quality of mentoring to be the single most important determinant, for good or ill, of their success, and also the comparative effectiveness of mentoring programs as opposed to other structured forms of professional development. Meanwhile, the number of faculty maintaining SoTL as a primary or valued secondary field of research, and/or holding significant SoTL-related administrative roles (such as director at one of the now nearly ubiquitous teaching and learning centers), has increased dramatically, as witnessed by many present contributors. The concept and practice of mentoring has been an easy wagon to hitch to the rising SoTL star. Growing awareness of SoTL research and institutional resources on the part of graduate students and faculty also prompts demand from below, resulting in new forms of mentee-driven administrative collaborations as well as fully home-grown mentoring efforts.

The stakes with academic mentoring extend well beyond individual professional success. Entrusted to the academy are two crucial functions: to advance knowledge, and to ensure the renewal of a capable citizenry. Higher education represents one of the few channels through which intellectual talent can be directed efficiently toward human benefit, and not squandered on enterprises indifferent or injurious to general welfare. Whether it can sustain this mission depends on many things, including its ability to attract and retain high-caliber recruits. While successful mentoring can never be more than part of this formula, it provides what nothing else can, a sense of immediacy, connection, and career "doability." Mentors can say, both literally and by demonstrating their investment in the relationship, "you're on the right path. Keep moving ahead. I will help get you there." This book is intended to support all parties as they continue to walk the mentoring continuum.

# PART ONE

# ORIGINS

# With a Little Help from My Friends: The Role of Peer Mentoring in Graduate Student Teaching Assistant Development

*Michael Amlung, Elizabeth A. Simpson,
Melissa Dengler, Brian Stone, Grace Williams, and
Denise P. Domizi*

Mentoring plays a crucial role in the academic, professional, and personal development of graduate students, in the context both of scholarly research and of teaching. In this chapter, we discuss the role of mentoring in supporting the teaching-related training of graduate students. Particular attention is given to the unique benefits and challenges that accompany peer mentoring, which involves graduate students working together to improve each other's teaching skills. In the sections that follow, we describe several examples of peer mentoring and discuss research on peer mentoring's effects on teacher training. We then identify potential challenges and barriers that can affect the success of peer-mentoring programs. Finally, we highlight some practical considerations related to implementing peer mentoring programs to complement existing teaching assistant (TA) training activities.

Before we begin, it is helpful to briefly describe the authors' backgrounds in teaching and mentoring. Several of us (Amlung, Dengler, Simpson, and Stone) taught undergraduate classes as graduate TAs, and attempted to increase the amount of teacher training offered in our department. Each of us also served in the role of peer mentor for incoming TAs in psychology. All authors carried out research on the University of Georgia (UGA) Department of Psychology peer-mentoring pilot study, discussed below. Finally, as the Coordinator for the Scholarship of Teaching and Learning at UGA, Dr. Domizi has coordinated TA development programs, including serving as a faculty mentor for UGA's Preparing Future Faculty program.

## Who Are Teaching Assistants and What Do They Do?

Teaching assistantships are common funding sources for graduate students in a variety of disciplines. They allow graduate students to pursue their degrees with free or reduced tuition, and typically with a stipend. In return, departments can meet their need for affordable teachers and achieve the flexibility necessary to accommodate fluctuating course enrollment in the face of restricted budgets.

Specific duties of TAs vary by course, discipline, and institution. The typical TA position involves serving in a supporting role than can include assisting the instructor of record with grading, holding office hours or extra help sessions, course management, occasional guest lectures, and leading discussion or breakout sessions. STEM disciplines often employ laboratory assistants, who are assigned instructional duties in a laboratory section (including computer labs). Teaching and laboratory assistants may support a single course each semester, or multiple courses. Finally, graduate students may also be assigned to serve as instructors of record for an entire course, typically having autonomy for teaching and assigning grades. In English, for example, many graduate students serve as instructors of record from very early in their graduate careers, especially if the institution maintains an introductory composition requirement. Such departments tend to have well-established pedagogy courses that graduate students take before or during their first semester teaching. In other disciplines, such as many of the natural and physical sciences, it is unusual for a student to be classified as instructor of record. Many departments prefer to ease their students into teaching, first as teaching or laboratory assistants, and then selecting exemplary students to serve as instructors of record.

Regardless of the type of appointment, TAs must balance the duties of their teaching positions with other responsibilities, including research, coursework, and other program requirements. It is therefore important to consider how we can better prepare TAs for their teaching responsibilities, to maximize their success both in the classroom and in their future careers, and to increase their confidence and skills in dealing with challenges as they arise.

**The Need for Additional TA Training**

Though teaching by TAs is common, many feel unprepared for their teaching responsibilities and report a lack of structured teacher training (see, e.g., Barnes and Randall 2011; Golde and Dore 2001). A survey of over 32,000 graduate students found that teaching-related training/preparation/supervision was rated substantially lower than other aspects of graduate training (Fagen and Suedkamp Wells 2004). It is often assumed that because TAs were good under-graduate students themselves, they will also be good teachers (Staton and Darling 1989). Fagen and Suedkamp Wells (2004) note that, "TAs are thrown into teaching environments in a sink or swim manner" (84). Dishearteningly enough, this sink-or-swim analogy is appropriate. Many TAs may not feel ready to tackle even the basic responsibilities of their positions, and as teaching responsibilities increase (e.g., serving as instructor of record for an entire course), this lack of preparation may be amplified. It is unfair for TAs to find themselves in this position and it is also unfair to the students they are teaching. One TA described teaching as analogous to jumping out of an airplane: "there's only so many things you can do on the ground" (Dudley 2009, 10). Though we agree that encouraging TAs to begin teaching early in their graduate training allows them to compile a record of teaching experience and also to show evidence of improvement prior to entering the job market, we do not believe that going in blindly is the best strategy.

So what can be done to address this seemingly pervasive lack of preparation? Some amount of teacher training is of utmost impor-tance prior to any substantial teaching responsibilities. Indeed, many graduate institutions offer pre-semester orientation programs, which are intended to give TAs the basic skills necessary to begin their teaching responsibilities. Topics typically covered during these orientation sessions include information about institutional policies related to teaching, guidelines/suggestions for interacting with students in class and during office hours, recommendations for grading student work, and an orientation to on-campus teaching resources (e.g., testing or disability resource centers). However, the length, content, and effectiveness of these orientation programs vary widely across institutions. In addition to pre-semester orientations, many departments have a formal program or seminar in which TAs are encouraged to enroll during their first semester of teaching. Such programs may take place over one or more days (Hardré and Burris 2010), a few weeks (Silva, Macián, and Mejía-Gómez 2006), or over the course of one or more semesters (Rushin et al. 1997; Smith 2001). Finally, additional training may also be available in the form stand-alone workshops on specific teaching topics. These departmental or institution-wide training opportunities are certainly helpful for TAs, but one-on-one and small-group interactions are also important. TAs appear to be aware of this: when asked how their training could be improved, TAs consistently suggest offering increased opportunities for teaching-related mentorship (e.g., Bomotti 1994; Jones 1993).

Supervising faculty members are one source for mentoring. Graduate students at teaching-focused institutions—whose schools are likely to have faculty who are willing and able to dedicate time to teaching-related activities—likely have largely positive mentoring experiences with faculty. However, the vast majority of graduate TA positions are in research-focused departments in which faculty mentors may give little teaching-related feedback to TAs (Prieto, Scheel, and Meyers 2001). This may be due to the fact that faculty at research-focused institutions are accustomed to a system that values scholarship (e.g., publications, grants) more than teaching (Boyer 1990). The relative value placed on scholarship and teaching at these institutions is evident across numerous domains, including institutions' mission statements (e.g., Morphew and Hartley 2006), the lack of adequate incentives for supporting teaching (e.g., Shannon, Twale, and Moore 1998), and differences in faculty pay (e.g., Binder et al. 2012). Indeed, faculty at institutions that value research more than teaching may be ineffective teaching mentors for graduate TAs (Boyer 1990). This may be due in part to the perception of faculty that—based on their own experiences—they would be doing their students a disservice by encouraging them to devote time to teaching and related activities (e.g., Robinson and Hope 2013). However, this perspective overlooks two important facts. First, graduate students' research skills also benefit from teaching experiences (Feldon et al. 2011), and second, graduate students are likely to end up at institutions with different priorities from the ones graduate faculty know and expect (Austin 2002). Nonetheless, most graduate students will likely receive at least some teaching training from faculty mentors.

One successful program that emphasizes small-group interactions is the Preparing Future Faculty (PFF) program.[1] This program is designed to provide graduate students with opportunities to observe and experience faculty activities that are both teaching-focused and research-focused. Importantly, graduate students participating in PFF programs are paired with faculty mentors who provide feedback on their teaching and other insights about the nature of an academic career. Several reports have documented the many benefits of PFF programs (DeNeef 2002; Phelps 2010); however, participation in PFF activities at some institutions may be limited to only a small cohort of TAs. As such, we believe that complementing faculty/supervisor and small-group–based training with collaborative learning experiences involving larger groups of TAs is an important and largely unexplored approach. This type of preparation is what we refer to as peer mentoring.

**Peer Mentoring: Definitions and Examples**

Mentoring has been defined as a "pairing of a more skilled or experienced person with a lesser skilled or experienced one, with the agreed-upon goals of having the lesser skilled person grow and develop specific competencies" (Murray 1991, 4). Mentors care about the success of their protégés, and provide career advisement, leadership, and support. The connection formed between mentors and protégés, including a sense of protection and security for the protégé, is also an important component of the experience (Gibson 2003). There are many different types of mentoring. A mentor may be vastly more experienced than a mentee, and therefore the mentee may gain more from the relationship than the mentor. For instance, some graduate programs provide structured faculty-student mentorship for graduate TAs (Meyers and Prieto 2000). Peer mentoring, on the other hand, refers to interactions between individuals with a similar level of training that extends beyond simple peer support and includes focused guidance, resource sharing, and problem solving. In general, programs that focus on facilitating peer mentoring among graduate students are rare. In the following paragraphs, we discuss examples of structured and informal peer-mentoring programs described in the literature.

Several kinds of formal, structured peer-mentoring programs have been implemented across a range of academic disciplines. For instance, Files and colleagues (2008) developed a facilitated peer-mentoring program for medical instructors that was designed to boost academic productivity. Heinrich and Oberleitner (2012) describe a multi-year peer-mentoring program with the goal of enhancing scholarly productivity in a nursing school setting. Peer mentoring has been successfully used to combat academic and professional stress among nursing students (Li et al. 2011). In the domain of business and organizational research, peer mentoring has been shown to increase collaboration and sharing of organizational knowledge (Bryant and Terborg 2008). Similarly, Parker, Hall, and Kram (2008) reported that peer coaching positively contributed to professional development in MBA students. Elsewhere, peer mentoring has been incorporated into graduate programs in education (e.g., Dorn, Palpalewis, and Brown 1995), gerontology (e.g., Webb et al. 2009), accounting (e.g., Jackling and McDowall 2008), and as a university-wide initiative (e.g., Holley and Caldwell 2012). Together, these examples illustrate the positive effects of structured peer-mentoring programs on productivity, collaboration, and academic success.

Structured peer-mentoring programs whose aim is specifically to enhance graduate TA teaching development, however, are less common. Peer-mentoring activities in college writing programs have been documented by two research groups (Martin and Paine 2002; Barr Ebest 2002). In a case study by Barr Ebest (2002), novice TAs were paired with senior TA peer mentors. The teams met regularly throughout the year to discuss progress, and mentors conducted classroom observations of TAs, analyzed syllabi and assignments, and reviewed graded papers. Silva, Macián, and Mejía-Gómez (2006) provide another example of a highly structured, year-long peer-mentoring program for TAs in a foreign language graduate program. Three to four advanced TAs dedicated 30 hours per term to peer-mentoring activities, including consultations, observations, and organizing workshops. Importantly, they found that protégés often sought assistance for non-teaching-related aspects of graduate student life, such as balancing multiple roles and responsibilities.

Even in the absence of structured peer-mentoring programs, TAs often engage in informal, unstructured mentoring activities with fellow graduate students (see, e.g., Austin 2002; Meyers and Prieto 2000). TAs turn to each other for guidance, support, and knowledge, and often forge their own informal mentoring relationships (Wulff et al. 2004). What does this type of informal peer mentoring look like? Drawing examples from our own training, we all have had the unfortunate experience of getting negative feedback on course evaluations at the end of a course. One psychology TA, struggling with negative feedback on course evaluations, was advised by a peer mentor to try midterm course evaluations. The TA took this advice, made improvements to the course mid-semester to address students' concerns, and received higher teaching evaluations as a result. Another TA was having difficulty conveying a particular psychology concept to students, who found it frustrating and difficult to understand. Rather than trying to tackle this problem alone, the TA sought advice from a group of fellow graduate students, who helped to brainstorm solutions. The TA successfully carried out one of the suggested activities and the students shared an "Aha!" moment. These examples illustrate how informal peer mentoring can help TAs address common teaching challenges.

## Research on Peer Mentoring: Motives and Outcomes

Scholarly research on the role and effectiveness of peer mentoring in TA development is limited. Below, we briefly review the available literature on peer mentoring, with a focus on motives for seeking peer mentoring and the benefits and outcomes for both the TAs and their mentors. Throughout this section, we also discuss findings from a pilot study in which graduate TAs in a psychology department at a large research university ($N = 108$) completed an anonymous survey that assessed frequencies of various teaching-related mentoring activities, motivations for engaging or not engaging in mentoring, and teaching-related benefits gained from these experiences.[2] Generally speaking, we found that TAs engaged in peer mentoring improved their teaching skills, and did so to a greater degree than those relying exclusively on faculty mentoring.

TAs may seek out mentoring experiences for a variety of reasons. Peer-mentoring relationships are viewed as safe places, in which TAs feel they can be honest and open (Bonilla, Pickron, and Tatum 1994). We speculate that the advantage of peer mentoring in this regard may be due, in part, to faculty members being in a position of power relative to their students, whereas peer-to-peer mentoring does not involve such an imbalance. Peers are also often more accessible than faculty, partly because the TAs' offices are typically segregated from faculty offices, limiting opportunities for chance encounters and informal discussion (Wulff et al. 2004). In our pilot study, TAs were asked to identify the most common reasons they sought teaching-related peer mentoring. The most frequently cited were that their peers seemed to understand/relate to their situation (97% of respondents), and that peers seemed willing to help (91%). Other common reasons included seeking peer mentoring in order to save time (84%)

and to receive social or moral support (81%). The most common reasons that TAs sought help from faculty (not including their major professor) were for feedback on their teaching (44%), for advice on teaching careers (34%), and to build professional networks (31%). We also examined common reasons for avoiding faculty-based mentoring for teaching. Perceived conflicts between teaching and research roles prevented many TAs from approaching their major professors (41% of TAs cited this as a primary reason). TAs also had the perception that they would be a burden (34%) and did not think faculty would be willing to help (31%).

There are numerous benefits to peer mentoring, which thus far have only been documented anecdotally (e.g., Holley and Caldwell 2012). One benefit is that peer mentoring allows TAs to gain new techniques. For example, one of us recalls a conversation with a peer mentor concerning a student who was not actively contributing to classroom discussions. Being relatively inexperienced, the TA felt that he had exhausted every technique he knew to encourage the student to participate. The more experienced TA shared additional strategies from her own experience—including using low-stakes writing and classroom response systems—that proved successful in the classroom. Interdisciplinary peer-mentoring groups that span academic departments also expose TAs to different perspectives they may not have previously considered. For example, another one of us recalls talking with a peer in an English department about how to help students who were struggling with writing papers. This experience led to an exchange of sample rubrics and other materials related to evaluating student writing.

Peer mentoring may also serve as a valuable source of professional development for future instructors. Recent graduates, when asked about the most pivotal events in their preparation for teaching careers, cited peer mentoring as playing a crucial part in positively contributing to their professional development as teachers (Smith 2001). Peer mentoring may also increase TAs' preparedness and competitiveness on the job market, improving their collaborative and cooperative skills as well as their teaching. Importantly, peer mentoring is also beneficial to mentors, providing them with an opportunity to critically reflect on their own teaching (Barr Ebest 2002). Mentors are then better prepared to serve in mentoring roles in the future, regardless of whether they pursue teaching-focused careers or not (Noonan, Ballinger, and Black 2007). In fact, research suggests that individuals who were mentored are likely to mentor others at a later time (Hunt and Michael 1983).

In our study, TAs rated their peer-mentoring experiences as significantly more beneficial than mentoring received from faculty, though each type of mentoring provided unique benefits. The most common benefits that our TAs reported receiving from peer mentoring were examples of teaching materials (e.g., lecture slides, in-class activities, assignments), advice about effective teaching practices, and social support and encouragement.

## Challenges to Peer Mentoring

Despite clear potential benefits to both mentors and protégés, peer mentoring programs face a variety of potential barriers and challenges (for a recent discussion of this issue, see Holley and Caldwell 2012). Some challenges are practical in nature, while others stem from institutional or departmental cultures regarding teacher training. From a logistical standpoint, one of the most common challenges to any form of mentoring is time. Both faculty and graduate student TAs are incredibly busy and find themselves with ever-increasing responsibilities and deadlines. In addition to providing research mentoring to their graduate students, faculty members often have added administrative, service, and other professional obligations. As a result, some faculty may be reluctant to devote time and energy to mentoring graduate TAs. Student-led peer-mentoring initiatives, like the one described below, may circumvent some of these faculty time constraints. From the standpoint of the protégés, first-year students are similarly overwhelmed with coursework, beginning their research programs, and learning to perform their TA duties. With these competing responsibilities, incoming TAs may feel that they lack sufficient time to improve their teaching. However, novice TAs should be informed that forming peer-mentoring relationships with senior students may actually save time and reduce stress.

Many graduate programs are also operating with diminishing resources, including smaller budgets, heavier teaching loads, and greater competition for physical space. Implementing a formal, department-wide TA training program, therefore, may not be feasible. While some forms of peer mentoring require departmental contributions (e.g., a faculty or staff member to serve as a facilitator, funds to invite guest speakers), informal peer mentoring can be low-cost, if not free. For example, a student-led peer-mentoring group may only require access to a classroom for regular meetings. While refreshments are a nice addition to meetings (and may have the added benefit of increasing attendance among hungry graduate students), our experience is that participants are typically willing to pitch in food and drinks in a potluck format.

For TAs at research-focused institutions, one common challenge to seeking teaching training is the perceived conflict between their roles as researchers and teachers. Silva, Macián, and Mejía-Gómez (2006) note that it is common for TAs at research-focused institutions to receive conflicting messages regarding the relative value of teaching and scholarship. Faculty supervisors and thesis advisors at these types of institutions may appear to value teaching, but then actively discourage spending time building these skills (Barr Ebest 2002). As already mentioned, this may be due to institutional priorities that privilege scholarship over teaching, or to the failure of faculty to consider the types of institutions in which their graduate students are most likely to teach in the future. Thus, some TAs find themselves caught between explicit messages supporting teaching and implicit messages and actions implying that it is less important than scholarship (Wulff et al. 2004). Silva, Macián, and Mejía-Gómez (2006) further suggest that peer mentors may help reduce this tension, since they provide a valuable model for effectively balancing these roles. More experienced TAs are "able to find time and energy to dedicate to both activities" (Silva, Macián, and Mejía-Gómez 2006, 243). Our pilot data supports this: nearly all respondents indicated that other graduate students better understood and related to their situations, including the challenges of balancing multiple obligations. We believe that supporting peer-mentoring programs may contribute to larger cultural changes in the value and visibility of teaching.

**Practical Considerations for Increasing Peer Mentoring**

In this section, we discuss several practical considerations related to increasing peer mentoring, both through formal (i.e., structured pairings) and informal (i.e., fluid pairings, unstructured) programs, to improve TA training. These "best practices" are drawn from examples of peer-mentoring programs that have been described in the literature (e.g., Silva, Macián, and Mejía-Gómez 2006; Martin and Paine 2002; Barr Ebest 2002) as well as our own experience with creating a peer-mentoring organization for TAs in psychology.

Although largely anecdotal, we think they are a useful starting point for implementing a new peer-mentoring program.

*A Case Study: The Psychology Educator Development Association*

Like many large research universities, the University of Georgia (UGA) relies on graduate students to fulfill its instructional mission. Each semester, TAs in the UGA Department of Psychology assist professors with courses or serve as instructors for their own courses. The department offers several teaching-centered professional development opportunities, including a seminar for incoming TAs and an advanced teaching practicum course. However, graduate students in the department (including several authors of this chapter) desired additional training beyond what was then offered. This led to the founding of an informal student-led organization named the Psychology Educator Development Association (PEDA).[3] The organization maintains a diverse calendar of monthly meetings, guest speakers, course planning roundtables, and periodic social activities. PEDA also organizes group travel to regional teaching-related conferences. As participants, we noticed that one of the primary advantages of PEDA was the increased collaboration and communication among the graduate student peers that occurred via informal discussions outside of regularly scheduled events. Incoming graduate students, in particular, used PEDA to connect with advanced TAs in the department with shared interests in teaching. Importantly, the pairing of mentors and mentees in PEDA was a fluid process, allowing TAs to seek support and advice from multiple mentors.

Creating a peer-based teaching organization, such as PEDA, was complicated by the lack of practical recommendations in the TA development literature. One notable exception is the Appendix in Silva, Macián, and Mejía-Gómez (2006, 248–49), which provides a list of guidelines for implementing their structured peer-mentoring program. Silva and colleagues first describe the requirements for serving as a peer mentor, including positive teaching evaluations, at least one year of teaching experience, strong organizational skills, and evidence of the ability to create and adapt a variety of teaching materials. The authors then describe the different roles that a peer mentor might assume, including helping new instructors transition from orientation workshops to the real classroom, assisting TAs with crafting lesson plans and other teaching materials, conducting periodic teaching observations, and providing mentees with detailed feedback to help improve teaching.

*Format and Structure*

As the examples described elsewhere in this chapter demonstrate, peer mentoring can take many forms. Some graduate programs may take an informal approach, as we did with PEDA, fostering communication and collaboration among TAs in the department without placing any restrictions on the nature of these interactions. Other departments may favor a more structured TA mentoring program, such as that proposed by Silva, Macián, and Mejía-Gómez (2006), in which a small number of advanced TAs are selected to serve as mentors for novice TAs in the department. The choice of structure and format depends on several factors, including the amount of time and resources available to support mentoring and the level of initiative and motivation among potential participants.

We believe that both options can be worthwhile, with each offering unique benefits and challenges. In our experience with PEDA, the informal format was useful in that we were able to shift our focus to teaching topics that were most timely for our members. For instance, if some of our TAs were struggling with facilitating classroom discussion, we devoted our next meeting to that topic. Informal mentoring may also require less time and resources than structured alternatives (e.g., mentors and mentees do not have to commit to a fixed number of hours per week to meet). However, informal programs necessarily demand greater initiative and planning by participants to make the program successful. Mentees also need to be more motivated to seek out and schedule training with peer mentors. If a department does not have a critical mass of graduate students who are interested in leading the initiative, then an informal format may not be ideal. Structured programs, on the other hand, have the advantage of holding participants accountable for devoting meaningful time and effort to mentoring activities. Structured mentoring programs may also produce greater benefits for some TAs—particularly first-year TAs, who would otherwise be unlikely to seek as much support from their mentors, but who require help in prioritizing teaching amongst their other responsibilities. Nonetheless, in both types of programs, it is beneficial for TAs to teach individual lessons and get constructive, personalized feedback from experienced teachers. Ideally, there should be a period of transition in which novice TAs gradually take on more responsibilities throughout their graduate training, receiving guidance and mentorship along the way.

## Identifying Mentors

The selection of experienced TAs to serve as mentors for novice TAs is an important first step, and can be carried out either by the novice TAs themselves or through a more formalized matching process (e.g., surveying both mentors and mentees and matching them based on mutual goals). The pairing of mentors and protégés can be fluid, as in our case with PEDA, or more static, such as in a structured mentoring program (e.g., Silva, Macián, and Mejía-Gómez 2006; Barr Ebest 2002). At a minimum, it is critical that both mentors and protégés share a commitment to improving teaching and professional development. Among the qualities Silva, Macián, and Mejía-Gómez (2006) associate with strong peer mentors are good teaching evaluations, strong communication and organizational skills, experience observing teaching, evidence of implementing a variety of activities in the classroom, and sufficient time to devote to mentoring. It may also be useful for mentors and protégés to have similar topical interests in teaching. For example, mentees may wish to select mentors who have previously taught a course they are currently preparing to teach. In addition, some mentors may be particularly good at certain aspects of teaching, such as successfully leading students to work in teams, carrying out engaging class demonstrations, creating effective learning assessments, or using technology. In this way, mentor-mentee pairs may be based on the skills mentees hope to develop and the skills mentors have already mastered. Finally, some protégés may be more comfortable seeking out mentors who are similar to themselves in some characteristic, such as gender, ethnicity, or being a non-native English speaker (Holley and Caldwell 2012).

## Timing and Duration

Another important consideration when implementing a peer-mentoring program is the appropriate timing and duration of the experience. Catching new TAs early in their careers is important, as this is a phase in which they are establishing their identities as teachers and beginning to solidify aspects of their teaching style (Wise 2011). Moreover, providing opportunities for mentoring early includes peer mentors as an integral part of the department's support structure for teaching (Silva, Macián, and Mejía-Gómez 2006). The first few semesters of graduate school are also when students are learning time management strategies that will allow them to effectively balance multiple teaching and research obligations. Encouraging new TAs to participate in teaching-related training may also help counter negative views toward teaching (i.e., viewing teaching as less important than scholarship) before these attitudes are fully engrained. In our view, exposing novice TAs to examples of high-quality teaching early in their careers provides a model for TAs to follow throughout their training. Nonetheless, the opportunity for mentoring in later training stages (i.e., when TAs take on more significant instructional responsibilities for laboratory/discussion sections or as instructor of record) is also important for generating new teaching strategies and further refining teaching skills to assess and improve student learning.

Prior implementations of peer mentoring have varied widely in the duration of the experience, with many structured programs taking place across multiple semesters (e.g., Barr Ebest 2002; Martin and Paine 2002; Silva, Macián, and Mejía-Gómez 2006). Importantly, although less durable peer-mentoring relationships may have a meaningful impact on TAs, empirical research suggests that sustained training is necessary to ensure improvements in teaching practices (e.g., Rushin et al. 1997; Richardson and Placier 2001). Ideally, mentors would be flexible in the amount of time they are available to each mentee, allowing for individual differences in training needs. Both parties should discuss the unique goals for the mentoring experience and plan for a sufficient amount of time to achieve goals. At minimum, such mentoring should occur for one semester—or for the duration of a single course—since different challenges will arise at different points across the semester (e.g., designing syllabi prior to the start of the semester, creating midterm assessments and projects, utilizing course evaluations at the end of the term to further refine the course for the future).

*Seeking Institutional and Other Support*

Support from departmental and institutional sources increases the likelihood of a peer-mentoring program having long-term success. For departments that rely heavily on TAs to meet instructional needs, coordinators of peer-mentoring programs should emphasize the benefits of improving TAs' teaching skills (e.g., improved quality of undergraduate instruction). In our work with PEDA, we approached the department administration and secured financial support for a group of TAs and instructors to attend regional teaching conferences. Our department also provided funds for group registration for online workshops related to teaching. Program facilitators may also want to ask the department for physical space for mentors and mentees to meet. Silva, Macián, and Mejía-Gómez (2006) discovered that the peer mentors in their pro-gram needed office space to meet with the new TAs. Departments may also be willing to set aside space for a teaching lab or resource room to further support the mentoring program. TAs might use this space to compile teaching materials and other helpful resources.

Another potential resource, if available, is a campus teaching and learning center. Our experience is that teaching center staff genuinely want to help graduate students improve their teaching, but may not know about all of the activities in every department on campus. In our case, we found that the Center for Teaching and Learning at UGA was eager to recommend topics for our meetings and to connect us with distinguished teaching faculty across campus who were willing to speak during our group meetings. Finally, teaching centers may also be a useful source for financial support for campus TA development initiatives.

## Summary

Teaching is a lot of work, but can also be very rewarding, especially when it is a shared experience. In our view, peer mentoring provides an important supplement to existing faculty-based training for graduate TAs. Both our pilot study and our experiences with PEDA suggest that the majority of TAs share this view. For example, the majority of TAs in our study indicated that they would likely take advantage of structured peer-mentoring programs if such programs existed. Programs that support peer mentoring may not only foster growth among TAs, but may also improve undergraduate instruction, given the large number of courses taught by graduate TAs. Such programs will also better prepare graduate students to transition into faculty positions and other mentor roles once they complete their degrees.

**Notes**

1. Additional information on the Preparing Future Faculty program is available online at http://www.preparing-faculty.org.

2. Preliminary results of this study were previously presented at the 2012 meeting of the American Psychological Association (see Amlung et al. 2012).

3. For additional information about PEDA see Rizel 2012.

**Works Cited**

Amlung, M., M. Dengler, E. Simpson, B. Stone, G. Williams, and D. Domizi. 2012. "The Role of Peer Mentoring in Psychology Teaching Assistant Development." Poster presented at the 2012 Annual Convention of the American Psychological Association, Orlando, FL.

Austin, A. E. 2002. "Preparing the Next Generation of Faculty: Graduate School as Socialization to the Academic Career." *The Journal of Higher Education* 73 (1): 94–122.

Barnes, B. J., and J. Randall. 2011. "Doctoral Student Satisfaction: An Examination of Disciplinary, Enrollment, and Institutional Differences." *Research in Higher Education* 53 (1): 47–75.

Barr Ebest, S. 2002. "Mentoring: Past, Present, and Future." In *Preparing College Teachers of Writing: History, Theories, Programs, Practices*, edited by B. P. Pytlik and S. Liggett, 211–21. Oxford: Oxford University Press.

Binder, Melissa, Janie Chermak, Kate Krause, and Jennifer Thacher. 2012. "The Teaching Penalty in Higher Education: Evidence from a Public Research University." *Economics Letters* 117 (1): 39–41. doi: 10.1016/j.econlet.2012.04.021.

Bomotti, S. 1994. "Teaching Assistant Attitudes Toward College Teaching." *Review of Higher Education* 17 (4): 371–93.

Bonilla, J., C. Pickron, and T. Tatum. 1994. "Peer Mentoring Among Graduate Students of Color: Expanding the Mentoring Relationship." *New Directions for Teaching and Learning* 1994 (57): 101–13.

Boyer, E. 1990. *Scholarship Reconsidered: Priorities of the Professoriate*. Princeton, NJ: Princeton University Press.

Bryant, S. E., and J. R. Terborg. 2008. "Impact of Peer Mentor

Training on Creating and Sharing Organizational Knowledge." *Journal of Managerial Issues* 20 (1): 11–29.

DeNeef, A. L. 2002. *The Preparing Future Faculty Program: What Difference Does It Make?* Washington, DC: Association of American Colleges and Universities.

Dorn, S. M., R. Palpalewis, and R. Brown. 1995. "Educators Earning Their Doctorates: Doctoral Student Perceptions Regarding Cohesiveness and Persistence." *Education* 116:305–14.

Dudley, M. G. 2009. "Jumping Out of an Airplane: A TA's Perspective on Teaching Effectiveness." *Eastern Education Journal* 38 (1): 1–10.

Fagen, A. P., and K. M. Suedkamp Wells. 2004. "The 2000 National Doctoral Program Survey." In *Paths to the Professoriate: Strategies for Enriching the Preparation of Future Faculty*, edited by D. H. Wulff and A. E. Austin, 74–91. San Francisco: Jossey-Bass.

Feldon, David F., James Peugh, Briana E. Timmerman, Michelle A. Maher, Melissa Hurst, Denise Strickland, Joanna A. Gilmore, and Cindy Stiegelmeyer. 2011. "Graduate Students' Teaching Experiences Improve Their Methodological Research Skills." *Science*, August 19, 1037–39. doi:10.1126/science.1204109.

Files, J. A., J. E. Blair, A. P. Mayer, and M. G. Ko. 2008. "Facilitated Peer Mentorship: a Pilot Program for Academic Advancement of Female Medical Faculty." *Journal of Women's Health* 17 (6): 1009–15.

Gibson, S. K. 2003. "Being Mentored: The Experience of Women Faculty." *Journal of Career Development* 30 (3): 173–88.

Golde, C. M., and T. M. Dore. 2001. "At Cross Purposes: What the Experiences of Doctoral Students Reveal About Doctoral Education." Philadelphia, PA: a report for the Pew Charitable Trusts. http://www.phd-survey.org.

Hardré, P. L., and A. O. Burris. 2010. "What Contributes to Teaching Assistant Development: Differential Responses to Key Design Features." *Instructional Science* 40 (1): 93–118.

Heinrich, K. T., and M. G. Oberleitner. 2012. "How a Faculty Group's Peer Mentoring of Each Other's Scholarship Can Enhance Retention and Recruitment." *Journal of Professional Nursing* 28 (1): 5–12.

Holley, Karri A., and Mary Lee Caldwell. 2012. "The Challenges of Designing and Implementing a Doctoral Student Mentoring Program." *Innovative Higher Education* 37 (3): 243–53. doi:10.1007/s10755-011-9203-y.

Hunt, D. M., and C. Michael. 1983. "Mentorship: A Career Training and Development Tool." *Academy of Management Review* 8 (3): 475–85.

Jackling, B., and T. McDowall. 2008. "Peer Mentoring in an Accounting Setting: A Case Study of Mentor Skill Development." *Accounting Education* 17 (4): 447–62.

Jones, J. L. 1993. "TA Training: From the TA's Point of View." *Innovative Higher Education* 18 (2): 147–61.

Li, H. C., L. S. Wang, Y. H. Lin, and I. Lee. 2011. "The Effect of a Peer-mentoring Strategy on Student Nurse Stress Reduction in Clinical Practice." *International Nursing Review* 58 (2): 203–10.

Martin, W., and C. Paine. 2002. "Mentors, Models, and Agents of Change: Veteran TAs Preparing Teachers of Writing." In *Preparing College Teachers of Writing: History, Theories, Programs, Practices*, edited by B. P. Pytlik and S. Liggett, 222–32. Oxford: Oxford University Press.

Meyers, S. A., and L. R. Prieto. 2000. "Training in the Teaching of Psychology: What Is Done and Examining the Differences." *Teaching of Psychology* 27 (4): 258–61.

Morphew, C. C., and M. Hartley. 2006. "Mission Statements: A Thematic Analysis of Rhetoric Across Institutional Type." *Journal of Higher Education* 77 (3): 456–71. doi:10.1353/jhe.2006.0025.

Murray, M. 1991. *Beyond the Myths and Magic of Mentoring*. San Francisco: Jossey-Bass.

Noonan, M. J., R. Ballinger, and R. Black. 2007. "Peer and Faculty Mentoring in Doctoral Education: Definitions, Experiences, and Expectations." *International Journal of Teaching and Learning in Higher Education* 19 (3): 251–62.

Parker, P., D. T. Hall, and K. E. Kram. 2008. "Peer Coaching: A Relational Process for Accelerating Career Learning." *Academy of Management Learning and Education* 7 (4): 487–503.

Phelps, R. E. 2010. "Transforming the Culture of the Academy through 'Preparing Future Faculty' Programs." *American Psych-*

*ologist* 65 (8): 785–92.

Prieto, L. R., K. R. Scheel, and S. A. Meyers. 2001. "Psychology Graduate Teaching Assistants Preferences for Supervisory Style." *Journal of Graduate Student Teaching Assistant Development* 8 (1): 37–40.

Richardson, V., and A. Placier. 2001. "Teacher Change." In *Handbook of Research on Teaching*, edited by V. Richardson, 4th ed., 905–47. Washington, DC: American Educational Research Association.

Rizel, R. J. 2012. "Learning How to Teach." *gradPSYCH*, November. http://www.apa.org/gradpsych/2012/11/learning-teach.aspx.

Robinson, T. E., and W. C. Hope. 2013. "Teaching in Higher Education: Is There a Need for Training in Pedagogy in Graduate Degree Programs?" *Research in Higher Education Journal* 21:1–11.

Rushin, J. W., J. De Saix, A. Lumsden, D. P. Streubel, G. Summers, and C. Berson. 1997. "Graduate Teaching Assistant Training: A Basis for Improvement of College Biology Teaching and Faculty Development?" *American Biology Teacher* 59 (2): 86–90.

Shannon, D. M., D. J. Twale, and M. S. Moore. 1998. "TA Teaching Effectiveness: The Impact of Training and Teaching Experience." *Journal of Higher Education* 69 (4): 440–66.

Silva, G. V., J. L. Macián, and M. Mejía-Gómez. 2006. "Peer TA Mentoring in a Foreign Language Program." *International Journal of Teaching and Learning in Higher Education* 18 (3): 241–49.

Smith, K. S. 2001. "Pivotal Events in Graduate Teacher Preparation for a Faculty Career." *Journal of Graduate Teaching Assistant Development* 8 (3): 97–105.

Staton, A. Q., and A. L. Darling. 1989. "Socialization of Teaching Assistants." *New Directions for Teaching and Learning* 1989 (39): 15–22. doi: 10.1002/tl.37219893904.

Webb, A. K., T. Wangmo, H. H. Ewen, P. B. Teaster, and L. R. Hatch. 2009. "Peer and Faculty Mentoring for Students Pursuing a Ph.D. in Gerontology." *Educational Gerontology* 35 (12): 1089–106.

Wise, A. 2011. "Supporting Future Faculty in Developing Their Teaching Practices: An Exploration of Communication Networks Among Graduate Teaching Assistants." *International Journal of*

*Teaching and Learning in Higher Education* 23 (2): 135–49.

Wulff, D. H., A. E. Austin, J. D. Nyquist, and J. Sprague. 2004. "The Development of Graduate Students as Teaching Scholars: A Four-year Longitudinal Study." In *Paths to the Professoriate: Strategies for Enriching the Preparation of Future Faculty,* edited by D. H. Wulff and A. E. Austin, 46–73. San Francisco: Jossey-Bass.

# Graduate School–Facilitated Peer Mentoring for Degree Completion: Dissertation-Writing Boot Camps

*Jan Allen*

Most of the existing research and literature on mentoring emphasizes the mentoring dyad and specifically the roles, responsibilities, effective functions, and potential pitfalls and dysfunctions in faculty–graduate student or senior faculty–junior faculty relationships.[1] There has been much less attention to peer mentoring as an effective means to provide academic and psychological support in the graduate student experience.[2] In this chapter, I will make a case for the important role that graduate students have as peer mentors, including the ways that peer mentors make distinct and unique contributions to the support and advancement of their fellow students. I also will describe ways that the Graduate School (and other central offices or disciplinary departments) can promote peer mentoring and peer support communities that facilitate degree completion. To a large degree, I base my comments and suggestions for peer mentoring programs on my faculty and administrative experiences with programs at the University of Tennessee, Columbia University, and Cornell University.

For several decades, since at least the 1980s, there has been general agreement and research evidence that graduate students are more successful when they have supportive and effective mentoring (Allen forthcoming; National Academy of Sciences 1997; Nicoloff and Forrest 1988; Ulke-Steiner, Kurtz-Costes, and Kinlaw 2000). Yet over the past decade or so, the increasing expectations for faculty teaching and student engagement, research, publishing, securing research funding, and engaging in university service and shared governance have continued to make it difficult for faculty to provide consistent and effective mentoring to all graduate students in their programs. As a result, mentoring accessibility and effectiveness can be highly variable across individual faculty and programs.

Given the evidence that good mentors can have a critical impact on students' confidence, competence, degree completion, and career advancement, it is ironic that, at the point that students may feel the most anxiety and pressure to complete their degree—when they are tasked with the one responsibility, to write a thesis or dissertation, that students have never done before (save the very few who seek a second research master's or doctorate)—we as faculty send the message, "Now go away and write. Contact me when you have a chapter (or two or all of them) ready for me to read. Good luck with that." Whatever sense of community, camaraderie, and support that new student orientation events, or taking coursework with one's entering cohort, or passing the qualifying exams to enter into the ABD club have engendered, the independence expected of most students—especially in the humanities and social sciences—at the thesis and dissertation stage only increases the stress and isolation reported by graduate students as they begin to write, in the last months or years of graduate school.

The research and literature focusing on peer support that does exist has emphasized the psychological and social support provided by peers in graduate school. There has been little attention given to the role of peers in academic support and degree completion. Johnson and Huwe (2003), in their comprehensive book on mentoring in graduate school, describe peer mentoring as an "alternative mentor form." Peer mentoring is a "lateral relationship in which a fellow graduate student provides career-enhancing and psychosocial functions to another student" (179). Another alternative form, peer-group mentoring, consists in "a group of peers who agree to meet regularly for the purpose of providing role modeling, networking, and psychosocial support" (179). In what ways, then, do peers, as individuals or in groups, function in a mentoring role?

## Peer Mentoring Contributions

Peers function as mentors by providing supportive relationships, empathizing through shared experiences, and offering social networks in ways that faculty cannot, especially in the ways described here.

*Mentoring always involves a relationship* that extends beyond simply an advising role (Allen forthcoming). And although a faculty mentor can provide advocacy, guidance, and financial and other critical forms of support, many roles are beyond the boundaries of appropriate faculty-student relationships. For example, peers, whether as individuals or in groups, have far more opportunities for academic conversation and nonacademic socializing outside the classroom, office, and lab than would generally be considered appropriate for faculty-student interactions. Peers can go to restaurants and bars together. They are more likely to travel to and room together at conferences. They share offices and occasionally residences. In contrast, there are many fewer situations where faculty-student pairs engage and socialize in these ways and settings.

*Peers provide lateral exposure and perspective.* Peers experience in real time the same or similar issues related to the graduate school experience. Peers who share an advisor or the same program faculty can offer advice based on their direct experience with the work style, temperament, and expectations of the shared advisor and faculty. Further, even the most supportive, communicative, and empathetic advisor shares experiences and advice reflecting their own graduate school experience years or decades in the past, and most often at a different institution. To paraphrase Heraclitus, peers step in the same river.

*Peers are important for the social network they provide* beyond academic support. One of the many differences between the undergraduate and the graduate experience is that students' focus and work narrow in significant ways in graduate school. Especially beyond the coursework stage, graduate students have a much smaller academic world. At the thesis- and dissertation-writing stage, especially in the humanities and social sciences, students engage primarily with one faculty chair/director/sponsor. When that relationship is fraught with conflict or excessive expectations, students may forget one of the most important (but often uncommunicated) rules of graduate school: "You are *not* your thesis or dissertation. It is your *work*. It is *not you*. You remain a worthy person deserving of care and support. And this includes taking care of yourself." Even in constructive, healthy student-faculty relationships, students benefit from multiple sources of support and information.

*Graduate students have multiple needs that multiple mentors can meet.* Distinguishing the research on mentoring in business from research on mentors in higher education, Lyons, Scroggins, and Rule (1990) identified three functions in the "peculiar intimacy" of mentoring essential to a successful experience in graduate school.[3] First, mentors transmit formal scientific knowledge and skills (see Reskin 1979). Second, mentors help their students understand and practice the "rules, values and ethics of the discipline, or what Phillips (1979) accurately called 'the lore and mysteries of the profession'" (Lyons, Scroggins, and Rule 1990, 279). And third, mentors praise and encourage their students to build confidence (Alleman, Cochran, and New 1984; Blank 1988). More recently, Johnson and Huwe (2003) identified additional functions of a mentor, listed comprehensively in Table 2.1.

Fischer and Zigmond (1998) have identified four areas of "survival skills" that graduate students must develop to succeed in graduate school and beyond. All four categories reflect information and skill-building that mentor are expected to provide to their students: (1) basic skills, including navigating and thriving in graduate school; (2) communication skills, including presenting and publishing research; (3) skills for finding employment; and (4) advanced skills (including teaching, writing funding proposals, and managing people). Central to all these skills is the core ability to act responsibly and professionally. No one faculty mentor has either the time or the ability to fulfill all of the various needs that students may require or expect. So students are encouraged to have multiple mentors for multiple purposes, offering information and expertise in different domains; this includes finding and using supportive, informative mentors among their peers.

*Peers likely have no supervisory or evaluative function* with other graduate students. Leadership and managing functions, yes. But supervisory and evaluative roles with their peers are appropriate only in extraordinary and controlled circumstances. So, as with secondary faculty mentors, students' boundaries with peers can extend beyond those with a faculty mentor who is also in the advisor/chair/sponsor role; peers can offer even more candid advice on a myriad of topics. One benefit of peer mentors over faculty members has been described in the context of students' community of practice (Wenger 2013). In writing support groups, peers have no authority or power over each other; to have an effect, they must negotiate and persuade their fellow writers: "The language of negotiation is simultaneously shaping the writer as other group members challenge her to defend her ideas, to respond authoritatively to questions about her work, and to position herself as a scholar. By responding … a writer is practicing for later engagement with the rest of her discipline" (Phillips 2012, 6). This safe

| Function | Provided by Faculty Mentor | Provided by Peer Mentor |
|---|:---:|:---:|
| Is accessible and available | x | x |
| Provides encouragement and support | x | x |
| Shares mutual trust and respect | x | x |
| Offers essential information and advice | x | x |
| Models professional traits and behaviors in intentional, visible ways | x | x |
| Provides introduction to colleagues in the discipline and profession | x | |
| Willing to self-disclose | x | x |
| Is selective based on match of important factors (research topic and approach, work style, temperament, expectations, etc.) | x | |
| Provides constructive feedback, evaluation, and appropriate challenge | x | x |
| Advocates for student in the program, field, discipline, profession | x | |
| Provides help with navigating program politics | x | x |
| Helps to provide exposure and visibility of the student's work | x | |
| Provides protection and defense from challenges by others | x | |
| Provides acculturation/socialization into the discipline/profession | x | |
| Encourages student's development from protégé to independent scholar and colleague | x | |

TABLE 2.1. Mentor functions. *Sources:* Adapted from Johnson and Huwe 2003, Kram 1985, and Kram and Isbella 1985.

environment with peers helps students to prepare for and transition into the role of independent scholar and researcher.

*Peers can discuss the "underground folklore" of the graduate program.* This information is seldom in writing, yet is as invaluable guide to graduate school success. As an assistant professor, one year away from my own graduate experience, I developed and gave my graduate students a one-page document called the "Underground Guide to Graduate School." It included all the tips and advice I wish I had known sooner than I did in graduate school—for example, "Submit your IRB protocol as soon as you can; even experienced researchers report that the approval process takes longer than expected." Each year my list grew longer as my graduate students added their own advice for new students. Within five years the underground guide had become a standard part of the department's graduate handbook (and retained its name for two decades to prompt students to read it). In addition, peers share advice on how to navigate departmental and institutional bureaucracy. And although information about faculty work styles, temperament, and eccentricities won't be codified in a departmental graduate student handbook ("Don't ask both Dick and Cheryl to be on your committee. They are close friends and always vote as a block. If one doesn't vote to accept your dissertation, it's guaranteed that the other won't either."), peers share information about departmental politics and personalities that faculty should never discuss with students.

*Peers can refer their fellow students to university and other resources* with greater ease, acceptance, and sometimes credibility. There are "dark sides" to mentoring. Sometimes there is a mismatch in work styles, expectations, or temperament. Some faculty neglect or exploit their students. Sometimes there are boundary violations, unwelcome attraction issues, or other conflicts. For students experiencing dysfunctional mentoring relationships, peers are often their first recourse for advice, support, and referral to campus resources (for example, the Ombuds office, Graduate School, or counseling center).

*There are reciprocal benefits in peer mentor relationships,* just as there are with faculty-student mentoring relationships. With peer mentoring, advanced students gain confidence by sharing their knowledge and experience with new graduate students; the former develop and refine their own skills as mentors in advance of completing their degree and beginning to mentor their own undergraduate and graduate students (or new colleagues).

To illustrate these roles and contributions of peers as mentors, I describe below some peer mentoring models that vary from institution to institution based on student needs and institutional resources. These programs focus on academic success, psychological support, and degree completion, with peer mentoring as a central component. I first describe programs with which I have direct experience; I also describe programs at Stanford and the University of Pennsylvania, both among the first of their kind among U.S. graduate schools and boasting documented effectiveness. Finally, I conclude with recommendations for developing programs that encourage peer support and mentoring for degree completion.

## Developing Future Faculty as Teacher-Scholars at the University of Tennessee

For me, the idea of peer mentoring for degree completion came about quite by accident. In 1996, my colleague at the University of Tennessee, Sky Huck, and I founded and directed for six years the Developing Future Faculty as Teacher-Scholars Program, an interdisciplinary, campus-wide mentoring program for master's and doctoral students who held Graduate Teaching Assistant and Graduate Teaching Associate positions. The former served as TAs working with a faculty member; the latter were responsible for their own classes. Each year in the mentoring program, we formed mentoring teams of six to ten graduate students, facilitated by a faculty member from a department different from that of any member of the team. The primary focus was on professional development and support for students' instructional roles and responsibilities. In addition, the faculty mentor for each team also facilitated discussions and provided resources to help students prepare for making fellowship applications and grant proposals, writing and publishing their research, making effective conference presentations, addressing ethical and legal issues in higher education, and entering the academic and professional job market. The program began with five primary objectives: (1) to improve the quality of instruction provided to undergraduates by graduate students; (2) to elevate the status of teaching in the minds of graduate students who would soon join faculty ranks; (3) to increase team-building skills among graduate students regardless of whether they would become faculty members or take positions in business, private research, NGOs, the government, or elsewhere; (4) to provide a year-long mechanism through which faculty who are recipients of the university's Outstanding Teaching Award can share their insights about teaching, learning, and student engagement with graduate students; and (5) to develop and share the model with other colleges and universities to adapt and use (Gaia, Corts, Tatum, and Allen 2003).

In our initial plans for the mentoring program, the goal had been to find outstanding faculty, with strong credentials in both teaching and research, who were known to be effective graduate mentors. They would guide their teams, share their knowledge and experience, and inspire their graduate students for future faculty and professional roles. What we never anticipated was the peer mentoring and support that developed among team members. Students shared their own knowledge and experiences about teaching undergraduate students, securing graduate funding, getting papers and conference presentations accepted, and resolving challenging situations with their advisors and mentors. When a faculty mentor had to miss a bimonthly team meeting, the students provided the necessary facilitation and leadership for their team. At the end of the first year, as we prepared to select another 100 or so students for the next year's mentoring program, students from our inaugural group began to ask, "Wait, are you cutting us loose? We want to continue in the program." So some of the teams continued to meet beyond their first year, facilitated by one or more of the group members. In addition, our plans for the subsequent years of the program included the co-facilitation of each team by a faculty member and a mentoring team member from the previous year. These Mentoring Fellows served as peer mentors and provided some of the strongest, most effective contributions to the program for its duration.[4]

### Dissertation- and Proposal-Writing Boot Camps at Columbia University

At Columbia University, beginning in 2008, doctoral students were invited to participate in an intensive week-long dissertation-writing boot camp.[5] Our boot camps were designed, using Simpson's (2013) later terminology, to be "outward-focused" rather than "inward-focused" activities. The former are part of a more comprehensive effort to provide writing support across programs and through multiple approaches, while the latter often "lack strategic planning and explicit discussion of program goals with students and university stakeholders" (Simpson 2013, 2).[6]

Our specific goals at Columbia were to

- help students identify and use effective strategies to become more productive writers;

- encourage students to develop a strategic plan that includes daily goals, effective writing habits and strategies, interim deadlines, and a target completion date;
- provide an environment conducive to writing, with space for individual writing and team meetings, with food and beverages throughout the day;
- create a writing support community for students that would continue to provide peer support and coaching beyond boot camp.

Twelve to fifteen students, each from a different doctoral program, were assigned to a boot-camp group. Throughout the year we offered three-day, five-day, six-day, and eight-day versions of the boot camp during semester, spring, and summer breaks. We provided distraction-free writing space from 9:00 AM to 5:00 PM, with team meetings, facilitated by the Graduate School associate dean for PhD programs, at the start and end of each day. During lunch we offered optional presentations by the facilitator and professional development staff. The day after the first boot camp ended, one of the participants emailed: "My entire team met today at an undisclosed location and wrote all day long." Another student wrote: "It was an incredible experience that continued for us once the official boot camp ended. We're gathering to write and use the good habits we learned in boot camp."

From both the formal assessment and anecdotal information, we knew that our boot camp had been successful. Students reported that while the advice and encouragement, guest speakers over lunch, and nonstop food buffet were all appreciated, the most valuable part of boot camp was the opportunity to be part of a writing community that continued the conversations and support. Following the first boot camp, we began to schedule weekly "Write-In" events, where students could return and write together as a group. As word spread, we opened the Write-Ins to all graduate students who wanted a quiet writing space, not just those who had participated in boot camp.

In designing and implementing our Columbia boot camps, we were helped by developers of two of the programs that preceded us and who also have reported outcome data. The University of Pennsylvania is credited with having the first dissertation boot camp, developed collaboratively by Penn's Graduate Student Center, Graduate School of Education, and Weingarten Learning Resources

Center in 2005. The creators describe their two-week event as one that "motivates students using intense, structured writing time" combining "components of structure, accountability, advising, comfort, and community" (Mastroieni and Cheung 2011, 4). Writing is mandatory from 9:00 in the morning to 1:00 each afternoon, with optional writing time until 5:00 PM. On the first day of the event, Learning Resources Center staff present a workshop with tips on time management and staying on schedule. Up to 25 students participate in each boot camp. A 2008 survey of Penn Boot Camp alums revealed that 70% of the "campers" felt the event helped them to meet their writing goals; the majority of respondents had a dissertation defense within three months of their boot camp participation (Mastroieni and Cheung 2011, 6).

Stanford University followed the University of Pennsylvania in 2008, with a Dissertation Boot Camp (DBC) focusing on "reinforcing the writing process through opening and closing workshops, scheduled follow-up discussions, individualized one-hour tutorials, daily writing logs, and multiple check-in points" (Lee and Golde n.d., 2). Stanford's DBC events are intended to help students write more and develop greater awareness of the writing process. A 2010 survey of former Stanford participants revealed that over 30% reported that their boot camp experience helped them finish their dissertation one or more quarters sooner than anticipated, which reflected actual dollars saved by the students in tuition or by their department in tuition and stipend costs. A majority of students also reported that their writing skills and practices had improved as a result of their DBC experience. The authors attributed the DBC's effectiveness to writing consultations that were available to students during DBC and to helping students understand the "collaborative and community-based" nature of writing rather than pursuing writing goals in isolation. Students benefit from multiple forms of collaboration, such as "conversations with advisors and writing consultants and feedback given by writing support groups, peers at conferences, reviewers in journals, and book editors," (Lee and Golde n.d., 4).

## Boot Camps for Dissertations, Theses, and Proposals at Cornell University

Cornell University began offering dissertation-, thesis-, and proposal-writing boot camps in Spring 2013. (Details about those events are included in Appendix A; Figure 2.1 below shows the daily schedule for a six-day event.) In addition to facilitators from the Graduate School, we utilize writing consultants, statistical consultants, and data/information management consultants who are available to meet with boot campers during the event. Concurrent with each on-site boot camp, we also offer a concurrent "Virtual Boot Camp" for students away from campus. And incorporating Stanford's model, there are also "After Dark Boot Camps" for students with lab, teaching, and employment responsibilities during the day.

Following each boot camp, there are regular follow-ups via email to offer support and encouragement. We host monthly "Re-Boots" that provide space, food, and additional support for the ongoing community of writers who attended boot camp. Coinciding with our first boot camp, the Graduate School began funding a Graduate Writing Consultant program through Cornell's Knight Institute for Writing in the Disciplines, which offers one-hour consultations (individual sessions or a series) by trained graduate peers. We also offer a daily Write-In (8:00 to 11:00 AM, Monday through Friday) at Cornell's Graduate Student Center so that students working on any writing project can write in a designated space with free coffee and tea. Finally, as part of this suite of writing support mechanisms for graduate students, we send out biweekly emails with writing strategies, advice, and encouragement to over 10,000 graduate student subscribers through our Productive Writer listserv.

## What the Organizers Learned at Boot Camp

From the initial Dissertation Boot Camp at Columbia to subsequent events at Cornell, I have come to recognize a number of outcomes, some expected and some unanticipated, about boot camp.

Students recognize and appreciate the *diversity of disciplines and programs* represented among, for instance, the mentoring teams at the University of Tennessee, where groups were populated with no more than one member from any one graduate program. For several reasons students find value in this. One rule of boot camp is, "What Happens at Boot Camp Stays at Boot Camp!" We promise confidentiality in our discussions. Facilitators and graduate student peers in the group agree at the outset that we will not report or repeat participants' comments to their advisor or program faculty. Students can speak candidly about their struggles, fears, or problems, even those concerning their advisor, and their comments

**Day One (Friday)**

| | |
|---|---|
| 7:30–9:00 | Breakfast available; optional writing time |
| 9:00–11:30 | Orientation and introductions |
| 11:30–12:30 | Lunch available |
| 11:30–3:30 | Writing time (Students are encouraged to write in 45- to 90-minute blocks without interrupting their writing.) |
| 3:30–4:00 | End-of-day check-in group meeting |
| 4:00–7:00 | Optional writing time |

**Day Two (Monday) and Day Three (Tuesday)**

| | |
|---|---|
| 7:30–9:00 | Breakfast available; optional writing time |
| 9:00–10:00 | Group meeting to share daily goal and any obstacles |
| 10:00–12:00 | Writing time |
| 12:00–1:00 | Lunch |
| 1:00–3:30 | Writing time |
| 3:30–4:00 | End-of-day check-in group meeting |
| 4:00–7:00 | Optional writing time |

**Day Four (Wednesday) and Day Five (Thursday)**

| | |
|---|---|
| 7:30–9:00 | Breakfast available; optional writing time |
| 9:00–9:30 | Group meeting to share daily goals and any obstacles (optional for individuals; facilitator included if/as needed) |
| 9:30–12:00 | Writing time |
| 12:00–1:00 | Lunch available (optional mini-lecture and discussion on related topic: managing stress, maximizing time and energy for greater productivity, tools for managing data and notes, thesis/dissertation submission guidelines) |
| 1:00–3:30 | Writing time |
| 3:30–4:00 | End of day check-in group meeting (optional for individual students; facilitator included if/as needed) |
| 4:00–7:00 | Optional writing time |

**Day Six (Friday)**

| | |
|---|---|
| 7:30–9:00 | Breakfast available; optional writing time |
| 9:00–9:30 | Group meeting to share daily goals and any challenges (if needed) |
| 9:30–12:00 | Writing time |
| 12:00–1:00 | Lunch (with celebratory cake and ice cream) Awarding of completion certificates and T-shirts |
| 1:00–2:00 | Group meeting to finalize plans for "Taking Boot Camp Home" (i.e., to maintain writing pairs, small group, or large group writing support beyond Boot Camp) |
| 2:00–5:00 | Optional writing time |

FIGURE 2.1. Six-day boot camp schedule.

remain within the group. Students also report their surprise at how many of their own experiences and struggles are shared by other students in different disciplines. Music and psychology students have the same anxiety about never finishing. Engineers and historians alike have advisors who don't make their expectations clear. Both art historians and anthropologists don't know when to stop writing. And almost none of the students anticipate how long getting feedback can take. At boot camp we frequently hear, "I didn't know anyone else had *my* problem." Many of the writing pairs or small groups that splinter into permanent writing communities maintain this interdisciplinary composition, for the support and confidentiality that non-departmental peers provide.

Another kind of diversity among the team members is that students are at different stages of dissertation writing. With more resources we might have created different events for students at the beginning, middle, or close to the end of writing. As it turned out, students benefit from this mix. Students at the beginning of writing learn from their more experienced peers, who discover they have advice to share, which serves as a confidence-booster.

And finally, students appreciate the opportunity to socialize, beyond boot camp and apart from their academic writing, with peers outside their graduate programs. When students are in the final months or years of their degree program, they are hesitant to be seen socializing by their program peers. Taking time away from research and writing with boot camp peers helps students to maintain much needed life-work balance.

Students report that the best part of boot camp is what happens after the intensive experience ends. Five- or six-day events seem to provide the optimal amount of time for students to really bond as a *support group and writing community*. I usually see this group formation and bonding by day three or four in the boot camps. In the most recent session, I saw the supportive community emerge within the first few hours. As students were introducing themselves, giving a two-minute presentation of their research and describing the obstacles and challenges they face, one student began to describe her struggles with her dissertation writing and conflicts with her advisor. After a few minutes of listening to her anguished description of her lack of progress, one of the other students in her group said, "We've got this. We'll help you get through this. We'll find a way out of this for you." (At the end of the boot camp, the congratulatory cake had a new inscription: We've got this!)

Our first Dissertation Boot Camp at Columbia University taught us the value of ongoing *communal writing space* for graduate students. We began to reserve a room for "Write-Ins," advertised first to our boot camp alums. But some students, because of work schedules or family commitments, were never able to attend a week-long event, so we soon invited the entire graduate student population to join the Write-In community. For these come-and-go sessions, we asked students to sign in with their name and writing goals. On their way out, they indicated how long they wrote and whether they accomplished their goals. We wanted this simple sign-in/sign-out procedure to create accountability to this ad hoc writing community and underscore their commitment to writing and degree completion.

*Multiple approaches and models can be effective.* Some elements of boot camp are difficult to plan for and some student needs can't be anticipated. In some boot camp models, space is reserved, food is provided, and students write for the duration of the event. Other models engage campus writing consultants to meet with participants during the event; consultants work with participants on organization, thesis statements, shaping arguments, presenting evidence, sentence structure, voice and style, and editing strategies. At Cornell, we also schedule time for statistical consultants and for data/information management specialists to come to our events and meet with students by their request. And on the last day, in a session we call "Taking Boot Camp Home," students commit to a writing schedule and strategies, including continuing to write with a virtual or in-person writing buddy or group as they work to complete their thesis or dissertation.

*Careful consideration should be given to the size of the group.* We try to admit as many students as possible to our events, yet eight to twelve students seems to be the optimal group size to allow introductions on the first day and sharing of goals, strategies, and obstacles during the team meetings. Maria Gardiner at Flinders University in Australia hosts a wonderful two-day writing productivity program and deals with the issue of group size by having half of the students introduce themselves, their research, and their challenges on the first day, while the others introduce themselves on the second day. Although the purposes of this event are somewhat different from a week-long boot camp, at Cornell we have divided a group of 20 into two groups of 10 and staggered the start times, one in the morning and one in the afternoon; this works well to support bonding and group formation, insofar as it promotes an authentic rather than a hurried and obligatory exchange.

*A skilled facilitator contributes to the development of the peer community.* The facilitator welcomes the group of boot camp participants by email prior to the start of the event. These messages set expectations, explain some of the logistics, and, for our events, prompt students to begin a productivity and reflection log at least a week before the start of boot camp. During the event, the facilitator welcomes participants, guides the introductions and orientation to the program, and continues to facilitate the daily goal-setting and check-in meetings, at least through the second or third day. The facilitator then checks with the group members to decide when they are ready to meet, guide, and support each other in their group times without the facilitator's help.

Among the Graduate Schools hosting boot camps, some use staff from the Graduate School or writing center as facilitators. In some cases facilitation teams include two or more assistant/associate deans, writing instructors, and consultants. In my experience as facilitator, I draw heavily on my 20 years as a faculty member advising and supervising graduate students as well as what I have learned from students across dozens and dozens of disciplines and programs in my role as a graduate school associate dean for 15 years. And selfishly, I enjoy boot camp for many reasons, not the least is that each boot camp is like a six-day focus group: I learn a great deal about students' experiences as graduate students as well as about the careful and effective mentoring by our faculty.

At Cornell we have recently begun to invite advanced graduate student "alumni" of previous boot camps to facilitate one of the boot camp groups (usually the proposal- or thesis-writing students). Students have been both enthusiastic and effective in their facilitator role. There are, of course, pros and cons to using faculty, administrators, and students. It can be an enormous time commitment for all. And because students are paid or given an honorarium for their time (faculty and administrators are "volunteers"), advanced students create an extra expense—though one that is well worth the cost, because students identify with their peer-facilitator, and advanced students are developing and using valuable skills in managing groups, on-the-spot problem-solving, and providing appropriate encouragement and support for (sometimes) struggling students. I believe students can feel intimidated by or be less candid with faculty than with Graduate School staff or other students;

however, when Cornell's Director of Graduate Studies in History hosted a semester-break boot camp for students last year, and invited faculty to participate and write for the week along with the doctoral students, the faculty "jumped right in" to share their struggles and obstacles in the group meetings. And often the students were the ones offering their advice and support to the faculty!

While deciding who has the expertise and availability to facilitate, consider other important qualities of effective facilitators. First and foremost, facilitators "think on their feet." When students describe their challenges, the facilitator responds with a solution or strategy. "I find that what works for many students is...." "How do you think your advisor would respond if you...?" "Here's a strategy to try; if it works for you, make it a habit." When students express fear or anxiety, facilitators are prepared with stress-reducing suggestions or referrals to campus resources. This dialogue will continue throughout boot camp, and the facilitator's ability to help students move forward in the face of anxieties and other obstacles is one of the most critical, and daunting, responsibilities. Simultaneously, effective facilitators are able to hold back when needed and instead of offering advice, ask, "Does someone have a strategy to suggest or a similar experience to share? What works for some of you?"

Different institutions use various boot camp models (briefly described in Appendix B), with shared goals: to create intellectual and psychological support within a peer-writing community to promote degree completion. Writing boot camps provide much-needed community-building and, even more, an opportunity for graduate students to reflect on their skills and identity as writers and scholars. We emphasize that being the *authors* of their dissertations gives them the *authority* to critique, argue, and write with a confidence perhaps not heretofore available or possible for them. And we provide a set of strategies to develop their confidence and skills as both authors and scholars.

There are positive outcomes, both planned and unplanned, at boot camp. Each event provides new information for the planners that can be incorporated into future events, resources, and training. Our boot camps at both Columbia and Cornell have prompted individual academic programs to create writing space and communities for their own students. For example, as mentioned above, Cornell's History program started a winter break boot camp for history and anthropology doctoral students (the two programs share the same building). These events, both campus-wide and program-specific, build writing and support communities, offer training in writing and other skills needed for successful academic and other professional careers, and encourage and develop peer mentors to both competently and confidently serve as sources of academic and psychological support for fellow graduate students.

**Notes**

1. The author wishes to thank vice provost and dean of the Graduate School Barbara Knuth at Cornell University, former GSAS dean Henry Pinkham at Columbia University, and former chancellor Bill Snyder, former provost John Peters, and former dean of the Graduate School C. W. Minkel at the University of Tennessee for their enthusiastic support and engagement in our mentoring and boot camp programs at their respective institutions.

2. Throughout the chapter I used the term *graduate student* to refer to both graduate and professional students, i.e., those in doctoral, research master's, and non-research master's and other professional programs.

3. The phrase "peculiar intimacy" is from Phillips 1979.

4. A detailed guide to program elements and outcomes can be found in Gaia et al. 2003, and in Allen, forthcoming.

5. Following our second boot camp, during which one of the humanities doctoral students announced, "I wish I had known all this when I was writing my dissertation proposal three years ago," we added proposal-writing boot camps for students at the proposal/prospectus stage.

6. Lee and Golde (2013) have proposed a comparable model of "Writing Process" as opposed to "Just Write" events. In the former, students have the opportunity to consider their writing process, identify and use effective strategies, and overcome the challenges that delay progress in conversation with fellow boot campers, facilitators, and writing consultants. "Just Write" events, conversely, support students' writing productivity by providing space, food, and structured time. Other support, such as writing consultants, presentations on writing topics, and encouragement to reflect on the writing process, is minimal.

**Works Cited**

Alleman, E., J. Cochran, and I. New. 1984. "Enriching Mentoring Relationships." *Personnel and Guidance Journal* 62:329–32.

Allen, J. forthcoming. *The New Faculty and Graduate Mentor.* Sterling, VA: Stylus Publishing.

Blank, M. A. 1988. "Mentoring and the Process of Becoming a Teacher." PhD diss., University of Tennessee, Knoxville.

Fischer, B., and M. Zigmond. 1998. "Survival Skills for Graduate School and Beyond." *New Directions for Higher Education* 101: 29–40.

Gaia, C., D. Corts, H. Tatum, and J. Allen. 2003. "The GTA Mentoring Program: An Interdisciplinary Approach to Developing Future Faculty as Teacher-Scholars." *College Teaching* 51 (2): 61–65.

Johnson, W. B., and J. Huwe. 2003. *Getting Mentored in Graduate School.* Washington, DC: American Psychological Association.

Kram, K. E. 1985. *Mentoring at Work: Developmental Relationships in Organizational Life.* Glenview, IL: Scott Foresman.

Kram, K. E., and L. A. Isbella. 1985. "Mentoring Alternatives: The Role of Peer Relationships in Career Development." *Academy of Management Journal* 28:110–32.

Lee, S., and C. Golde. 2013. "Completing the Dissertation and Beyond: Writing Centers and Dissertation Boot Camps." *Writing Lab Newsletter* 37 (7–8): 1–6. https://writinglabnewsletter.org/archives/v37/37.7-8.pdf.

Lee, S., and C. Golde. n.d. *Starting an Effective Dissertation Writing Group: Stanford University Hume Writing Center Graduate School Workshop.* Palo Alto, CA: Stanford University.

Mastroieni, A., and D. Cheung. 2011. "The Few, the Proud, the Finished: Dissertation Boot Camp as a Model for Doctoral Student Support." *NASPA Knowledge Communities*, Fall, 4–6.

National Academy of Sciences. 1997. *Adviser, Teacher, Role Model, Friend: On Being a Mentor.* Washington, DC: The National Academies Press.

Nicoloff, L., and L. Forrest. 1998. "Gender Issues in Research and Publication." *Journal of College Student Development* 29 (6), 521–28.

Lyons, W., D. Scroggins, and P. B. Rule. 1990. "The Mentor in Graduate Education." *Studies in Higher Education* 15 (3): 277–85.

Phillips, G. M. 1979. "The Peculiar Intimacy: A Conservative View." *Communication Education* 28:339–45.

Phillips, T. 2012. "Graduate Writing Groups: Shaping Writing and Writers from Student to Scholar." *Praxis* 10 (1): 1–7.

Reskin, G. R. 1979. "Academic Sponsorship and Scientists' Careers." *Sociology of Education* 52:129–46.

Simpson, S. 2013. "Building for Sustainability: Dissertation Boot Camp as a Nexus of Graduate Writing Support." *Praxis* 10 (2). http://projects.uwc.utexas.edu/praxis/index.html/index.php/praxis/article/view/129/pdf.

Ulke-Steiner, B. Kurtz-Costes, and C. R. Kinlaw. 2000. "Doctoral Student Experiences in Gender-balanced and Male-dominated Graduate Programs." *Journal of Educational Psychology* 92: 296–307.

Wenger, E. 2013. "Communities of Practice: A Brief Introduction." http://wenger-trayner.com/theory.

**APPENDIX A: Creating, Implementing, and Evaluating Boot Camp**

**Preparing for Boot Camp**

Several months before the start of boot camp, identify appropriate space. The environment should include writing space with one or two students per table. (We prefer tables that can accommodate two students; these pairs often end up continuing as writing buddies, virtually or in person, after boot camp ends.) Comfortable chairs can't be overrated. At one of our boot camps, students suggested we replace the end-of-event T-shirt with a seat cushion and suggested that, instead of the "I Survived Dissertation Boot Camp" slogan on the shirt, it would not be inappropriate to embroider the seat cushions with "Keep Your Butt in this Seat and Write!" (We agreed with the need for the cushions; we remain undecided about the proposed slogan.) Space is needed for group meetings of 12 to 15 students, plus facilitator(s). There also should be space for food service (breakfast and lunch, as well as refreshments throughout the day). Some students prefer to work through meals; they get their food and return to their table to continue to write. Other students want the break for eating and socializing. (It's only during these breaks that students are allowed to use phones and check email.) For about half the days of boot camp, we schedule a group lunch and offer a 20- to 30-minute presentation and discussion on a pertinent topic, such as developing editing skills, working with advisors, managing time, or staying healthy. We include a visit from the thesis/dissertation manager or a reference librarian who talks about information management tools relevant to students' work. These lunchtime group meetings are optional; students may also use the time to write.

In addition to individual work and group meeting spaces, and space for buffet-style food service, we created a "Stress-Free Zone" with "Re-charge Stations" to our most recent boot camp. The Zone was simply a corner of the room that included de-stressing activities: Play-Doh, crayons and drawing pencils, small hand weights, and craft materials. And because there is evidence that people who are appreciative or grateful for something or someone are more resilient and healthy, we provided cards, envelopes, and postage to encourage our boot campers to write a thank-you note during their break from writing. Posted signs indicated, "No Stressful Conversations Here," "Just Breathe," and "Relax ... Take a Break." Some students found the Stress-Free Zone very helpful. (We added the Zone when, during the initial orientation, as students were talking about the struggles and challenges they were facing, the student seated next to me leaned in and whispered, "Listening to this is making me so anxious, I think I'm going to throw up.")

Along with the space considerations, we include amenities and accessories ranging from the essential to the thoughtful. Only once has our space included enough electrical outlets, so determine in advance if you'll need to bring extension/surge-protector cords. An environment where tables can be placed against the walls, rather in the middle of the room, helps to avoid tripping hazards from the maze of cords. We provide table tents preprinted with students' names and graduate programs; these remain in place to identify students' work space for the week. We place the name placards in dollar-store picture frames; students can keep the frames and insert their end-of-event certificate when boot camp concludes. And although we bring in breakfast and lunch each day, we also keep a large bowl of (mostly) healthy snacks on hand with several beverage choices throughout the day. An extra thoughtful touch is the presence of a massage therapist who gives hand and neck massages midway through the event (boot camp becomes known as Dissertation Spa on that day).

## Publicizing Boot Camp and Soliciting Applications

Through our Graduate School website (https://www.gradschool.cornell.edu/thesis-and-dissertation/cornell-proposal-thesis-and-dissertation-writing-boot-camps) and weekly email events calendar, we announce upcoming boot camp dates and the application deadline. After the first boot camp, word spread as students encouraged their colleagues, and faculty encouraged their students, to attend. In reviewing applications, we are especially interested in identifying students who are ready to begin writing or are already in the writing stage of their dissertation. A surprising number of students who apply are within a month or two of their deadline to submit a complete draft to their advisors or committees. As mentioned earlier, these students add "stage" diversity and are among the most highly motivated of our boot campers. We try to accommodate everyone who applies, including creating separate teams of 10 to 12 and staggering the start time or day; different groups work in the same space, share meals, and socialize during breaks as one large group.

At least a month before the event, we let participants know they have been selected to participate. We send logistical details (dates, times, and location), including the ground rules: We expect students to attend each day, to attend all required team meetings (usually once in the morning and again in the afternoon), and to submit paperwork (brief assignments, such as daily goals and progress) each day. We also ask participants to begin keeping a writing log at least a week before the start of boot camp, recording on a log sheet we provide their daily goals, daily word count, and thoughts about their writing process and progress as well as any obstacles they encountered. We let participants know that breakfast, lunch, and snacks will be provided, including vegetarian options, and that they are welcome to bring their own food as well. Following the practice at the University of Pennsylvania, we have experimented with requiring a deposit to reserve a spot in boot camp. At Columbia University we asked students to give us a $50 check in a sealed envelope, which we held. If students completed Boot Camp, we returned the sealed envelope. (Organizers at Penn now tell students that their account will be charged the deposit amount if they fail to complete boot camp.) At Cornell we don't charge a deposit; we keep a wait list in case someone has to drop out prior to the start of boot camp, so we always have a full cohort of at least 12 in each group.

### Boot Camp Week

Students consistently report that the best schedule involves starting boot camp on a Friday. The Friday introduction and orientation provides students with a good sense of what will be expected of them in their upcoming intensive week. They use the weekend to find and organize needed articles and books for their writing goals for the subsequent five days.

The first half-day of boot camp begins with the facilitator describing the purpose and goals of boot camp, previewing the week's schedule, and sharing expectations for students' engagement and commitment to their writing, progress, and peers. Students introduce themselves in three to five minutes (name, program, point in program, schedule for completion, and so forth). After this round of introductions, and following a short break (if needed), the facilitator asks students, one by one, to announce their writing goal for the day. Students also write their daily goal on an easel to make them public. The facilitator also invites students to share any obstacle or challenge they have encountered with their writing or progress to completion. The facilitator suggests strategies to address and overcome the obstacle (a tip sheet listing 30 such strategies, "The Boot Camp Way," is available from the author). After this session—two to three hours, depending on the size and engagement of the group—students are free to write.

Our daily schedule is shown in Figure 2.1 above. The groups proceed through the week based on individual and team needs. After the first day there is a daily minimum of four hours of writing, with extended optional hours each day. Most students write during all the available optional sessions. By the third day, groups decide how many group meetings each day they need (zero, one, or two) and whether the facilitator is needed to meet with them. Most often, groups choose to meet once a day and invite the facilitator to join them. On the last day, several important things happen. Cake and ice cream are served with lunch, to celebrate the productive week. Students are awarded certificates and T-shirts ("I Write Therefore I Finish" in Latin). Very important is the last group meeting, in which students complete a "Strategic Plan for Taking Boot Camp Home" and commit to maintain their good writing habits and progress, using their peers for support and as resources. This support can take any of several forms. For example, our first boot camp of 14 participants (four of whom have graduated) includes a pair who continue to meet in a department office to write together three days a week. Another group of three meets every Friday afternoon, with one of them sharing pages in advance and then discussing what is working, or not, about his or her writing process; the other two provide feedback on the content.

### Assessing Boot Camp Effectiveness

We evaluate our boot camp planning and implementation in several ways. Midway through boot camp we offer a one-page "taking stock" opportunity for students to let us know (anonymously) what is working and not working for them during boot camp. We request more comprehensive feedback at the end of the event. As part of the application, we ask students to share their expectations for boot camp and indicate the degree to which they struggle with setting and meeting deadlines, overcoming procrastination or perfectionistic tendencies, staying motivated, avoiding writer's block, and getting timely and useful feedback on their writing. We tailor a final evaluation form using the expectations the students conveyed in the application. We also ask students to indicate (on a Likert scale) which aspects of boot camp were most effective in helping them to manage or overcome the challenges above (setting and meeting deadlines, overcoming procrastination, etc.) The final evaluation also asks students to describe changes in their writing approach, habits and attitudes that they believe will support their writing and degree completion. This instrument is distributed on the final day of the event, and most students complete it thoroughly. We then send it electronically to students a month later, asking if they have additional insights and feedback to share as they have tried "to take boot camp home" and continue their writing productivity and accomplishments.

### APPENDIX B: Dissertation-Writing Boot Camps and Retreats

*Boston College, Office of Graduate Student Life* (since 2011)
  http://www.bc.edu/content/bc/offices/gsc/about/programs/
  dissertation-boot-camp.html

Dissertation Boot Camp at Boston College is a three-day event each semester for ten doctoral students. The event includes "intense, focused writing time" with "structure and motivation to overcome typical roadblocks in the dissertation process."

*Claremont Graduate University, Writing Center* (since 2007)
  http://www.cgu.edu/pages/8913.asp

Claremont offers weekend events once a month, with all-day "quiet space with no distractions or interruptions" as a "writing retreat for graduate students who must balance their dissertation writing with the demands of home and work." Claremont also offers a week-long boot camp with "guest faculty, peer speakers, and 35 hours of quiet writing time."

*Lehigh University, Graduate Life Office* (since 2008)
  http://gradlife.web.lehigh.edu/programs/boot-camp

Lehigh offers a two-day (weekend), "entirely distraction-free" event for up to 25 students. The $25 cost includes "four meals, a refocusing yoga exercise, chair massages to reduce stress, and all supplies." A 10-minute motivational speech on the first morning is designed to increase students' focus and productivity.

*Loyola University Chicago, Graduate School* (since 2008)
  http://www.luc.edu/gradschool/pcap/dissertationbootcamp/

Loyola offers two week-long sessions each summer for doctoral students. The two facilitators, a faculty member and an assistant dean, "coach Ph.D. candidates on strategies for writing success, offer tales from those who made it to the other side ... and support hard work and time devoted to writing."

*New Mexico Institute of Mining and Technology, Writing Center* (since 2011)
  http://www.nmt.edu/academic-affairs-section-list/344-title-v-ppoha/4586-boot-camp

New Mexico Tech offers a week-long event, twice a year, for 12 students writing their theses or dissertations. Coffee and snacks are provided, as well as a "focused writing environment with an element of peer pressure [that] motivates better than writing alone."

*Northwestern University, Graduate School and Writing Center* (since 2011) http://www.tgs.northwestern.edu/documents/professional-development/Boot_Camp_CFP_2012_December.pdf

Northwestern offers a two-week event with "required writing from 9:00 AM to 1:00 PM, optional lunchtime workshops, and optional individual writing consultations."

*Princeton University, Writing Center* (since 2009)
http://www.princeton.edu/writing/university/graduate/

Princeton provides "quiet space and the camaraderie of a writer's community" that includes workshops and debriefing sessions for doctoral students.

*Stanford University, Writing Center* (since 2008)
https://undergrad.stanford.edu/tutoring-support/hume-center/writing/graduate-students/dissertation-boot-camp

Stanford offers 10-day events (four hours per day) for up to 12 students working on a dissertation, thesis, or other academic writing project. The program helps them "learn to write more productively and often to produce better writing" by providing space, routine, peer motivation, and writing consultants. Stanford also offers "After Dark" (5:00 to 9:00 PM) and "Before Dawn" (7:00 to 11:00 AM) versions of their boot camps.

*University of Chicago, Graduate School* (since 2011)
http://grad.uchicago.edu/training_support/dissertation_writing_skills/dissertation_write_in/

Chicago's Dissertation Write-Ins are five-day workshops for up to 20 graduate students, "to help break through personal procrastination habits and make good progress on writing." Participants write four hours a day with an additional three hours of optional writing time. During spring break there is a concurrent Thesis Write-In for master's students.

*University of North Carolina at Chapel Hill, Writing Center* (since 2010)
http://writingcenter.unc.edu/dissertation-boot-camp-resources/

UNC–Chapel Hill offers a week-long event (9:00 AM to 1:00 PM) to help students "set writing goals, practice disciplined writing habits, learn new strategies, and connect with other dissertation writers."

The cost to students is $20.

*University of Pennsylvania, Graduate Student Center* (since 2006)
   http://dissertationbootcampnetwork.wordpress.com/dissertation-bootcamps/

University of Pennsylvania's boot camp, credited as the first in the nation, "was developed to help students progress through the difficult writing stages of the dissertation process." The biannual, two-week long events for up to 20 students provide "structure and motivation to overcome typical roadblocks in the dissertation process."

*University of Wisconsin, Graduate School and Writing Center* (since 2011)
   http://grad.wisc.edu/pd/dissertation/bootcamp

The University of Wisconsin offers a week-long event for 18 students selected on the basis of their "anticipated time to degree completion, the importance of boot camp at stage of project, and broad disciplinary representation." (The first boot camp drew 84 applications.) The event includes "structured writing time for at least six hours a day, one-to-one conferences, daily writing exercises, and optional lunchtime workshops."

*West Virginia University, Writing Center* (since 2011)
   http://tlcommons.wvu.edu/GraduateAcademy/WritingAndResearch/

West Virginia University offers two one-week events each summer, one for students in the humanities and social sciences and another for students in the physical/life sciences and engineering. The program "combines workshops, peer review, individual consultations, and dedicated writing time."

# Subject Matter *Plus*: Mentoring for Nonacademic Careers

*Paula Chambers*

If you are a faculty member advising doctoral students and/or postdocs, the fact that you picked up this book and turned to this chapter reflects well on you, because it indicates that you are interested in being a better mentor to your advisees, and even willing to consider developing your mentoring skills around the sometimes difficult, sensitive issue of nonacademic careers. You are exactly the person for whom this chapter was written. Others may also benefit—faculty development professionals in particular may want to recommend it to advisors—but this chapter is written for faculty members who would like to be better equipped to mentor doctoral students and postdocs around nonacademic careers and to support them towards a wider range of possible outcomes.

Most professors do not even attempt to tackle nonacademic careers in their mentoring. And candidly, why should they? There are compelling institutional reasons not to. Most students in doctoral programs are there because they want academic careers. As a career academic yourself, you know firsthand how much effort, persistence, and round-the-clock dedication it takes to build such a career. You (and I too) believe deeply in the academic enterprise, in the merit of your research, and in the importance of developing quality intellectual talent to nourish your discipline into the future. And you are expected to enhance the reputation and ranking of your department and institution by helping your students get placed into full-time faculty positions. Given those imperatives, one might reasonably question the wisdom of taking on the nonacademic careers piece at all. Even those who are eager to take it on often feel ill-prepared.

49

You probably don't have much nonacademic work experience yourself, and as a responsible intellectual, you have a keen appreciation for expertise, and understandably gravitate towards subject areas where you feel fairly confident in your knowledge. You imagine there must be careers outside the academy where your students' knowledge and abilities would be welcomed, but the specifics are elusive. There are many barriers.

Thankfully, you do not have to know everything about nonacademic careers in order to be a good mentor in this area. You do not have to use special nomenclature, have hordes of contacts in business and industry, know how to write a winning nonacademic résumé, or be able to reel off an exhaustive list of all possible nonacademic careers for PhDs in your discipline. Being a good mentor in this area is not about being a subject matter expert at all. It is mainly about being a genuine supporter of student well-being and an open-minded facilitator of forward motion toward diverse career goals.

You do not even have to be the sole or main source of mentoring for your advisees. The notion that one person should, or even *can*, serve as a one-stop shop for all-inclusive mentoring is considered preposterous anywhere but inside the academy. As one graduate student recently wrote, "Other people (non-PhDs) also don't have someone holding their hand when they apply for jobs, and get their ideas and advice from multiple sources, rather than from just one person (career services, family members, friends, etc.). You just can't expect there to be one person 'mentoring' you—this model only exists in academia, and frankly, I'm not sure it's such a great model there either!"[1]

So relax. You do not have to be perfect, or master a giant corpus of new knowledge, or assume total responsibility for your advisees' careers. All you have to do is learn a little new information and make a few adjustments in your mentoring. How much you want to learn and how many adjustments you are willing to make is up to you.

This chapter will help in the following ways. It opens with reflections on the question of who is responsible for providing graduate students with nonacademic professional development. Then I will describe the value of PhD skills outside the academy and point out specific skill sets that employers have suggested as recommended additions. Finally, I will give you practical strategies for how to become a better mentor in this area, describing each adjustment you might consider making. You will learn how to

- manage the messages you send, often inadvertently, to your advisees about career
- assess the "career climate" of your department
- make referrals to available resources
- support a broadening of knowledge and skills
- learn what to say to nonacademic employers.

For the record, when I speak of "PhDs," I mean to include ABDs as well, those who leave their programs without completing their dissertations. The terms "professors," "faculty," and "advisors" are used interchangeably and refer to any faculty member or researcher who has direct advisory or supervisory relationships with doctoral students and/or postdocs, and "advisees" is intended to include both students and postdocs. The focus of this chapter is on the doctoral advisor-advisee relationship in the research disciplines, but some of the guidelines presented here may be helpful for those advising master's students as well, and possibly for faculty in professional doctoral programs whose relatively insular, academically oriented cultures have much in common with programs in the research disciplines (e.g., Doctor of Divinity and Doctor of Management programs).

## Who Is Responsible?

You hardly need reminding about the state of the academic job market. Some disciplines are faring better than others, but overall, the number of tenure-track lines is decreasing and has been for a long time. Depending on which source you are consulting, 50–75% of all college and university teaching is now done by adjuncts. Humanities and social science PhDs in particular toil for years in contingent positions, many eventually leaving the field in despair because of low pay and lack of benefits or job insecurity. The persistent few who adjunct for a decade or more without ever getting on the tenure track do so at tremendous cost to themselves and their families, as they pass up opportunities to earn more income and benefits elsewhere. On the STEM side, it is common nowadays for a PhD to do two, three, even four postdocs, enduring years of low pay, low status, and poor working conditions with no assurance that they have a real shot at the academic jobs they want.

In short: the chances are high that most of your graduate students and postdocs, even the best and brightest, will end up outside the academy whether they want to or not.

Some argue that PhD programs should admit fewer students, to bring supply more in line with demand in the academic job market. I take the position that focusing exclusively on reducing doctoral admissions as the silver-bullet solution basically reduces doctoral education to high-class vocational ed. Getting a PhD is a rare and often beautiful experience that, globally speaking, very few are privileged to receive. It puts the student on the leading edge of what humans know and want to know. It makes the student an expert on a particular subject of interest. It is a transformative, life-changing experience, the significance of which cannot be reduced solely to the narrow, utilitarian agenda of "getting an academic job"—even though it is also true that the doctoral experience comes at a definite economic cost. Doctoral education should be accessible to as many who desire it as possible—yet there should also be *transparency* about likely employment outcomes afterward. Students who are embarking on doctoral study solely so they can be professors need to be counseled that the odds of that are slim. And frankly, drastic reduction in PhD student population is highly unlikely even if it *were* the answer. People tend to believe that if some education is good, more must be better, therefore *any* amount of education will be worth the investment because it will surely lead to greater employability and earning power. Even people who do not believe that, or do not think in those terms, or who *were* given clear job market information before enrolling, may well enroll anyway because they want the doctoral experience and want a *break* from thinking about career. (That was the case with me. I did not investigate the employment landscape for PhDs prior to entering my program because that was the last thing on my mind. I dove into doctoral study in order to *withdraw* from the working world, to forget all about jobs and careers and enjoy seven or eight blissful years of studying the subject I loved, hopefully with a professor job waiting for me at the end, but that outcome was so comfortably far-off that it did not beg scrutiny.) Consequently, my position is, reduce admissions if you must, but meanwhile, help those who are already in the system by providing them with at least some of the help they want and need.

Is it the department's bailiwick to do this? Which units on campus should provide graduate students with nonacademic career information and guidance? These questions are a matter of national debate within the graduate education community (e.g., at the Council of Graduate Schools' meetings, which I have attended every year since 2009). The ball of perceived responsibility bounces in these conversations between PhD-granting departments, the Career Center, the Graduate School, and occasionally elsewhere (postdoc office, library, alumni association). Many Career Centers and Graduate Schools have taken the issue to heart and are creating entirely new staff positions that have graduate student professional development as one responsibility or even as the primary responsibility. The recently retired president of the Council of Graduate Schools (CGS), Debra Stewart, in one of her last speeches in office, urged her members to take broader career preparation very seriously, because the accountability pressures that are now being brought to bear on undergraduate education "are *coming* to graduation education, no doubt about it."[2]

Since the graduate dean community is taking the issue so seriously now, it may be tempting for you, the faculty member, to view that as "enough" and locate the responsibility outside the department, certainly outside the offices of individual professors. But departments and programs are under increasing pressure to be part of the solution. Disciplinary associations are releasing statements about the need for doctoral-granting departments to do more to prepare students to compete for jobs that actually exist, and are also improving their own efforts in that regard. And, with funding from the Mellon Foundation, CGS recently launched a feasibility study focusing on tracking PhD career pathways *program by program*.[3] Accountability for PhD employment outcomes is indeed "coming" to doctoral programs.

Students and postdocs themselves feel very strongly that departments and faculty hold some responsibility. Ideas vary about exactly what that responsibility consists of, but the prevailing sentiment among advisees is that departments and faculty are at least somewhat responsible, because they have the most contact with the student and therefore the greatest impact, the greatest opportunity to make a positive difference. I agree. That is why it is so good that you are reading this chapter.

### The Value of PhD Skills Outside the Academy

The very things you spend your days conveying to students and postdocs—subject matter knowledge, research methods, teaching, writing, critical thinking, problem solving, etc.—are valued outside the academy to some degree or other in all employment sectors. Though only a small minority of nonacademic jobs require a doctoral degree, many nonacademic fields will happily absorb the skills and knowledge your advisees are developing, and the high-octane learning ability that most PhDs have is itself a major asset, allowing PhDs to absorb information quickly, develop clever solutions to problems and thus advance promptly in their post-academic careers, once they get started.

Subject matter aside, most PhDs graduate with the following skills, more or less, depending on the exact nature of their training, interests, and talents:

- research methods
- critical thinking
- analysis/synthesis
- problem identification
- information-gathering from primary and secondary sources
- written and oral communication
- content and curriculum development
- assessment/evaluation
- rapid learning

These skills are all extremely useful in a wide variety of post-academic careers. The odds are excellent that a person with these skills will make a discernible positive impact on whatever they are involved with.

If it troubles you to think of academic training being used in so many unknown contexts, think of it this way: by consigning the stuff you are teaching solely to the academic world, you are selling it short. The wide applicability of PhD skills is *the good news*. It supports the continuation of doctoral education without the imperative to tie the number of admissions to the number of tenure-track lines being created. Even if you feel that doctoral admissions *should* be limited, until the academy achieves that, it owes to those who have already been admitted a broader vision of their futures and of the value of the programs in which they have enrolled. It owes them a sense of meaning in their accomplishment, and it owes them a helping hand toward getting situated afterwards.

Though I would never suggest that employers should dictate the content or purpose of doctoral education—an obviously terrible idea—I do gently suggest that their voices should at least be heard when they make requests. Some of the things employers are asking for are arguably quite compatible with the learning and professional development goals of doctoral education. In April 2012, CGS released a groundbreaking report titled "Pathways Through Graduate School and Into Careers" (http://pathwaysreport.org), one finding of which was that employers feel PhDs need more of the following skills:

- teamwork
- project management
- creating and delivering oral presentations
- delivering outcomes on time and on budget
- communicating with lay audiences

None of that, in my opinion, runs counter to the traditional goals of doctoral education. What on earth could be bad, for example, about students working in teams at various points in their pro-grams—such as on class assignments, service projects, even perhaps dissertation research (collaboration being already common in STEM dissertation research)? Which academic projects could *not* stand to be better managed? Could there be an idea or a concept that is valuable in print but somehow not worth communicating orally? Is on-time delivery of research results, chapter drafts, and other scholarly work-products somehow antithetical to the academic enterprise? And even in the most specialized, obscure line of research inquiry, is there really *nothing* that can be presented engagingly to lay audiences?

Moreover, how would those skills not be helpful even in an *academic* career?

Another window on what employers want is provided by labor market information companies that analyze the content of nonaca-demic job postings and identify patterns and trends. One such company, Burning Glass Technologies (founded by PhDs, I might add), recently looked at the employability of college graduates with liberal arts degrees and found that demonstrated experience in *any* of the following eight skill domains greatly enhances the employability of those graduates:

- marketing
- sales
- social media
- graphic design
- data analysis
- computer programming
- IT networking
- business knowledge

Liberal arts graduates with even *one* of those skills alongside their academic degrees were qualified for many, many more positions than those without (Burning Glass Technologies 2013). The study did not look at PhD graduates, but it is not much of a stretch to imagine that the same principle applies to them as well.

For these reasons, I offer a modest proposal: the ideal doctoral program graduate should emerge as "Subject Matter *Plus*." Any of the above-listed skills—even just *one*—can and should be added alongside the traditional learning outcomes already served by the PhD program. That is how a doctoral graduate can be as *versatile* as possible, with a broad range of employment options and powerful skills that are useful both inside and outside the academy. Exactly how to add those skills is discussed below.

### Adjustment #1: Manage Your Messaging

Graduate school is stressful. First-year graduate students are dropped into a strange, intense academic environment where ambitions and expectations are suddenly much higher. They discover there are many rules they must learn—cultural rules about what is valued and what is not. Some students are thrown into radical self-doubt during coursework. They were accustomed to being at the top of pretty much every class they had ever taken; now, in their doctoral programs, they can see that everyone else is extremely smart too, making them merely average, ordinary, not special. This observation can be deeply disorienting.

In this pressure-cooker environment, you and your departmental colleagues are their most important sources of vital information and feedback. Fellow students a year or two farther along are another source, but faculty have the imprimatur of the institution. You, the professor, seem like their number one source of everything they need most: guidance as to what to study, recognition for their work, information about academic culture, and clues as to how well they are doing. As students progress through coursework and approach the dissertations, their need for professorial attention and approbation may seem to diminish—but really, they need it more than ever. Those who want to stay in the academy and become permanent fixtures in your discipline need it even more. Their future careers may seem to them largely dependent on you: your endorsement of their research, your contacts (and your willingness to speak to those contacts on their behalf), your ability to validate or dismiss the merits of their scholarship. When you look upon a student, both physically and by examining their work, you are embodying, perhaps without realizing it, what I call the *professorial gaze*. Your eyes, your voice, your body language convey your feelings, beliefs, and values and thus have tremendous impact on students. This is particularly true in the humanities and qualitative social sciences, where subjective judgments carry more weight and are, in fact, required to assess the quality of work. The professorial gaze is extremely powerful in those disciplines but can also be quite powerful even in STEM.

The idea that professors have a big impact on students is nothing new. However, an unseen dimension of this impact concerns career planning. The messages students receive from you about careers have enormous influence on their perceptions of what careers are available and desirable for people like them. In many cases, your ideas practically *become* their ideas. What you mention is what they know. What you feel and believe, they sense. I'm not saying students are complete blank slates—some of them do have specific nonacademic careers in mind for themselves—but the majority are hoping for academic careers, and the 6–10 years it will take them to earn the doctorate will likely reduce, rather than expand, their vision of nonacademic options and the desirability thereof. If you think that academic careers are preferable, or (worse) that an academic career is the only acceptable career and that "the best students do get jobs" (ergo, those who don't are losers), that is what they will think too, especially if they get the same message from multiple professors.

The further students progress in their programs, the more they become aware of their dicey chances at the tenure-track job they may have hoped for. Consequently, you can safely assume that many if not most advanced doctoral students and postdocs are struggling with doubt about their careers, even if they are not telling you about those doubts.

On a deeper level, the message that one's career is all-important and defines who a person is, is itself a major influence on student well-being around this issue. When identity is too closely wedded to career, the emotional health hazards are great. In the Versatile PhD community, there have been many times over the years when grad students have voiced extreme stress about their careers, sometimes to the point of considering suicide. Those in the greatest pain are those who feel *afraid to speak with their professors about nonacademic careers*, in most cases because the professor has made it clear, explicitly or implicitly, that s/he holds negative views of those careers and the students who pursue them. Granted, there may be other things going on with these students that are not under anyone's control, but consistently, the running theme of "you *are* your career" attaches far too much importance to the whole subject of career and unhealthily skews student self-esteem toward that one issue.

I will never forget the time in my own doctoral program (Rhetoric and Composition, Ohio State, 1996–2000) when I interviewed several staff members at my institution about their careers. One of them insisted to me, with surprising intensity, "I don't have a career. I have a *job*. My job does not define who I am. I define myself by my family and my volunteering. [She taught literacy skills to homeless kids on weekends.] That's where the real Joanne is. Not here." I was floored. Never before had I questioned my professional-class assumption that of course everyone has a "career" and of course their careers define who they are. It was one of the healthiest career-related moments of my entire life, and certainly the only time anyone in the academy ever suggested that my personhood is more important than any career choice I might make. More people should say such things. You should say such things.

The separation of self-esteem from career has been richly discussed in the Versatile PhD community. One member recently wrote,

> I bought into the idea that a tenure-track job was the only sure path to happiness, the only real measure of whether or not I was a "success" by the standard of the academy, my advisors, or colleagues. What I didn't appreciate at the time and what I have had to learn through a series of ups and downs, is that the only thing that matters in this lifetime is the quality of our character and whether or not we are working each day to be our best selves. I am now in the process of becoming a physician assistant, something that wasn't on my radar at all when I was a graduate student in the humanities and something I wouldn't have ever allowed myself to consider on the path toward getting my PhD.

So—reflect for a moment on the relationship between career and identity in your own life. To what extent does your career define you? Have you ever felt a need to resist over-identification with your career? Has there been any cost to you or your loved ones of your commitment to your career? Even if the costs have been worth it, it is still healthy and appropriate to note that there probably *have* been costs, and to encourage others to avoid whatever mistakes you may have made in this area.

Being aware of the impact you have on student notions of career enables you to consciously counteract the gravitational pull students feel to believe they will be officially seen as losers if they do not secure academic jobs. They feel the pull from every corner of their experience in the academy: remarks made in seminars, casual conversations in the hallways, disciplinary discourse at conferences and in journals, text on departmental websites highlighting academic placements of PhD graduates but not mentioning nonacademic placements at all. Even the high workload and pressure to publish as early as possible is a tremendous source of gravitational pull towards that belief. The pressure to be super-productive as a PhD candidate or early-career postdoc is necessary precisely because what used to be considered a good level of scholarly output is no longer good enough. The unspoken message is, everybody has to work really hard, and even then, not everyone will make it. Those who don't make it are losers. It's "The Hunger Games" and there are very few winners.

Remember that when you look at students, they viscerally feel it as the professorial gaze. Your words have tremendous impact. Your words about careers, even facial expressions and little casual throwaway remarks, communicate volumes about your belief system and the academic belief system. Observe and gently train yourself to adjust the things you say to your advisees. Certain things are commonly said by well-meaning professors who do not realize that their utterances are actually having a negative impact. Examples include responses like these to students who voice an interest in nonacademic careers:

"But you're so bright. You have such potential."

"I just hate to think of all the time and energy you've spent being wasted."

"You owe it to yourself to at least go on the market."

And so on. Do you see the disparagement in those statements, both of the student and also of the nonacademic world? All strongly imply that the only good career is an academic career. The first statement additionally implies that nonacademic careers do not require intelligence, that most people working outside the academy are unintelligent, and that whatever "potential" one might have outside the academy is trivial compared to the potential to hit the highest of all highs: to have an academic career and make a mark on the discipline. The second implies that the only reason to go through a doctoral program is to have an academic career—thus reducing the PhD experience to mere vocational training. The third implies that of course the student cannot possibly be truly excited or hopeful about a non-academic career, and thus, not to go on the academic job market equals not pursuing what must be their true dream. Of course you want your students to pursue their dreams, right? Right ... but their dream may not be the same now as when they first came to you. Research has shown that a significant percentage of doctoral students (at least in STEM) change their career goals about three years into their programs (Fuhrmann et al. 2011); on experiencing the academic world and seeing what their professors' lives are like, they change their minds about wanting to be professors (Sauermann and Roach 2012).

Here are some things *to* say (ideally early and often), phrased as if to the student:

- "*Explore both academic and nonacademic careers.* Read widely and ask around to get a sense of different academic and non-academic careers. Even if you do end up in an academic career, remember it may be in a different type of institution. Explore other types. Join the Versatile PhD community and use the PhD Career Finder on the Versatile PhD site to learn about nonacademic careers. Gathering information on a wide range of careers will not lessen you in my eyes. In fact, tell me if you find anything interesting!"

- "*Start preparing for a range of careers as early as possible in your program.* Even if you feel certain that you want an academic career, the academic job market is so bad that even the very brightest students should have more than one career in mind. By the time you pass your exams and begin work on your dissertation, you should at the very least be aware of two or three nonacademic careers that might appeal to you. By the time you finish, you should have a nonacademic résumé as well as a CV and have taken concrete steps to explore and prepare for at least one of those careers. Being informed and prepared in this way will not make me think any less of you. I will be proud of you."

- "*There are good resources available to you about nonacademic careers. Use them.* Watch for professional development workshops and events and attend them. Do not feel anxious that I might see you there. I want you to go."

- *"Observe yourself and your feelings while going through the program.* Research has shown that grad student career goals often change mid-program. You may think you want an academic career right now, but you may change your mind later on. It's okay. As you go through the program, notice which activities you gravitate towards, and why. Watch in particular your procrastination behaviors (I know you procrastinate; we all do). Those observations contain major clues about what kind of career might be best for you."

- *"Keep records of everything you do.* Count actual numbers of papers written, lessons delivered, experiments completed, service commitments fulfilled, etc. Focus on practical accomplishments and list both what you did and what was the practical result. This will help you write your nonacademic résumé later on and may even help you write your vita."

- *"If I am ever an obstacle to you, work around me.* I am a career academic. As such, there is much that I do not know about nonacademic careers. I want to help you, but I may not always be able to. Feel free to develop additional mentors who can. No matter how close we become or how much you respect me and my research, *you* are in charge of your career. Do not let fear of my disapproval be an obstacle. It is more important that you approve of yourself."

That last point in particular may strike you as strange. Of course you are not an obstacle in your students' lives. Why would you characterize yourself that way? Well, let me tell you. A major running theme in confidential discussions among graduate students and postdocs is *fear of disappointing the advisor.* Many, many students are afraid to talk to their professors about nonacademic careers. They fear being judged as less intelligent, less committed, less worthy of professorial time and trouble. In some cases their fear is misplaced; in other cases it is not. To deliver that last point to students is a deeply ethical thing to do. It allows for the possibility that you might have a blind spot or two. It places the student squarely in charge of his or her career and encourages critical thinking on the part of the student.

Even if you stop reading right here and just convey those messages to students, you will already be a better mentor.

### Adjustment #2: Assess the Career Climate in Your Department

Another factor that influences student attitudes and emotional well-being is what I call the "career climate" in the department. What cultural messages do doctoral students receive during their programs about nonacademic careers for PhDs? To get at that, consider doing a one-time exploratory research project that will take no more than a couple of hours and will tell you a lot about your students' likely state of mind. Investigate the following:

*Career Climate Departmental Assessment*

To what extent does the department offer nonacademic professional development opportunities to doctoral students specifically, such as panel discussions with post-academic PhDs or workshops on job search skills (e.g., converting your CV to a résumé)?

1. not at all
2. one event per year
3. more than one event per year

To what extent does your department promote on-campus professional development resources located outside the department, for instance, through the Career Center, the Graduate School, or other units?

1. not much; department mostly keeps to itself in that respect
2. now and then, when there is an easy opportunity to do so, but there is no systematic effort
3. regularly and systematically: department makes sure all grad students know about these resources

To what extent does your department tell doctoral students about books and websites relating to nonacademic careers for PhDs?

1. not much; department keeps no list and trusts students will ferret these out on their own
2. now and then, when there is an easy opportunity to do so, but there is no systematic effort
3. regularly and systematically: department has a list and gives it to all grad students

What does the department know about where its recent PhD graduates got placed?

1. little or nothing
2. some academic placements are known but nonacademic placements are unknown
3. all academic placements are known but nonacademic placements are largely unknown
4. all academic placements are known and nonacademic placements are somewhat known
5. *all* placements are known

What systems are in place for collecting that information?

1. voluntary reporting only; department knows only what graduates or faculty tell them
2. exit survey, but it is not mandatory and/or it only asks about academic placements
3. exit survey that is mandatory and elicits information about all types of placements
4. exit survey that is mandatory, includes all placements, and asks the student how well the department did at providing them with nonacademic professional development

How is PhD placement information stored?

1. no one seems to know
2. in a place where one person has access to it
3. in a place where multiple people have access to it, or where many have access but it's not clear how to find it
4. in a place where everyone has easy access to it, including students

Assign a point value for each question: one point for #1 answers, two points for #2 and so on. The maximum score is 22, and the minimum, 6. What is your department's score?

18–22: The career climate in your department is very positive for nonacademic careers. Doctoral students are getting the clear message that nonacademic careers are acceptable to the department and respected as much as academic careers.

15–17: The career climate in your department is generally positive. Doctoral students are getting the message that nonacademic careers are okay for those who want them.

11–14: The career climate in your department is superficially positive but generally negative. Doctoral students get the message that lip service must be paid, but really academic careers are best. Many doctoral students, particularly advanced students, are likely to feel a fair amount of anxiety about their careers.

6–10: The career climate in your department can be characterized as very negative. Doctoral students are getting the message that only academic careers are acceptable, and probably feel afraid to express interest in nonacademic careers. Some students are probably experiencing extreme stress about their careers after graduation.

Just knowing these facts about your own department will instantly make you a better mentor. The career climate in your department has a huge influence on your students' emotional states around this issue. Knowing what messages students are getting allows you to serve as a much-needed counterbalance—and also allows you to become an advocate for positive change.

### Adjustment #3: Make Referrals to Available Resources

You don't need to be super-knowledgeable about nonacademic careers, but you should be able to guide students to good career-related resources, both on campus and elsewhere. Start by learning about the resources on your campus. Maybe someone in your department has already made a list, but that's doubtful, so you are probably the first faculty member in your department to actually take the time to do this (you're a pioneer!). "Resources" on campus can mean almost anything: a collection of books and information about nonacademic careers for PhDs, self-assessment tests, notebooks or electronic files of model résumés, online resources such as databases and job boards, even a real, live counselor who can meet with them. Some places to start include the Career Center, the Graduate School, and, if there is one, the Office of Postdoctoral Studies. All three of those units may or may not have nonacademic career resources for graduate students. Ideally you would start with a web search, but also make actual phone calls, to verify information and ask questions. Websites alone are not always as descriptive or complete as they could be. You want to truly understand these resources so that you can make *good, appropriate, solid* referrals.

Next, make an effort to explore online resources not specific to your institution. As a starting point, does your university subscribe to Versatile PhD? What other online resources does your university subscribe to that might be helpful to grad students? For example, many university career centers subscribe to Vault (*aka* Career Insider), Going Global (for international careers), and other online resources. Though not targeted specifically to graduate students as Versatile PhD is, these sites nonetheless provide information that may not be easily available elsewhere. Nonprofits worth checking out include AAAS (http://www.aaas.org), NYAS (http://www.nyas.org), and ACLS (http://www.acls.org), all of which have good information relevant to PhD careers. And don't neglect "the Google." A simple search for "astronomy careers," for example, will likely yield some worthwhile sites that you might want to tell your students about.

Finally, look to your own disciplinary association and see what career resources it provides to members. Some associations are wading into nonacademic careers by developing web-based career resources tailored to their members. Many graduate students do not know about these resources, even if they are members of the association. I have presented at discipline-specific conferences where a majority of the graduate students in the audience had not, until my presentation, been aware of the nonacademic career resources that their own association prepared for them. It is facile to assume that the associations are no help and nothing has been provided.

Here's a clever time-saver: ask an advisee to work with you with this project (collaboration!), especially an advisee who has expressed interest in nonacademic careers. That person will be very motivated and will benefit directly from doing the legwork. Break it down into phases with deadlines (delivering outcomes on time!). Suggest that the student present your joint findings to the rest of the department in a brown bag lunch session or some other occasion (oral presentation skills!). Or at least consider sharing the resulting resource list with other faculty and grad students in the department. Controversial? Perhaps. Helpful to students? Absolutely.

## Adjustment #4: Support a Broadening of Knowledge and Skills

Every discipline has its own body of knowledge and research

methods, many of which constitute "skills" both inside and outside the academy. STEM students frequently learn laboratory research techniques, database construction, statistics, coding, and more in the course of conducting their research, and humanities students learn how to identify, retrieve, interpret, and utilize a wide variety of textual and visual materials and media. All of those skills are valued outside the academy. Yet as explained earlier, what really opens a student's nonacademic prospects—particularly in the humanities—is the addition of skills and bodies of knowledge that are less common among scholars in their discipline and that are valued outside the academy. Again: Subject Matter *Plus*.

Knowledge can be broadened by taking a class or two outside the discipline, or participating in a special program designed to impart knowledge. For example, when a humanities student takes Intro to Statistics or Business 101, or joins the Entrepreneur's Club on campus, it adds whole new domains of knowledge and measurably increases their employment options. When that knowledge is tangentially related (or even, in some cases, intimately related) to their scholarship, all the better, because then it can be utilized in their dissertations or at least in seminar papers. Not every dissertation research project can include research methods that will broaden student skills, but in cases where that is possible and not harmful, it is certainly advisable.

Skills can be broadened through service. Encourage your advisees to take on service projects that will develop practical, marketable skills such as the ones listed above. Then express interest in those projects and praise them for their accomplishments. If you are dead set against allowing anything of this nature to intrude upon your advisees' scholarship per se, surely you can cede their *service* time as territory where such broadening can take place.

If you are managing and advising postdocs, please have a conversation with each one in which you go over together the written description of the postdoctoral position, paying particular attention to the skills and knowledge that it promises to develop in the appointee. Ask the student whether s/he has been getting enough exposure to those things, and if not, make specific, concrete adjustments to improve the situation. Ask the postdoc if s/he has developed any new interests during this appointment and if so, is there anything not in the original job description that s/he would like to learn? Then try hard to find a way to deliver on that as well. Many voices in the Versatile PhD community have testified about postdoctoral appointments that turned out completely different from how they were described, PI's who behave inconsiderately towards their appointees, and the relentless pressure on postdocs to drop all activities outside the lab (just a few examples). If a postdoctoral appointment is "training," then do your best to improve and increase the training your postdocs receive, in accordance with their interests.

Though I am well aware of time concerns ("How can advisees simultaneously prepare for academic and nonacademic careers? They need all their time just to be ready for today's *academic* job market.")—and also of the possible incendiary impact of my suggestion that the research disciplines should be more "practical" ("Isn't the deep value of academic research precisely that it need *not* be concerned with practical implications?")—it is indeed my considered recommendation that you support a broadening of advisee's skills and knowledge, particularly when an advisee has actually expressed interest in nonacademic careers. Encourage them to broaden their knowledge base and acquire new skills that are not normally in the standard tool kit of your discipline. It is better for the advisee.

### Adjustment #5: Learn What to Say to Nonacademic Employers

You know how to write academic letters of recommendation. It would be extremely helpful to your students if you could learn how to handle conversations with nonacademic employers as well, should they call. In the Versatile PhD community, references from advisors are a perennial topic of interest. It comes up every few months at least and is the subject of much hand-wringing. The question is often along the lines of, "How can I ensure that my advisor will give me a good recommendation if I choose to apply for nonacademic jobs?" or, "Is my professor even capable of giving a good nonacademic reference, especially when s/he is disappointed that I am going the nonacademic route?" Many students fear that either you won't know what to say to the employer, or that you might even be tempted to *undersell* them because you would rather see them in an academic career. A positive, supportive mentoring relationship from the beginning will eliminate the latter concern, because your support will have already been demonstrated and the advisee will have no reason to fear that you might sabotage their chances. But a little effort on your part will make you able to give them good references when you are called upon to do so. Your willingness and readiness to speak positively to prospective employers is a great gift you can give to your advisees.

When the time comes, here are some things to do.

- As a preparatory exercise, reflect on the student and the accomplishments and attributes that you like best or admire most about the advisee. Write those down and think of specific incidents where they demonstrated each quality. Reflect further on the *practical* side of those incidents. How did the advisee make a positive impact in that moment? Did his attention to detail catch a ghastly error? Did her cleverness save time or money, or lead to a better outcome? Did he brighten up the work environment just by helping other people feel good? Did her promptness give you peace of mind that all of her deadlines would be met? Did he realize on his own that he would need to change strategies for how to solve a problem, and was he right? All of these things are examples of good workplace behaviors, very much valued in the nonacademic world, and they do not always come across in application materials. Practice describing the student in this way to someone off campus (your spouse, a friend, a relative) and ask for feedback on how it sounds. What about your description made a good impression on the listener? What might make it stronger?

- Encourage advisees to tell you what kinds of positions they are applying for and why. The more you know about the position, and the advisee's interests, the better you will be able to testify to your advisee's ability to excel in the position.

- Ask the student to let you know whenever they get an interview and it goes well. That would be your cue that you might be called at some point. Without an interview, there is no point thinking about it, because the interview always comes first. No interview, no call. Truthfully, they may not call you even if the student does get an interview and it does go well. Not all employers check references. When the student gets an interview and it goes well, ask to see the résumé and cover letter they submitted for the position, so you will know exactly how the student has represented him- or herself to the employer. If you have questions or concerns about the résumé, ask the advisee about it even though it may feel awkward to do so. It will make this process infinitely easier for you, and better for the advisee, if you are clear on the facts when you speak to the employer. By working through any questions about the student's accomplishments ahead of time, everything the employer knows about this applicant will be singing in harmony: the résumé and cover letter, and now the things they are hearing from you.

- When the student alerts you that the prospective employer is seriously interested and likely to start calling references, look at the résumé again and think of facts or impressions that you would be able add but that are not already there. For example, "Candace says X on the résumé but I think she is selling herself short there. She's even better at X than she takes credit for" (and give an example). Or, "Yes, all of that is true, and I can tell you something he didn't say. Jamal is one of the hardest-working people I have ever known" (or whatever your positive observation is).

Here are some attributes that nonacademic employers love and want, in addition to specific skills listed in the job ad and earlier in this chapter. Many are ones with which PhD students are often particularly well equipped:

√ self-motivation
√ problem-solving ability
√ ability to *define* problems and get to the root of the issue
√ teamwork
√ deadline-consciousness
√ detail-consciousness
√ budget-consciousness
√ pleasant personality
√ dedication
√ eagerness and ability to learn
√ responsiveness to email and phone communications
√ genuine *interest in the position—and in leaving the academy*

That last point is an important one. Nonacademic employers are often concerned about PhD applicants because they worry the person is just taking a temporary gig and will leave the minute they get a faculty position. You can do your advisee a huge favor by assuring the prospective employer that while the advisee definitely has the intellectual chops to be a successful academic, he or she is genuinely eager to work in a different kind of setting—ideally a setting *just like the specific setting in question*. Mention anything about the advisee's ambitions that match the organization you are speaking with: "he's always been interested in finance"; "she's always wanted to help people and I think she will be more satisfied in your nonprofit than here in the ivory tower"; "his temperament is just too pragmatic and proactive for university life. I think he would excel in a fast-paced environment like yours and be very happy there." Say it however you like, but that's the idea: use your honest impressions of the student to emphasize the fit between the student and the position or organization. Do not lie. Do think deeply about the student and actively search for qualities or attributes that would play well outside the academy. Some of these qualities or attributes (e.g., friendliness, responsiveness to email) would also play well inside the academy; the two lists need not be mutually exclusive.

### The Ultimate Adjustment?

In these days of shrinking higher education budgets and increasing pressure for "accountability" (meaning placement), it is less and less clear what higher education in general, and doctoral education in particular, will look like in the future. Some PhD programs are augmenting traditional doctoral coursework with skills training and work experiences; others are experimenting with reducing enrollments and increasing the amount of funding provided for each enrollee, to reduce graduate student debt; still others are experimenting in other ways with changes that can serve both traditional and nontraditional goals. The doctoral program of the future may look quite different from how it looks today. We don't know. Whatever the future holds, it does seem that faculty who actively support a broadened range of possible employment outcomes for doctoral graduates will be on the right side of history. The ultimate adjustment, I think, in mentoring for nonacademic careers, is to place student well-being absolutely first in your consciousness: ahead of your research, ahead of institutional rankings, and ahead of the future of the discipline. This chapter has introduced some specific strategies for how to adapt your mentoring to the current era; you may develop your own strategies as well (and if you do, I would sincerely like to hear about them). No matter what adjustments you choose to make, the end result should be that graduate students feel comfortable talking with you about all of their career possibilities. With practice, and with genuine curiosity on your part, you will feel increasingly comfortable with those conversations yourself. The fact that the skills and knowledge you are teaching your doctoral students *are* valued outside the academy is excellent news, because it frees doctoral education from the overly-specific vocational purpose of preparing university faculty, liberating it to be potentially a richer, more intellectually diverse, more possibility-*opening* experience than the traditionalists in your department may believe it to be.

## Notes

1. All quotes from graduate students and postdocs are taken from the discussion forums of the Versatile PhD website (http://versatilephd.com), which I founded, and are used with permission.

2. Remark made by Stewart during her plenary address at the Western Association of Graduate Schools meeting, March 31, 2014, in Fargo, North Dakota.

3. Reported on the CGS website, https://www.cgsnet.org/cgs-launches-project-study-feasibility-tracking-phd-career-pathways.

## Works Cited

Burning Glass Technologies. 2013. *The Art of Employment: How Liberal Arts Graduates Can Improve Their Labor Market Prospects.* Boston: The author.

Fuhrmann, C. N., D. G. Halme, P. S. O'Sullivan, and B. Lindstaedt. 2011. "Improving Graduate Education to Support a Branching Career Pipeline: Recommendations Based on a Survey of Doctoral Students in the Basic Biomedical Sciences." *CBE–Life Sciences Education* 10: 239–49.

Sauermann, H., and M. Roach. 2012. "Science PhD Career Preferences: Levels, Changes, and Advisor Encouragement." *PLoS ONE* 7 (5): 1–9. doi: 10.1371/journal.pone.0036307.

### APPENDIX: Suggested Readings

Basalla, Susan, and Maggie Debelius. 2015. *"So What Are You Going to Do with That?" Finding Careers Outside Academia.* 3rd ed. Chicago: University of Chicago Press.

An extremely useful book for humanists and qualitative social scientists interested in nonacademic careers. Step-by-step guide to identifying possible career paths, preparing to enter those fields, and applying for positions. Written with a friendly, accessible tone. Many examples of PhDs who have succeeded outside the academy.

Bolles, Richard Nelson. 2013. *What Color Is Your Parachute? A Practical Manual for Job-Hunters and Career-Changers*. Berkeley, CA: Ten Speed Press.

A bestseller for good reason, this book has helped many thousands of people in its long life, including many academics. Nice balance between inner work (assessing yourself, observing your psyche) and outer work (preparing your résumé, navigating the job search process). New editions appear regularly.

Council of Graduate Schools and Educational Testing Service. 2012. "Pathways Through Graduate School and Into Careers." Report from the Commission on Pathways Through Graduate School and Into Careers. Princeton, NJ: Educational Testing Service. http://www.pathwaysreport.org.

A hugely important study urging greater transparency about career paths after earning an advanced degree.

Fiske, Peter S. 2001. *Put Your Science to Work: The Take-Charge Career Guide for Scientists*. Washington DC: American Geophysical Union.

As essential for scientists as *So What Are You Going to Do with That?* is for humanists. Shows a broad range of career options for scientists, helps the student self-assess, and provides excellent practical guidance on the job search process, including some tips on the academic job search. Highly recommended.

Fuhrmann, C. N., D. G. Halme, P. S. O'Sullivan, and B. Lindstaedt. 2011. "Improving Graduate Education to Support a Branching Career Pipeline: Recommendations Based on a Survey of Doctoral Students in the Basic Biomedical Sciences." *CBE—Life Sciences Education* 10 (3): 239–49.

A recent study showing how biology grad students' career goals change during graduate school.

Lovitts, Barbara E. 2001. *Leaving the Ivory Tower: The Causes and Consequences of Departure from Doctoral Study*. Lanham, MD: Rowan and Littlefield.

A detailed study of why graduate students leave their programs without finishing. While many in academe place the blame on the student, this study points to institutional factors and suggests ways to increase retention and completion.

Newhouse, Margaret. 1993. *Outside the Ivory Tower: A Guide for Academics Considering Alternative Careers.* Cambridge, MA: President and Fellows of Harvard University.

A classic on a par with Bolles, out of print but available used. Relevant to all disciplines.

Robbins-Roth, Cynthia, ed. 2006. *Alternative Careers in Science: Leaving the Ivory Tower.* 2nd ed. Burlington, MA: Elsevier Academic Press.

A self-described "scientist gone bad" describes how she went "from the bench to the boardroom" and presents a dazzling array of non-research career options for scientists, each described first-hand by someone who has gone that route. Great for scientists interested in careers away from the bench.

Stephan, Paula. 2012. *How Economics Shapes Science.* Cambridge, MA: Harvard University Press.

Not a "how to" career book, but rather a cogent, lively analysis of the financial side of university-based scientific research—its costs and benefits, writ large—illustrating why fewer new STEM PhDs will get academic jobs today than they would have in earlier eras.

# Graduate Mentoring against Common Sense

## *Ron Krabill**

**C**ommon Sense

If common sense is the detritus of accepted truth from past eras (Gramsci 1972), then graduate students who want to engage in public scholarship have layers of sediment to work their way through during graduate school. This common sense is institutional in character. It makes claims about how one should be professionalized and, in so doing, sets the boundaries of what actions can be included as part of the profession. Its reach extends far beyond any single university, discipline, or academic association, deeply coloring the ways in which faculty imagine themselves and how they should train the next generation of scholars. Thus graduate mentoring becomes a key location in which the common sense of academia—with all its contradictions and inconsistencies—is used to discipline (in Foucault's expansive sense of the term) graduate students even as it is being passed on to them.

What are the key moments when the received knowledge of graduate training works to limit students' ability to engage in public scholarship? How might faculty mentor against the grain of this common sense? If the kind of work showcased in this volume is to flourish, what are the ways that faculty mentors can not only get out of the way of such work (which is sometimes necessary) but also help to encourage and facilitate this kind of research?

* Originally published in *Collaborative Futures: Critical Reflections on Publicly Active Graduate Education*, ed. Amanda Gilvin, Georgia M. Roberts, and Craig Martin (Syracuse, NY: The Graduate School Press, 2012), pp. 285–99. Reprinted with permission of the author.

One place to start to deconstruct the common sense of graduate training is to look for the statements that we often hear repeated in the context of graduate mentoring—many of us may have repeated the phrases many times ourselves—that caution students against engaging in public scholarship. A variation of these statements can also be found after a student has begun a public scholarship project; in this instance, the caution is against the student going "too far." As Gramsci understood, common sense always holds internal contradictions, as well as seeds of accuracy, in tension with the layers of collective lived experiences over many years. In other words, what any social group understands as common sense cannot be simply dismissed as wrong because it reflects parts of the lived experiences of that group. Common sense is not inaccurate. It is just not accurate enough, because it fails to take into consideration the institutional and systemic forces that shape those experiences.

So our task here is to examine those moments when graduate mentoring reinforces academia's common sense that public scholarship is the wrong path for a graduate student to pursue. The fact that those moments may sometimes contain good advice for the individual student complicates our task, but it does not make it impossible. Indeed, common sense is arguably at its strongest when what is seen as good advice for the individual perpetuates the inertia of the institution.

*Public scholarship is great, but wait until you have a tenure-track job to do it.*

Along with its (arguably) more common variant directed at assistant professors—wait until you have tenure—this phrase perpetuates the belief that engagement in explicitly public, and especially political, projects can only be conducted after you have climbed the academic hierarchy to a certain sufficient point. For the graduate student, it says that you should just get through graduate school as quickly as possible, after which you can start the real work of the academy. The fact that acquiring a tenure-track job—possibly the narrowest choke-point in academic careers—is immediately followed by the call to wait a bit longer, until you have tenure, is indicative of the statement's danger. While a tenured position reduces the immediacy of the publish-or-perish imperative and protects positions from (some) political attacks, reaching that point takes a minimum of 10–15 years in many fields. To expect graduate students and junior faculty to spend that amount of time practicing more traditional research, then shift gears intellectually and methodlogically into public scholarship, underestimates both the potential depth of public scholarship as a research practice and the power of repetition to ingrain more traditional practices and academic common sense. Meanwhile, the future of the traditional tenure-track job remains increasingly uncertain; graduate mentors should prepare their students for emerging academic markets that may look very different from today's university, much less the university of the twentieth century (Newfield 2008; Schuster and Finkelstein 2006).

*Public scholarship takes too long and is too complicated to complete for your dissertation.*

There is no doubt that one of the biggest practical obstacles to public scholarship is the time required to do it right. As the projects described in this volume attest, building relationships with partners outside of the university, building in sufficient feedback loops for the information you gather (whether you do that through performance, data, or deep hanging out), and allowing for the different timelines of various stakeholders all make public scholarship more complicated and time-consuming than a more traditional dissertation. The pressure on departments to confer graduate degrees within a certain period—a metric that often figures into national rankings—increases the demand to choose more streamlined paths to degree completion. And students' own justified desires to finish graduate school and move on to faculty or other positions drive this pressure as well, even as a weak economy and limited job opportunities cause some students to delay the actual date of completion. Graduate mentors thus need to help their students develop a realistic sense of the scope of their projects while simultaneously developing different kinds of support—financial, intellectual, and temporal—to focus on their research. Crucial in this formula is a mental shift that must occur among graduate mentors, departments, and funding agencies: a recognition that public scholarship is exactly that—scholarship— rather than an extension of service or teaching or extracurricular activity, even as it often incorporates these elements as well.

*Public scholarship is fine, but you need to do it in addition to, rather than in place of, more traditional research.*

This statement grows out of two related concerns with public scholarship: first, that it involves so many collaborators that it becomes difficult to claim as your own work when applying for jobs; and second, that it isn't recognized as "real" scholarship and therefore you need to have both types of research in your repertoire. Each of these claims again raises the question of public scholarship's legibility to broader audiences and common-sense assumptions about what counts in academic professions. Graduate mentors need to assist students to author papers and participate in professional conferences and workshops that lay claim to their scholarship *as scholarship*, while maintaining full integrity in their collaborations. Perhaps more essentially, mentors need to learn how to find outlets for their students' work that acknowledge public scholarship as a form of knowledge production equal in validity to the single-authored paper or presentation.

The second concern, that public scholars should have both modes of research in their repertoire, seems infinitely reasonable at first blush, and in fact publicly engaged scholars almost always operate within both modes at different moments in any given project. However, graduate mentors need to be vigilant that this does not become another form of academic speed-up, where junior scholars are expected to produce research in both modes at a far greater scale than either their mentors or their colleagues creating more traditional forms of research outputs. In other words, the solution to making public scholarship legible must not simply be to duplicate the public work in traditional forms. Such an approach runs the risk of nullifying the very strengths of public scholarship and burning out our best, most committed early-career scholars.

*Public scholarship is great if you don't mind teaching at a school that isn't as good.*

Leaving aside the obviously problematic formulation of "a good school"—which in this phrasing is assumed to be defined explicitly through its embrace of more traditional modes of knowledge production—this statement fails to acknowledge the degree to which public scholarship actually allows graduate students to stand out from the crowd in many applications. Due to the success of organizations like Imagining America and Campus Compact over the past decades, public scholarship and its fellow travelers, community-based and service learning, have become keywords in the mission statements and strategic plans of many universities across the higher educational spectrum. The logics of public scholarship may not have fully permeated faculty cultures at high-prestige schools (or most others, for that matter), and many of these changes in promotional language serve as thinly veiled tropes for business as usual. Nonetheless, public scholarship by graduate students can garner significant positive attention for both their institutions and their careers, further improving job opportunities. More importantly, if we truly believe that integrated public scholarship improves the insights garnered by our research, then public scholarship will also strengthen the more traditional lines of our academic work and strengthen job candidacies accordingly.

However, a second strand of academic common sense is at play in these assumptions around what makes a school good—namely, that the prestige of the school or the perceived quality of the faculty positions it offers is an objective measure of job satisfaction for those who would hope to land jobs at that institution. While the resources of high-prestige institutions often outstrip those of more modest reputation—an issue of significant import to faculty and graduate students alike—where those resources are directed also impacts the kind of work one can accomplish at various locations. Take my own position as an example. I am a professor at a "satellite" campus, Bothell, of the University of Washington (UW). Common metrics for academic jobs would see my position as a secondary one, lesser than that of my colleagues at the "flagship" campus in Seattle. We have slightly higher teaching loads and very different teaching structures, and certainly higher demands for institutional service. Yet for the type of work I do—collaborative, publicly engaged, interdisciplinary media and cultural studies—having a foot in both the R1 tri-campus university system of UW and the innovative community of scholars at UW Bothell has been the best of both worlds, both in terms of intellectual engagement and in terms of material resources.

For publicly engaged graduate students, determining which colleges and universities hold the promise of being a good school, or providing a good job, requires an additional layer of investigation to move beyond common-sense assumptions. Rather than viewing this as an additional burden, graduate students looking toward faculty positions can also redefine the kinds of institutions that might make for a good professional trajectory, opening up their career possibilities to places and programs that would otherwise seem too far off the beaten path to be viable. In other words, public scholarship can and should be understood to broaden a graduate student's future opportunities instead of being considered solely in terms of limiting and complicating the job market.

*Public scholarship is great, but you need to write about it in a way that makes it legible to traditional academics.*

This is perhaps the most pernicious advice passed on by graduate mentors, not because it is false, but because it so strongly illustrates the grounding of common sense in accurate but incomplete concerns. Of course public scholarship must be made legible to others, including those who may be hostile to the entire endeavor as well as those who may be sympathetic but uninformed. In this respect, public scholarship is no different than any other form of scholarship; one of the greatest challenges of academic life is to communicate complex, highly developed ideas in clear, concise ways for the benefit of others who have not focused the same energy on those ideas. Yet publicly engaged work should not carry this burden to any greater or lesser degree than more traditional modes.

The danger lies in an expectation that public scholarship win legitimacy by adapting itself to traditional forms of research. If the modes of producing knowledge differ in public scholarship, then the communication of that knowledge will necessitate, at least at times, a different format. Take, for instance, the newly arising field of digital scholarship (whether publicly engaged or not). The idea that knowledge generated through new forms of digital collaboration and engagement will best be expressed through a single-authored, peer-reviewed article in a printed journal with prestige from an earlier era seems unlikely, if not entirely implausible—not only because such an article will often be judged to be outside the scope of such a journal, but more essentially because the knowledge produced by such a project will be insufficiently captured by the journal's medium. Public scholarship thus needs to explore new modes of communicating the knowledge it produces, matching its means of production with its means of dissemination, consumption, and assessment (and often blurring the lines between these functions). While these new modes of expressing public scholarship may not be understood as quickly or as broadly as more traditional forms of scholarly publishing, they will sometimes be necessary to remain true to the work itself, the knowledge it produces, and the politics it embraces.

## Challenging Common Sense

If these preceding statements of well-intentioned advice represent the half-truths of graduate mentoring common sense, what are the proactive efforts that faculty mentors can take in conjunction with and in support of their publicly engaged graduate students? I would like to propose three approaches to mentoring that offer a way forward: first, graduate mentors should rethink the mentoring process as radically collaborative; second, graduate mentors should embrace and foster multiple possible professional trajectories for the graduate students with whom they are working; and third, graduate mentors should become active agents of structural institutional changes that will better support students engaged in public scholarship. In offering these approaches I want to emphasize that I am not claim-ing to have mastered them, or even in some cases to have previously embraced them. Rather, they seem to hold the most promise in overcoming the limitations of our profession's common sense and forging new directions for public scholarship and the academy as a whole.

### Radically Collaborative Graduate Mentoring

Much is made of the buzzword *collaboration* in today's academy; indeed, it is difficult to find a mission statement or strategic plan that does not invoke the term. We must therefore be clear what we mean by collaboration or, as I am arguing here, radical collaboration. The essence of radical collaboration is a displacing of the assumption that the graduate mentor holds greater knowledge or experience of the practices of public scholarship than his or her graduate students. While this may be the case, my experiences indicate that it often is not. Graduate students—particularly those who subsequently pursue publicly engaged scholarship—are often entering graduate school with previous knowledge and experiences of working with political issues, social movements, or community-based organizations, and as such they often bring to the table a deep political commitment to understanding those experiences with greater theoretical depth. Graduate students doing publicly engaged work often find themselves in a position of greater expertise than their mentors in crucial facets of their public scholarship, and this inversion of assumed expertise occurs much earlier in the student experience than with traditional models of graduate education. The radical collaboration of graduate mentorship is a bringing together of these experiences that sees great opportunity in such an inversion rather than attempting to subordinate the knowledge generated by engaged work outside of academic settings to the knowledge created by the academy. In this formulation, a graduate mentor becomes a guide through many of the opportunities and pitfalls of graduate school, but also remains open to learning of the opportunities and pitfalls of engaged work outside the academy, without reducing that work to a mere case study or test site for academic theory. To accomplish this, mentors often must rely on students at least as much or more than the reverse.

Such radical collaboration must also extend beyond the pairing of the faculty mentor and advisee. Graduate mentors should actively welcome the collaborators with whom publicly engaged students are working closely into the overall mentoring process. Integrating the community-based mentors of graduate students into their overall academic experience may blur the distinctions between a student's public-ness and their scholarship; such blurring, if welcomed by the student, may also serve to reduce the tension so many students experience balancing their academic and community-based commitments. Integrating community-based mentors can occur in a number of ways—they may attend academic presentations, serve some sort of evaluative role regarding the student's work, meet with the graduate mentor, and so forth—and could vary in terms of their formality or informality. For instance, one could imagine community-based mentors serving as outside readers for theses (as they sometimes do in the MA in Cultural Studies program I coordinate), or as part of a jury for arts-based exhibits or performances. But the integration I am arguing for is less dependent on its formality—for as we know, formalizing such relationships can often spell their doom—than on its flexibility in fully welcoming collaboration across multiple sectors often left out of the academic equation.

Radical collaboration does not mean that faculty mentors must subordinate themselves to the political or relational priorities that their students bring, becoming mere rubber stamps for students' projects. Faculty mentors do bring their own expertise, not only in the subject area within which they conduct their own research and teaching, but also within the academy as both social institution and intellectual project. Mentors need to help graduate students understand the limitations as well as the strengths of their publicly engaged work, how that work fits into existing literatures and academic fields, and how to make informed choices around the direction and extent of their public scholarship. Likewise, graduate students seeking to integrate public scholarship may not always like what they hear from their graduate mentors; they may receive feedback that seems to undercut their previous commitments and understandings of their own work, or pushes them in unforeseen directions. Radical collaboration calls for students and faculty alike to work through these moments with dedication and intellectual care, so that neither falls into the temptation of simply dismissing the other as naive or stubborn, or too far on one side of the (false) publicly engaged/scholarship divide.

Finally, radical collaboration can also mean getting out of the way. Paradoxically, sometimes the most supportive act a graduate mentor can take is to allow the graduate student to pursue publicly engaged scholarship the academic ends of which may not be immediately clear to the mentor. While mentors have a responsibility to express those concerns and frame the possible drawbacks to any given path a student may choose, they must also gauge the power they hold within the institution and adjust their "advice" accordingly, taking care not to overdetermine a student's trajectory. My experience has been that the political commitments of a student's publicly engaged work are often what sustain that student through graduate school; mentors therefore need to resist the temptation to purge such work from a student's repertoire in the name of academic expediency.

### Fostering Multiple (Possible) Professional Trajectories

The path to a career in academia that faculty know best is, of course, the path that they themselves took. As mentioned earlier, these more traditional trajectories are becoming less and less available in the current climate of higher education. But rather than stopping our analysis of the academy at the point of bemoaning what has been lost from older models (though this remains crucial at times), graduate mentors should also work with their students to imagine new trajectories that can carve out spaces for publicly engaged work both within and outside of the academy. A number of fellowship programs cater expressly to doctoral candidates exploring nonacademic careers; these programs were pioneered by the Woodrow Wilson Foundation in the 1990s and, most recently, include the new ACLS Public Fellows program (http://www.acls.org/programs/publicfellows). The wider scope of previous experiences with which many students now enter graduate school only increases the imperative for mentors to be informed regarding multiple possible career trajectories for their students.

For some students, this may mean future careers in organizations with more explicitly public or collaborative orientations than the academy: nongovernmental and community-based organizations, think tanks, arts and performance-based groups, K–12 education, and public policy groups, to name just a few. Although some disciplines have a longer tradition of directing graduates into these types of careers, faculty across disciplines tend to dismiss these trajectories as of less merit than the faculty positions that they themselves hold. However, these choices are not only Plan B for those who are unable to land academic jobs, as is often assumed by faculty, but the first choice for many new graduates and the aspirational choice of many current students. For one recent PhD graduate of the UW, a job at a major international human rights organization matched her desire to apply the theoretical work of her dissertation to ongoing, direct advocacy on contemporary issues. Yet some of her graduate mentors described their disappointment that she did not choose to "hold out" for a "real" job; they presumed that a faculty position was both her preferred choice and the more prestigious option. Sometimes these more subtle assertions of prestige and preference do more to indicate a mentor's lack of respect for publicly engaged work than any explicit attack. As graduate mentors learn to respect the knowledge and experiences generated outside of our institutions, we need also to respect the choices of our graduates who pursue professional trajectories that take them away from our own networks and professional comfort zone without seeing that as a failure of the department or a personal disappointment.

At the same time, graduate mentors must begin to imagine and shape new opportunities for both graduate education and post-graduate employment within the academy that not only permit but encourage publicly engaged scholarship. Such efforts can range from supporting professional organizations that promote public scholarship to working with faculty and graduate students within their own universities to make more visible the publicly engaged work already taking place. Mentors who are familiar with the professional networks of faculty working in the field and who give graduate students access to those networks represent an invaluable resource for graduate students entering the academic job market.

Similarly, graduate mentoring must also take seriously the concerns of individual students who see their career pathways—academic or otherwise—obscured by their involvement in public scholarship, rather than sacrificing those students on the altar of institutional change, as discussed below. In this category I include students who have done substantial publicly engaged work and then decide they want to refocus their efforts along more traditional lines of knowledge production, as well as students who are engaged currently in community-based work but resist making that work visible within their own scholarship. As much as we may seek to develop stronger profiles for our institutions as publicly engaged, we also need to respect the integrity of those commitments and the individuals who enact them. Not everyone can or should do public scholarship; the point is not to shift the traditional academic track to a publicly engaged one, but rather to make room for both tracks to be acknowledged as legitimate modes of scholarship.

### Becoming Agents of Institutional Change

Each of the two recommendations above requires primary implementation on the level of individual relationships between mentors and students, but each also hints at the need for a larger, systematic change on the level of institutions. For instance, if publicly engaged work is to be recognized as a legitimate form of scholarship, this requires not only that the individual mentor and student acknowledge it as such, but that other faculty and students (at both the home university and more broadly), institutional review boards, professional organizations, promotion and tenure processes, university and departmental ranking systems, and hiring committees also recognize it as such. While this is an undeniably tall order, it presents an immense opportunity to rethink higher education and its possibilities, particularly as these discussions are already taking place within the context of shrinking budgets, the privatization of public universities, and the commercialization and instrumentalization of education more generally.[1] Higher education is changing; public scholarship has the opportunity to shape that change.

Thus we return to the institutional nature of common sense and to Gramsci's conviction that no system of hegemony, including its common sense, is ever a closed circuit of power. There are always opportunities to subvert and challenge that common sense. If we are to contest common-sense assumptions around graduate mentoring in support of publicly engaged scholarship, then institutional space must be carved out for that work in order for the interpersonal mentoring relationship to thrive.

First and foremost, this means developing programs that encourage and recognize public scholarship as scholarship, both within specific colleges and universities and across the higher education sector. Imagining America's Tenure Team Initiative (TTI) attempts to do exactly this for junior faculty on the tenure track. While the TTI focuses specifically on reworking promotion and tenure documents and processes, its impact has been felt throughout the university in the form of heightened recognition of public scholarship in graduate education as well as in faculty research. Likewise, the University of Washington's Graduate Certificate in Public Scholarship seeks to acknowledge graduate students engaged in this work by supporting them with coursework in public scholarship, mentoring, conference funding, and the conferring of a formal certification. Imagining America's Publicly Active Graduate Education (PAGE) program brings together engaged graduate students from across many universities at their annual conference and in ongoing projects, as well as connecting participants to senior scholars. Many other programs on the master's level, like UW Bothell's Cultural Studies and New York University's Arts and Public Policy programs, explicitly encourage publicly engaged graduate research as part of their curriculum.

Other necessary institutional changes include the prioritization of funding structures for publicly engaged work, the explicit naming of community-based work in academic job advertisements (even if it is only one among a number of possible areas of concentration), and finding ways to tell our story that resist the rankings of departments and schools according to metrics like job placement (wherein only academic jobs count) or time to completion of degree (which, while an important statistic, can disadvantage departments encouraging public scholarship). The more public scholarship begins to appear across multiple documents and infrastructural systems within and across universities, the more it will become visible as a viable route for graduate students and faculty alike.

One particularly challenging institutional structure to address is the Institutional Review Board (IRB). While many faculty have learned the habit (or common sense) of avoiding the IRB whenever possible, public scholarship provides a useful moment to reassert the importance of a substantive engagement with research ethics. One of the most useful steps a mentor can do to support publicly engaged graduate students is to further educate the IRB on the ways in which public scholarship is indeed research, needs to be understood as such, and engages with the field of research ethics in important and meaningful ways. A graduate student I was advising once panicked when her application for IRB approval was returned, declaring that her project was not, in fact, research. While being released from IRB oversight was a relief for the student and conducting her project was simplified as a result, the lack of recognition of the project as research carries with it deeper institutional implications surrounding the marginalization of public scholarship. Avoiding the IRB and its approval processes may at times be expeditious, but such declarations shape the broader contours of what is understood to count or not count as scholarship. Particularly given public scholarship's deep engagement with the ethics of research and knowledge production, educating the IRB becomes a crucial step in fostering institutional change.

Graduate student funding must also be refashioned to provide greater support for those involved in public scholarship. Funding for students is too often tied to labor—whether teaching, research, or administration—that pulls them *away* from their publicly engaged scholarship, rather than supporting them *within* that work. While this dynamic rings true for most graduate students regardless of their involvement with community-based work, the results are particularly egregious for those students tackling the more time-consuming and unpredictable requirements of public scholarship. We must take care not to praise (and use for our own public relations campaigns) the hard work of student public scholars while simultaneously refusing to fund that work itself. Finding funding sources to actively support publicly engaged scholarship remains at the top of the priority list for graduate mentoring, as does providing students with further training in grant writing and other fundraising skills that may prove crucial in sustaining their public scholarship over a career.

Finally, graduate mentoring needs to resist the temptation to encourage publicly active students to engage in the speed-up of the modern academy without lending a critical eye to that speed-up. This may be the most difficult institutional change of all, as well as the most difficult to negotiate in individual cases. In an economic and professional atmosphere where finding jobs—whether academic or otherwise—becomes more and more competitive, reward systems all encourage graduate students to place productivity above all else. As we develop programs to recognize public scholarship, we would do well to avoid formalizing those programs to the point where they become yet another qualification or professional hoop that students must jump through as they pursue academic success. In other words, our efforts to make public scholarship more visible should avoid making some projects (or types of projects) visible at the cost of rendering other projects even less visible. Within this context, mentors need to work on institutional expectations that recognize and value the scholarship resulting from long-term, committed public engagements over flashier but less substantive partnerships, while also helping graduate students navigate the increasingly intense demands of their profession in a manner that allows them to develop a solid record of scholarship in a sustainable, integrative way.

Ultimately, graduate mentoring for public scholarship must tackle the systemic project of changing institutional norms and expectations to better encourage and recognize public scholarship. Without working on this larger project of institutional change—a project in which senior faculty have immensely more power than their junior colleagues and graduate students—the common-sense advice to the individual student to avoid or limit their involvement in public scholarship will remain salient and difficult for individuals to overcome.

### So, What's a Graduate Student to Do?

What seems, and perhaps once was, good advice for the individual may no longer be so. Part of what makes common sense so insidious is the way in which it blinds us to changing contexts, so that we continue to believe that enlightened self-interest remains on the side of common sense, failing to notice that the profession is making new space for the innovations of public scholarship. While the bulk of this essay has been aimed at ways for mentors to improve graduate mentoring, this conclusion briefly takes up the opportunities available to graduate students (and junior faculty) to improve the mentoring they receive. For if graduate students are in many ways more prepared for the rigors of public scholarship than their mentors, and mentoring does become a more radically collaborative process, then graduate students themselves will become central players both in transforming the one-on-one relationships of mentoring and in promoting the structural changes necessary to foster vibrant environments in which public scholarship can thrive.

First, seek the advice of all the potential mentors with whom you feel comfortable; do not limit yourself to a single mentor, or your formal program advisor. Be as entrepreneurial as you can in finding possible mentors who can address different parts of your overall interest in public scholarship. Contact supportive local and national organizations for suggestions. No one voice or perspective can grasp all the possible avenues for your own publicly engaged scholarship or career. And do not be surprised if the advice you receive from multiple mentors is contradictory; that most likely means that you are receiving a decent range of opinions.

Second, seek mentors outside of the academy who can help you keep perspective and stay grounded in your political commitments. Community-based mentors can be invaluable in helping you avoid taking yourself too seriously as an academic, while simultaneously reminding you of why you are engaged in the academy in the first place. Such mentors can also help keep your decision to work within academic institutions an active choice, rather than a default position based on your previous views of the world and your place within it.

Third, cultivate your relationships with mentors; continue to draw connections between your interests and projects. Suggest co-authoring a piece with mentors you feel have insights that would help flesh out work with which you are engaged. And keep the lines of communication open. Many mentors are working formally and informally with a large number of students; while you should respect their time, you should also be willing to assert yourself in order to stay on their radar. Keeping faculty invested in your projects and up to date on your progress will help them to be better mentors for you.

Fourth, insist on the radical collaboration for which I argue above. Pursue your public scholarship with commitment and confidence, and be willing to push back if necessary to carve out the space for the publicly engaged work that sustains you as a graduate student and as a person. Put the community-based mentors with whom you work in touch with your graduate mentors. Be willing to switch mentors if need be. And accept that sometimes the advice you receive from mentors within and outside the academy may be more accurate than you wish to admit.

Finally, and most importantly, do not wait until you reach some future stage of professional development to engage in the debates around public scholarship and its role within the university, whether they take place one-on-one with your mentors, within your cohort of graduate students, or within your department, your university, professional organizations, community partnerships, or amongst broader publics. These debates and the academic infrastructures they propose will shape the field—your field—for years to come. Take an active role in generating the insights that will challenge the assumptions of academic common sense and make our institutions more conducive to public scholarship in the future.

The notion that public scholarship is somehow less than fully realized scholarship, or that it distracts graduate students from the "real" work of research and getting "good" jobs, remains firmly ensconced in the common sense of academia. That common sense is not impenetrable, however, and effective graduate mentoring, when taking a radically collaborative form, can not only nurture a new generation of scholars but also educate existing faculties regarding the immense theoretical and empirical potential of public scholarship. It is to this task that we commit ourselves, together, as publicly engaged mentors and students.

**Notes**

1. See, for example, the work of EduFactory (http://www.edufactory.org/wp).

**Works Cited**

Gramsci, Antonio. 1972. *Selections from the* Prison Notebooks *of Antonio Gramsci*. Edited and translated by Quintin Hoare and Geoffrey Nowell Smith. New York: International Publishers.

Newfield, Christopher. 2008. *Unmaking the Public University: The Forty-Year Assault on the Middle Class*. Cambridge, MA: Harvard University Press.

Schuster, Jack H., and Martin J. Finkelstein. 2006. *The American Faculty: The Restructuring of Academic Work and Careers*. Baltimore, MD: The Johns Hopkins University Press.

PART TWO

# TRANSITIONS

# Mentors' Conceptions of Mentoring in Formalized Faculty Relationships

## *Susanna Calkins and Greg Light*

Senior faculty members often hold a position of critical influence at universities worldwide. Whether their voices are insistent or subtle, far-reaching or ad hoc, senior faculty members—especially those holding long-term or tenured appointments, or with important leadership positions at the institution—usually possess reputations, experience, and knowledge that can give their words and actions clout. As Mullen and Forbes (2000) have suggested, junior (still untenured) faculty members, often struggling to balance research and teaching demands, have long looked informally to senior colleagues for advice, wisdom, information, comfort, and feedback as they strive to meet the many demands they face. In a recent review of the international research literature regarding mentoring, Hobson and colleagues identify a number of benefits associated with supporting the professional development of early teachers, including "reduced feelings of isolation, increased confidence and self-esteem, professional growth, and improved self-reflection and problem-solving capacities" (2009, 209). In addition, a range of studies have indicated that mentors can help acclimate junior colleagues to the rigors and expectations of academic practices of teaching, research, and service (see Hobson et al. 2009).

Recognizing the value of such mentoring relationships, many colleges and universities in the U.S. and abroad have sought to establish more formalized mentoring arrangements for early-career faculty, who frequently struggle to keep up with their broad academic portfolio of scholarly research, teaching, or clinical demands and other professional obligations. More recently, formal faculty development programs focused on enhancing the teaching of younger faculty have included the use of senior colleagues as mentors (Kamvounias et al. 2008). Such mentors have provided observation and feedback, and supported junior colleagues in their acclimation to departmental culture in general, and with respect to the teaching role in particular. At the same time, they have helped inculcate collegiality and a sense of disciplinary ownership and identity in their mentees (Mathias 2005), and have built capacity in their mentees' understanding of teaching and learning (Smyth 2003).

Yet these senior faculty mentors—whether the role is formally assigned or voluntarily adopted—do not necessarily know how to mentor well, and the value of providing effective mentoring *for faculty mentors* has received insufficient attention. Many faculty simply draw on their own experience of being mentored (if indeed they received such mentoring as junior faculty or as graduate students), with mixed results (Calkins and Kelley 2005; Hobson et al. 2009). Furthermore, the different ways in which mentoring is understood by the mentors themselves is under-researched, and, unsurprisingly, the impact of different understandings on individual mentee development has not been conclusively demonstrated (Clutterbuck and Lane 2004; Zellers et al. 2008).

As Hobson et al. (2009) point out, a growing number of programs have introduced a reflective component into the mentoring process, so that mentors can consider, and potentially change, their approach to mentoring. However, mentors may nonetheless leave their general approach to mentoring intact, only tweaking for differences in individual mentees and not fully reflecting on their overall conception of what it means to be a mentor.

This chapter seeks to address a gap in our understanding of academic mentoring by investigating the nature and extent of variation in how senior faculty understand or conceive of the experience of mentoring junior colleagues. By analyzing and understanding how faculty mentors differ in their conceptions of the practice of mentoring, we hope to identify ways to promote critical reflection, learning, and meaningful professional development for both the mentors and their mentees.

## Methods

### Research Design

Our research explores how senior faculty, serving as mentors to junior faculty enrolled in a year-long faculty development program focused on teaching, conceived of mentoring. Taking an interview-based phenomenographic approach, we sought to identify the range of conceptions about mentoring held by our study participants (by "conception" we mean how an experience is described or understood by an individual). Phenomenography is a method for capturing how groups of people approach a given phenomenon, exploring how individuals understand, describe, or conceptualize that phenomenon (Micari et al. 2007). Phenomenographers thus seek to look at all the possible descriptions to capture the complete variation within that experience (Marton, Dell'Alba, and Beaty 1993). Specifically, we sought to understand the range of mentoring experiences as recognized by senior faculty serving as teaching mentors to junior faculty colleagues.

*Setting*

Our study was conducted over three years at Northwestern University, our home institution. At Northwestern, tenured and tenure-line faculty are expected to focus intensely on their research, and may only teach between one and four classes in an academic year. In their third year, tenure-line faculty undergo a review to assess their progress towards tenure, which they are expected to achieve by their seventh year. For nearly 14 years, faculty at the university's Searle Center for Advancing Learning and Teaching have been running the Searle Fellows program, a year-long faculty development program, for small cohorts of tenure-line faculty (15–18 participants a year) to help them develop their teaching. In our respective roles as director (Light) and associate director (Calkins) of the Searle Center, we have facilitated the program, working with both the Searle Fellows and their mentors.

*Participants*

Study participants were all senior faculty members who had agreed to serve as teaching mentors to junior colleagues enrolled in the Searle Fellows program. We had instructed each of the Searle Fellows to identify a senior colleague in their department (or in a closely related field) who would care about their professional development as teachers. Junior faculty were given the following criteria in selecting their mentors: They had to be able and willing to participate in at least some of the program events, discuss issues on teaching and learning, and provide feedback on a substantial teaching and learning project that the junior faculty member would develop during the year. Thus, most junior faculty selected mentors with whom they had a self-reported collegial relationship, although on three occasions we suggested mentors. A few Searle Fellows selected senior colleagues who were already serving as their mentors in some other capacity.

Across three years (2006, 2007, 2008), 22 out of 50 tenured senior mentors (44%) agreed to participate in the study. In the first year of the study, three subjects were recruited (from a cohort of 15) as a pilot sample with whom we could test the interview protocol. As the modifications made to the protocol based on the pilot were minor, we added them to the overall study sample. In the second year, 8 out of 18 mentors (44%) participated, and in the third year, we had 11 participants out of 17 (64%).

Each subject participated in the study in the same year that they served as mentors in the program. We interviewed each senior faculty member before the first program event of the year. Nine came from science and engineering fields; six came from medicine; five from humanities, social sciences and the arts; and two from other professional schools. Their teaching experience ranged from 6 to over 20 years. When we welcomed them as program mentors, all study participants informally indicated at least a passing interest in mentoring and did not openly express any negative opinions about mentoring.

*Procedure*

We interviewed each mentor once, prior to their involvement in the Searle Fellows program. The interviews were semistructured and lasted 30–50 minutes. To ensure that participants felt comfortable sharing their thoughts with us, we informed them that their responses would be kept confidential and that they could stop the interview at any point. We also assured them that we would assign them subject codes for our analysis and, if we used any of their comments in our research, we would conceal any identifying details, such as their educational backgrounds and areas of expertise. We used a semistructured interview protocol with 12 items, six of which focused on mentoring (the other questions focused on conceptions of teaching and learning and were used for a different study).

We first asked our participants to explain how they generally understood the concept of mentoring ("How do you understand the term "mentoring?"; "What does it mean to be a mentor?"). Secondly, we asked them to describe their perceptions of the qualities of a good or effective mentor, and to explain the role they believed a mentor should play in the mentoring relationship. These questions were designed to capture our participants' overall understanding of the concept of mentoring. Thirdly, we asked them to describe their experience serving as mentors ("Have you ever been a mentor in other contexts? What was that experience like?"). Lastly, we asked them to explain how they expected to interact with their junior colleague and whether they expected to learn or otherwise benefit from being a mentor ("Do you expect to learn or gain anything from being a mentor to your colleague?"). After each set of questions, we probed their responses carefully in order to get at the participant's underlying thinking about what it means to mentor a junior colleague in areas related to learning and teaching.

**Data Analysis**

The interviews were audiotaped, fully transcribed, and analyzed in several stages. In the first stage, one of us read through the interview transcripts to select passages in which the participants' discussed their ideas about the characteristics of a "good" mentor. We then independently read through the selected passages, mainly to determine whether the participants had a general idea of what good mentoring, as regards the kinds of characteristics suggested in the literature on mentoring—e.g., being approachable, accessible, knowledgeable, empathetic, generous with advice, encouraging, confidence-building, etc. (Clark, Harden, and Johnson 2000; Anderson and Shannon 1988). For example, if a participant indicated that a mentor should "be approachable and offer good advice," we noted that his or her description generally mapped onto characteristics widely associated with "good mentoring." If a participant was unable to generate a response or said he or she did not know what it means to be a "good mentor," we noted that as well. We then compared our responses. For this first stage, we had no disagreement and we readily achieved consensus for each participant.

In the second stage of the analysis, the phenomenographic stage, one of us read through the transcripts, identifying passages in which the participants described their understanding of mentoring, both generally and in the specific context of mentoring their junior colleague in the areas of learning and teaching. At this point, we both read through the excerpted transcripts and independently identified categories of description that seemed to express qualitatively different perspectives. We then discussed together the variation among responses that we had each noted. During this stage of our analysis, we independently found that variation in participant descriptions of how they view mentoring could be detected along three important features: (1) his or her role in the mentoring relationship; (2) the nature of mentoring; and (3) the process of mentoring. Across these three features, mentors reported two main aspects of variation in their thinking. The first aspect of variation concerned whether they felt the focus of the mentoring was on themselves as an exemplar for the mentee to follow (mentor-focused), or on the mentee developing an individual path (mentee-focused). In the second aspect of variation, mentors differed in terms of how passive or active they understood the process of mentoring to be. These two sets of variation in how mentors reported their thinking about mentoring led to four unique categories of description described below.

In the final stage of our analysis, we tested these findings by independently going back through each transcript with a view to the features identified, and the two aspects of variation within each feature, to ensure they described every participant. In doing so, we were able to locate each participant within the categories of description identified. We then compared our decisions, refining our analysis through our discussions of each individual. We were able to reach consensus in each case. Throughout the process, we reviewed the transcriptions in their entirety to keep the quotes in context.

## Findings

We adduce, first, how our participants characterize "good" or "effective" mentors; second, four different conceptions of mentoring in two overarching orientations; and third, the variation among these four conceptions.

### Characteristics of a "Good" Mentor

When asked to identify the characteristics of a "good" mentor, nearly all of the mentors indicated at least some of the characteristics that have been well documented in the literature. One indicated that he did not know what it meant to be a good mentor, but that he was willing to learn. Collectively, the others emphasized characteristics such as approachability and accessibility, as well as being knowledgeable and caring. For example, a professor of medicine remarked,

> Good mentors should be empathetic, should be objective. Should ... also temper with that [empathy] the ability to know when it is important to be tough, and when it is important to leave the person alone. When it is important to have the person just go and experience it themselves, and when it is important to just jump in and help out. (S1)[1]

Most mentors talked about the necessity of offering advice, being encouraging, and building self-confidence in their mentees. A comment by a professor of science illustrates this concept:

> Certainly an effective mentor has to be willing to listen, and be willing to listen on someone else's schedule, not just their own. And [the mentor] has to be able to offer thoughtful, reflective responses, rather than knee-jerk responses. And should be able to offer anecdotes or actual data or stories to back up their suggestions, rather than just say "this is my abstract view or radical framework about how teaching should occur." (G3)

Nearly three-quarters indicated that they had never been mentored formally, and five stated that they had never received any mentoring, except perhaps from a parent. For example, a communications professor commented:

> I must admit I don't have good concrete ideas of this since I was never mentored. But I guess I sort of adopted the idea that probably a mentor should be available for discussion about what he is doing in his teaching, answer questions, for me to give my advice when appropriate. (M4)

All 22 mentors expressed a general sense of good will about being asked to serve as mentors in the program. Each mentor also expressed a general interest in helping their mentees, although as we describe below, their understanding of what mentoring should consist of, and how active they needed to be as mentors, ranged considerably.

## Conceptions of Mentoring: Categories and Features

As described above, in our analysis of the excerpted transcripts, we identified four categories of description for the understanding of mentoring. As reported above, these understandings fell within two broad orientations—mentor-focused and mentee-focused—and differed in terms of how passive or active the relationship was viewed to be. These four conceptual understandings we call "the Model," "the Shepherd," "the Guide," and "the Companion" (see Table 5.1).

Mentors holding the mentor-focused orientation (the Model and the Shepherd) generally view their role to be the measuring stick for the mentee's success. The nature of mentoring is to encourage their mentees to closely follow in their footsteps (although they may also urge their mentees to avoid mistakes they had made earlier in their career) in order to achieve the same or better professional success and status as the mentor. The mentor seeks to mentor as he or she was once mentored, or otherwise reproduces mentoring that he or she observed in others. Mentoring here is often viewed as a necessary part of the job, although such mentors may see some external benefits of mentoring, such as seeing their image reflected in their mentees' work or professional comportment.

In contrast, mentors holding the mentee-focused orientation (the Guide and the Companion) regard mentoring as encouraging and helping mentees to develop their own voices and construct their own paths to success. Indeed, they define success for themselves in terms of how well the mentee has achieved this independence of voice. Mentors holding this orientation are often more reflective, seeking to learn from the mentee and the process of mentoring itself. They actively construct alternate ways of being mentored, and do not seek to recreate their own experience of being mentored.

Conceptions of mentoring also varied with respect to how proactive the mentors viewed the nature of the mentoring process to be; that is, how active or passive the mentors described their role in the relationship. For example, almost all of the mentors talked about offering advice to their mentees. However, some mentors described the process as more hands-on and engaged process (what we call "active"), while others waited for their mentees to approach them with a problem (what we view as "passive"). And, as will be seen, both active and passive understandings were found within each of the two main orientations. In addition, we found these two sets of variation suggested to varying degrees in all three features describing the mentoring conceptions.

## Mentor-Focused Conceptions of Mentoring: "The Model" and "the Shepherd"

Mentors holding mentor-focused conceptions of mentoring—the

**TABLE 5.1. Conceptions of mentoring.**

| Conception Features | Mentor-Focused | | Mentee-Focused | |
|---|---|---|---|---|
| | The Model (passive) | The Shepherd (active) | The Guide (passive) | The Companion (active) |
| How the mentor conceives of his or her role in the mentoring relationship | Opportunity to serve as expert academic resource, with expertise that can be reproduced | Opportunity to create mentee in mentor's own academic image, and/or to continue mentor's work | Opportunity to serve as a guide as mentee grows and develops academic self | Opportunity to encourage mentee to explore and develop mentee's academic self |
| | Assumes mentee will adopt the "right" voice (similar to mentor's voice) | Advises mentee to adopt "right" voice (similar to mentor's voice) | Expects mentee to develop his or her own unique voice | Challenges mentee to develop his or her own unique voice |
| | Views mentoring as a means to enhance mentor's reputation or to fulfill professional obligations | Embraces mentoring as a means to promote mentee's strength as extension of mentor's self-image | Sees mentoring as an opportunity for mentor to also learn from mentee | Values mentoring as an opportunity to also explore and develop mentor's own growth |
| | Views mentoring as modeling "right" academic values of the community to interested junior colleagues | Embraces mentoring as providing "right" academic values of the community to junior colleagues | Regards mentoring as assisting junior colleagues to find their own place in the academic community | Approaches mentoring as a means to challenge junior colleagues to construct their own unique space in the academic community |
| The nature of mentoring | Views mentoring as a fixed process; mentor reproduces real or assumed experience being mentored | Uses mentoring as a process to steer the mentee, reproducing mentor's real or idealized experience of mentoring | Approaches mentoring as a fluid process; open to ways of mentoring other than how mentor was mentored | Actively constructs new ways to mentor other than how mentor was mentored |
| | Assumes mentee will approach problems as mentor does | Persuades mentee to approach problems as mentor does | Hopes mentee will develop mentee's own solutions with mentor's guidance | Encourages mentee to construct new solutions with mentor's guidance |
| | Models the "right" path or what will lead to success | Directs mentee to follow mentor's "right" path to success | Understands many paths for mentee other than mentor's own path | Challenges mentee to create mentee's own path |
| The process of mentoring | May let mentee "fail" for not seeking or following mentor's advice | Expects mentee to take mentor's advice (the "right" way) | May let mentee "fail" in order to learn (opportunity for mentee's growth) | Actively encourages mentee to find and develop mentee's own solutions/try out new ideas and opportunities |
| | May offer "right" tips and strategies, but only when asked | Monitors mentee's progress, impressing his or her own solutions on mentee | May wait for mentee to approach after mentee grapples with problem first | Will approach mentee about his or her progress; may seek to deal with problem together |
| | Non-reflective and/or less invested in mentoring process | Partially reflective and highly invested in mentoring process | More reflective and somewhat invested in mentoring process | Highly reflective on and highly invested in mentoring process |

Model and the Shepherd—expect their mentees to approach problems as they do, essentially reproducing their own steps to success rather than allowing their mentees to define success for themselves. We classify these mentors broadly as "mentor-focused" because they focus on the role of the mentor in the mentoring relationship, rather than on the role of the mentee (see Table 5.1). These mentors tend to view mentoring as a didactic and somewhat fixed process, whereby they reproduce their own experience of being mentored. In this process, advice is often ad hoc, situational, and driven by simple tips. For example, an engineering professor commented:

> I think a mentor is somebody who hopefully has gone through sort of similar experiences that you are going through now, that you can go to and sit up and say, "Hey, this is what I am seeing, what did you do?" Somebody you can sort of get advice from their experience. (M3)

In this case, the mentor has an expectation that the mentee will follow his advice, and either reproduce the mentor's steps to achieve success, or follow the mentor's recommendation for a different path—but with that recommendation still based on what the mentor had concluded about his or her own experience, rather than the mentee's perceived needs. Essentially, any advice or recommendations stem from the mentor's sense of self.

The Model and the Shepherd differ primarily in the active or passive stance adopted in the mentoring relationship. Models tends to be *passive*, waiting for their mentees to approach with questions or concerns, usually not initiating contact or follow-up themselves. Models view themselves as figures to be emulated. Significantly, these mentors seem to assume that if they do not hear from a mentee, then there is nothing for them to do. As a communications professor explains, "I am not sure [what constitutes effective mentoring] since I haven't done it. [My mentee] usually doesn't come and ask advice about things..." (M4). In this case, the professor is aware on some level that he may not be a very effective mentor. In his view, mentoring begins with a mentee seeking out advice, rather than a mentor being proactive in the endeavor. Essentially, the lack of mentoring between him and his mentee stems primarily from his mentee's absence and lack of participation in the mentoring process (he "doesn't come and ask advice"), not from his own passivity.

In contrast to mentors holding the Model conception, mentors with the Shepherd conception tend to be more active and hands-on, frequently initiating contact with their mentees. They tend to expect a lot from their mentees, and at the same time, view their mentors as following their own recipe for success; a female engineering professor explains, "I want really [to be] friendly, to help them, to be very open, and to be supportive, but at the same time to be demanding" (S2). The active quality suggested in this quote sets the Shepherd apart from her more passive counterparts holding the Model conception. Mentors holding the Shepherd conception may seek to actively monitor their mentees' progress, to shepherd them along, and to check to make sure their mentees are following through on the mentor's advice.

Moreover, "reproductive" mentors—those who see their role as, in effect, self-replication—tend to give unambiguous direction as to what their mentees should do, or provide the "right" answer to a problem. For example, a professor of history noted, in response to the question about a mentor's responsibilities,

> [the mentee's] teaching has got to look a certain way if everything is going to go smoothly for her institutionally, right? Toward tenure and, you know, toward all those professional things. So, at some level, it's about making sure that there are these expectations, like them or not, that need to look a certain way and how are you going to do that? (S4)

Here, the mentor wants to ensure that his mentee's professional activities "look a certain way" in order to promote success in her career.

Generally, we found that mentors holding mentor-focused conceptions did not express any expectation that they might learn or gain anything from the mentoring process or from their mentees. Any perceived rewards come from the satisfaction of having aided the mentee's professional development, the perceived enhancement to their own profile or reputation, or the perception of having performed a necessary or required task for the department or institution. As the previously quoted engineering professor commented,

> I am a mentor, I am a teacher.... It is really important, because when you are speaking with all of my students [it's] interesting. All of them, they want to be like me, without exception. You know, for them, the dream is to be a professor, so you have a way that you attract the respect. (S2)

While in this case the professor was referring to mentoring her graduate students, she had referred to the process earlier in the interview as being similar to how she mentored early-career faculty. For her, the benefit of mentoring is to help her mentees be more like her, so that in effect their success will reflect her success.

### Mentee-Focused Conceptions of Mentoring: "The Guide" and "the Companion"

In contrast to those holding mentor-focused conceptions, faculty holding *mentee-focused* conceptions—the Guide and the Companion—consider the mentee to be the focus of the mentoring relationship. Mentoring is not about reproducing the mentor's journey but helping the mentee to create her own path.

Mentors holding these conceptions also reported being more open to learning, both from their mentees and from the experience of mentoring. One professor of medicine described the process of mentoring as "mutually enriching" (C4). Others view the process of mentoring as an important part of developing community, both in the department and in the discipline. For example, a different professor of medicine explained that for him, mentoring is "life fulfillment":

> One of the great joys and great pleasures is being in the company of wonderful, very bright, talented people who are making a contribution. So what I gain out of [mentoring] is ... life fulfillment. You know, here's a person who's a colleague, who's a friend.... We can enjoy the work together.... It's better than a hobby.... It's creative, it's fun. It's a contribution. (G4)

"The Guide" tends to be relatively hands-off, or passive, in the mentoring process. Like Models, Guides often advocate letting their mentees solve a problem on their own, and may wait to be asked before offering feedback or advice. Unlike Models, however, who may let a mentee "fail" for not soliciting or not following the mentor's advice, Guides are more likely to view failure as an important part of the mentee's professional development. Guides regard their mentees' understanding of their own strengths and weaknesses as an important part of their growth. As another engineering professor explains:

> And then there are also times where it just bothers me when

people want to reinvent the wheel, so, "Why don't we do it this way?" I think that could be a fault of mine where I step in and say, "Been there, done that, can't do it that way," instead of letting them try and learn for themselves. (G1)

This professor consciously refrains from intervening, even when he thinks his mentee is making a mistake. Thus, staying out of the way is a deliberate strategy that allows his mentees to work out a problem for themselves:

> Usually I have found that my inclination is to stop it because it is stupid, and I let them go and I am glad they did, because it was better; they really found the solution and they discovered things I had not anticipated. So it would have been wrong to have stifled that. (G1)

In contrast, Companions tend to be highly engaged and active participants in the mentoring process, making more effort to support the mentee and monitor his or her professional activities. Like Shepherds, Companions do not wait to be asked to give tough criticism and honest feedback to their mentees when necessary. They differ, to a critical degree, from the mentor-focused Shepherds in that they do not require the mentee to follow the mentor's established expectations for success. A science professor describes the act of mentoring as

> looking out for the person that you are mentoring and seeing to their professional development. And that means, if you see them doing something stupid, you are not afraid to tell them that and if you see an opportunity there, do something to help them to make the connection.... It is something that as a mentor you don't really want to say, because it is going to cause a little bit of pain, but nonetheless you have to, so that's what I mean by brutal honesty. (C3)

In this case the mentor actively wants the mentee "to make the connection" but is not trying to impose a specific formula or path to success even if it causes "a little bit of pain." Similarly, as a professor of medicine remarks, the mentor

> has to be willing to spend time to think about the needs of the mentee. [You] have to be willing to put time aside and to really get an interest [in] the activities of the mentee and just not be afraid and calling the mentee and saying "I think you

should consider this or do this," or "Why don't you change this?" (C2).

Here, the mentor is raising questions for the mentee to consider, after spending time reflecting on the mentee's interests and needs. The Companions often seek out their mentees when there is a perceived problem in order to work out the problem together, or to help their mentees find new solutions that are in the mentees' best interest.

More broadly, mentors holding mentee-focused conceptions of mentoring seem more reflective about what it means to be a mentor. They are open to constructing a different mentoring relationship— that is, to mentoring differently from how they were once mentored. They recognize that the mentee's experience is unique and may not fit their own. Such mentors believe they should challenge their mentees to excel, but allow them to find their own unique paths to excellence. The mentoring relationship often has a multi-level focus; mentors may discuss day-to-day practical problems with their mentees, as the mentor-focused mentors do, but they also address deeper, ongoing professional and career-related issues facing their mentees. As a music professor suggests, mentoring "happens when a person comes in and says, 'OK, I'm approaching my third year review…. What kinds of things do you think I should be doing differently in my work?'" (C1).

Rather than simply giving a set of steps that may have worked for themselves, mentee-focused mentors will concentrate on helping their mentees sort out their own path to success. They expect their mentees to develop their own unique voices, and to construct their own space within the academic community.

As indicated in Table 5.2, we found that 9 of 22 mentors (41%) held mentor-focused conceptions, with 5 (23%) holding the Model conception and 4 (18%) holding the Shepherd conception. We further identified 13 of 22 (59%) mentors as having mentee-focused conceptions, with 9 (41%) holding the Guide conception, and 4 (18%) holding the Companion conception. Almost two thirds ($N = 14$; 64%) appeared to view mentoring as a passive process, while one third ($N = 8$; 36%) viewed mentoring as a more active endeavor. There is no attempt here, however, to suggest that these numbers reflect larger patterns in academia; they are meant simply to describe our sample.

| Mentor-Focused | | Mentee-Focused | |
|---|---|---|---|
| The Model (Passive) | The Shepherd (Active) | The Guide (Passive) | The Companion (Active) |
| 5 | 4 | 9 | 4 |

TABLE 5.2. Participants by conception type.

## Discussion

Our phenomenographic analysis disclosed variation in how senior faculty understand mentoring of junior faculty as regards their teaching. This variation provided the basis for a framework that offered a way to capture nuances in the mentoring experience. However, as we mentioned above, our subjects consisted of faculty who (1) had agreed to serve as mentors in a year-long faculty development program, and (2) were willing to set aside time to be interviewed, implying at least a tacit interest in thinking about what it means to be a mentor. Thus, we are not seeking to generalize this framework to all senior faculty, or even to all senior faculty involved in mentoring programs. But we do think there are some lessons to be learned from capturing this variation among senior faculty who *care* about mentoring their junior colleagues.

First, we found it interesting that nearly half of our mentors would be considered mentor-focused, with nearly a third holding the Model conception. What does it mean for junior faculty when they are expected to follow a set path, and imitate their senior colleagues? Certainly, recent research suggests that female faculty, for example, are hindered and even excluded from achievement and advancement when they cannot (or choose not to) navigate the cultural norms of the department or field to which they belong (Maranto and Griffin 2011). Yet we must also wonder whether junior faculty feel inhibited in their professional decisions—are they curtailed from being more innovative? Standards and expectations for teaching, research, service, administration, and tenure are shifting—and senior faculty may be hurting their junior colleagues if they expect them to follow the same narrow path they trod, perhaps many years before. Moreover, the widespread tendency to simply reproduce perceived paths to success might undermine innovation in departments and institutions—a topic that could be more fully explored in future studies.

Secondly, we categorized nearly two thirds of our mentors as passive. This may reflect a lack of understanding about their specific role as mentors in the Searle Fellows program. Yet, since our questions were designed to elicit general conceptions of mentoring, as well as what it meant specifically to mentor their junior colleagues in teaching, this passivity may also suggest that some mentors may not know how, or may not be willing, to interact with their mentees in a more engaged way. They may also have felt reluctant to give advice to someone who is, after all, a colleague, albeit a much less experienced one. It may be, too, that at a research-intensive university like ours, where teaching is not privileged, faculty may feel uncomfortable giving advice about teaching, or believe if they do give advice about teaching, they will be leading their junior colleague astray— that is, off the bridge to tenure. This holds with Mathias's (2005) finding that in a UK higher-ed teacher development program, senior mentors who had to play dual assessment and evaluation roles for their junior colleagues did not consider themselves to be qualified experts in the area of "education." We think there is much to be done to help senior faculty recognize that they can learn to mentor effectively, especially if they are open to exploring best teaching strategies—including but not limited to effective peer observation, the constructive alignment of learning outcomes and assessments, innovative teaching methods, and effective mentoring strategies.[2]

Thirdly, we were pleased to discover also that more than half of our mentors were mentee-focused, focusing on their mentees' professional development as teachers. We were encouraged, moreover, to find that a third of the mentee-focused mentors held the Companion's conception. We contend that early-career faculty will thrive when paired with mentors who foster an environment in which they are encouraged to think through their needs, ambitions, and hopes, and to make reasonable decisions. The mentee-focused mentors served often as sounding boards, but did not specifically tell the mentees what to do—although on occasion the Companions might jump in and ask their mentees to give more sustained thought to their decisions and activities. For example, when referring to mentoring a junior colleague undergoing tenure review, a music professor commented,

> I think a mentor also has to be somebody who speaks up, who says without being asked, "I need to talk to you about something. It's really going to be a problem for you [in the tenure review process].... This isn't going to be easy for you to

hear...." I think there is that quality to it, so I think that is important to have. (C1)

## Conclusions

Taken together, these findings suggest that when serving as mentors, faculty should be asked—expected, even—to reflect critically on what it means to be a mentor, especially when mentoring junior colleagues. When involved in a formalized mentoring relationship, it is all the more critical that this reflection occur, because everyone involved may assume that *agreeing to be a mentor* means that one *knows how to mentor.* One way to foster this reflection would be to expose potential mentors to the variation between *mentor-* and *mentee-focused* conceptions, since research has shown that exposure to variation can enhance conceptual change and the adoption of more complex conceptions (McKenzie 2002).

The findings from this study provide a preliminary framework for understanding how senior faculty members may conceive of mentoring, particularly in regards to the teaching practice of junior faculty. Faculty development programs that systematically encourage reflection and critical inquiry in the mentoring process may help senior faculty develop a more sophisticated approach to mentoring. Faculty mentors could be encouraged to probe their understanding of mentoring through simple reflective exercises, informal conversations with other mentors, and discussions with their junior colleagues. Ultimately, helping faculty understand their own conception of mentoring may benefit their junior colleagues struggling to succeed in academia.

## Notes

1. Each quote is identified by the subject's unique classification code. Each code maps onto the conception types described in the chapter (M = Model; S = Shepherd; G = Guide; C = Companion).

2. For a fuller understanding of reflective teaching strategies, see Light, Cox, and Calkins 2009.

## Works Cited

Anderson, E. M., and A. L. Shannon. 1988. "Towards a Conceptualization of Mentoring." *Journal of Teacher Education* 39 (1): 38–42.

Calkins, S., and M. R. Kelley. 2005. "Mentoring and the Faculty-TA

Relationship: Faculty Perceptions and Practices." *Mentoring and Tutoring* 13 (2): 259–80.

Clark, R. A., S. L. Harden, and W. B. Johnson. 2000. "Mentor Relationships in Clinical Psychology Doctoral Training: Results of a National Survey." *Teaching of Psychology* 27 (4): 262–68.

Clutterbuck, D., and G. Lane, eds. 2004. *The Situational Mentor: An International Review of Competencies and Capabilities in Mentoring.* Burlington, VT: Gower.

Hobson, A. J., P. Ashby, A. Malderez, and P. D. Tomlinson. 2009. "Mentoring Beginning Teachers: What We Know and What We Don't." *Teacher and Teaching Education* 25:207–16.

Kamvounias, P., S. McGrath-Champ, and J. Yip. 2008. "'Gifts' in Mentoring: Mentees' Reflections on an Academic Development Program." *International Journal for Academic Development* 13 (1): 17–25.

Light, G., R. Cox, and S. Calkins. 2009. *Learning and Teaching in Higher Education: The Reflective Professional.* 2nd ed. London: SAGE.

Maranto, C. L., and A. E. Griffin. 2011. "The Antecedents of a 'Chilly Climate' for Women Faculty in Higher Education." *Human Relations* 64 (2): 139–59.

Marton, F., G. Dell'Alba, and E. Beaty. 1993. "Conceptions of Learning." *International Journal of Educational Research* 19:277–300.

Mathias, H. 2005. "Mentoring on a Programme for New University Teachers: A Partnership in Revitalizing and Empowering Collegiality." *International Journal for Academic Development* 10 (2): 95–106.

McKenzie, J. 2002. "Variation and Relevance Structures for University Teachers' Learning: Bringing About Change in Ways of Experiencing Teaching." In *Quality Conversations: Research and Development in Higher Education,* volume 25, edited by A. Goody, J. Harrington, and M. Northcote, 234–41. Perth, Australia: HERDSA.

Micari, M., G. Light, S. Calkins, and B. Streitwieser. 2007. "Assessment Beyond Performance: Phenomenography in Educational Evaluation." *American Journal of Evaluation* (28) 4: 458–76.

Mullen, C. A., and S. A. Forbes. 2000. "Untenured Faculty: Issues of

Transition, Adjustment and Mentorship." *Mentoring and Tutoring* 8:31–45.

Smyth, R. 2003. "Concepts of Change: Enhancing the Practice of Academic Staff Development in Higher Education." *International Journal for Academic Development* 8 (1/2): 51–60.

Zellers, D. F., V. M. Howard, and M. A. Barcic. 2008. "Faculty Mentoring Programs: Reenvisioning Rather than Reinventing the Wheel." *Review of Educational Research* (78) 3: 552–88.

# Taking Ownership of Your Mentoring: Lessons Learned from Participating in the Earth Science Women's Network

*Mirjam S. Glessmer, Amanda S. Adams, Meredith G. Hastings, and Rebecca T. Barnes*

**M**any academics, regardless of rank, often state that their career advancement was due in part to effective mentoring and the role of mentors in their professional development. Mentoring can take many forms— traditional one-on-one relationships, multiple mentoring, peer mentoring, and collective mentoring, among others. One-on-one mentoring relationships are prevalent in academia (MS and PhD advisors, postdoc advisors, tenure committees, etc.), yet these relationships do not necessarily lead to quality mentoring and can potentially fail the expectations and needs of the individual being mentored (the protégé). While some aspects of mentoring are still best served by formal mentoring relationships (i.e., a PhD committee advising the direction of a student's research), we favor a mentoring paradigm that empowers the protégé to actively expand his or her network and find the support needed—from different individuals, in different contexts, over different time spans—utilizing both informal and formal mentoring approaches to best serve individual needs.

Seeking and finding mentoring can be important for both career development and psychosocial development (Ragins and Cotton 1999). Mentors facilitate career development through sponsorship and coaching, and by providing challenging assignments, protection, and exposure (Kram 1985). Similarly, mentors provide psychosocial development through interpersonal aspects of the mentoring relationship, helping protégés increase their sense of competence, self-efficacy, and personal development (Ragins and Cotton 1999). Examples of positive career outcomes that have been linked to

113

mentoring include success in promotion (Scandura 1992), higher incomes (Chao, Waltz, and Gardner 1992; Dreher and Ash 1990), increased mobility (Scandura 1992), and greater career satisfaction (Fagenson 1989). The documented successes of one-on-one mentoring have led many institutions to adopt more formal mentoring programs in an effort to reach a wider range of participants. However, these more formalized relationships may not produce the same outcomes as informal mentoring relationships, particularly for women and other minorities.

The way most mentoring relationships develop can be unfavorable for these groups. Mutual identification and fulfillment of career needs serves as the basis for developing informal mentoring relationships, and mentors tend to select protégés that are younger versions of themselves, allowing them to contribute to future generations and avoid their own stagnation (Ragins and Cotton 1999). Perceived competence and interpersonal comfort are another important part of mentoring relationships (Allen, Poteet, and Burroughs 1997), which are often long term and adapt to the needs of the individuals (Ragins and Cotton 1999). However, one of the largest recognized barriers to the success and advancement of female students is a feeling of disconnection from others in their fields (Kemelgor and Etzkowitz 2001), due to an absence of female role models (National Research Council 2006). Many Earth Science departments, for example, have only one or two female faculty members (Holmes and O'Connell 2005). Such small numbers, below the critical mass to influence change and improve conditions (Etzkowitz et al. 1994), can create a sense of isolation. A lack of role models or understanding of the difficulties faced can make the workplace that much more challenging for women and minorities, particularly in the early stages of their careers. Additionally, when there is no critical mass, the few minorities in senior positions are not always perceived as viable role models; protégés look for mentors who can help them fit in to the institution, and women or minorities who are "the only ones" in their department do not impress protégés as people who can help them fit in (Chesler and Chesler 2002). Subtle bias also adds to the challenges faced by women and minorities in forming mentoring relationships. Moss-Racusin and colleagues (2012) conducted a study that evaluated the difference in how a candidate was evaluated for a lab technician position simply by changing the name (and thereby the gender) of the applicant. They found that the same applicant, when assigned a female name, was determined less competent, was offered a lower starting salary, and was less likely to be deemed a desirable protégé by reviewers.

While effective mentoring relationships can often be challenging for women and minorities to build, mentoring relationships organized by an institution do not necessarily mitigate this because mutual perceptions of competency and respect are less likely to be established in these relationships (Ragins and Cotton 1999). In fact, when mentors are assigned a protégé—particularly in programs where individuals chose to opt into formal mentoring to overcome their lack of informal mentoring—the mentors may view them as at-risk prospects who need the mentoring because they underperform; this is in stark contrast to development in informal mentoring relationships based on the protégé's potential (Ragins 1997). Additionally, in these highly visible, institutionally organized relationships, mentors are sometimes less likely to engage in mentoring activities such as sponsorship (e.g., recommending their protégé for an award or a leadership position), for fear that such behavior may be construed as favoritism (Ragins and Cotton 1999). These concerns and risks are often amplified when the protégé is of a different gender, race, and/or ethnic background than the mentor.

New models of mentoring have emerged in an effort to meet the challenges that women, minorities, and other underrepresented groups face in one-on-one mentoring relationships. Multiple mentoring, peer mentoring, and collective mentoring are models put forward by Chesler and Chesler (2002). Collective mentoring is institutional in nature, with an institution accepting responsibility to mentor a protégé via a collective group of mentors. This type of mentoring abandons the one-on-one relationship, but still relies on relationships defined by others. Both multiple mentoring and peer mentoring rely on the protégé being able to build a network of support. In multiple mentoring, the protégé seeks mentors for specific aspects of mentoring, but there are still clear roles of mentor and protégé. In peer mentoring, there is less distinction in professional level, and the mentoring focuses more on the support provided by peers who help each other overcome the same or similar challenges. In our collective experience, and as suggested by Etkowitz et al. (2000) and Ginorio (1996), early inclusion in a strong network provides a jump-start to a scientific career. One reason why it is especially important for women and minorities to form their own networks in science is that having a network gives them a place to reject outdated ideas of what a successful culture of science entails (Ginorio 1996). Additionally, the flexibility and informality of network-based mentoring allows for women to engage in mentoring in a way that best fits their personal needs (Limbert 1995). Hansford, Ehrich, and Tennent (2004) cite frequent problems that beset protégés in mentoring relationships, including a lack of mentor time and difficulty meeting with a mentor due to scheduling conflicts. Developing a network for mentoring, as we suggest below, helps overcome these challenges and provides for more flexibility. This is especially important for women, who may have less time availability due to family obligations (Biernat and Wortman 1991; Mason, Wolfinger, and Goulden 2013). Moreover, peer mentoring builds community by de-emphasizing the roles and hierarchy that often exist in mentoring relationships.

Academia by nature has a large number of mentoring relationships that develop as a result of position on the academic ladder; mentors may include master's and PhD advisors, postdoc advisors, tenure committees, and so forth. While the mentoring within those relationships has potential for improvement, it can be ineffective and risky to rely only on a small number of (perhaps randomly) assigned mentors to meet all the mentoring needs of a protégé. No matter how great a single mentor may be, it is wishful thinking to expect one individual to serve all the mentoring needs of a protégé (Tierney and Bensimon 1996).

The additional challenges of academics moving between institutions and positions, which may happen multiple times in their career, can make it even more difficult to find sufficient mentoring (Chelser and Chesler 2002) and may lead to the protégé feeling, or effectively being, abandoned. However, an informed and proactive protégé can use institutionally organized mentoring relationships to their advantage, if supplemented with other forms of mentoring.

As female earth scientists in the early stages of our careers (two of us are postdoctoral research associates, two of us are junior faculty), our participation in the Earth Science Women's Network (ESWN), a peer-mentoring network, has helped us overcome a number of barriers to success. Within this framework, we aim to provide guidance on such matters as how to determine the strengths and limitations of one's existing mentoring relationships; how to identify new mentoring relationships and utilize them to their full potential; and how to build a personal network that aims to meet all mentoring needs. Examples will be given from the Earth Science Women's Network, with the anticipation that these examples can be applied to a variety of disciplines and individual mentoring needs.

## Peer Mentoring and the Earth Science Women's Network

The mission of the Earth Science Women's Network is to promote career development, build community, provide informal mentoring and support, and facilitate professional collaborations among women in earth science–related fields. This is achieved through an international online network hosted on a password-protected community website (ESWNonline.org), as well as through in-person professional development and networking opportunities. A volunteer-based leadership board, comprised of ten early-career women (ranging from a graduate student to recently tenured associate professors), raises funds, supports and maintains the website and a job listserv (http://mailman.ucar.edu/mailman/listinfo/es_jobs_net), organizes professional development workshops (both gender-inclusive and those specifically for women), and arranges in-person networking activities at professional society meetings. Many individual members also organize and host smaller, local networking events.

Founded in 2002 by six early-career scientists, ESWN took shape through informal gatherings at professional meetings. The founding members recognized the benefits of informal peer networking and formed an email group, slowly adding to the list friends and colleagues, who in turn added their own friends and colleagues. As the group of women seeking out this peer mentoring grew, ESWN evolved from an email group to a sponsored listserv (2005) and then to a community website that sponsors discussions within a current total of 48 different interest groups (2013). Membership has grown mostly through word of mouth, ensuring that most members have a personal connection within the group. This, combined with the open and honest nature of our online discussion forums, has meant that even at ~1,700 members worldwide (as of February 2014) our group has retained a supportive and personal dynamic that leads to connections on a very individual level. Members include upper-level undergraduates, graduate students, postdoctoral researchers, junior and senior faculty, professionals in a range of environmental fields, and scientists working in research agencies, in academia, and in the public and private sectors. The majority of the members who responded to a 2013 survey are considered "early career" (i.e., 47% are graduate students or postdoctoral researchers). However, there are also women with more than 20 years of job experience, as well as women working outside of academia in nonprofits (4%), government labs (16%), and industry (3%). This diversity in career stage and job type allows for the network to provide opportunities for traditional mentoring relationships with women at different stages of their careers, as well as peer-to-peer mentoring within the same network. While ESWN was initially founded by atmospheric chemists, the membership has become inclusive of all the earth science disciplines and includes atmospheric scientists, geologists, hydrologists, ecologists, oceanographers, biogeochemists, planetary scientists, soil scientists, and many more. This breadth allows members who work across disciplines to avoid choosing which discipline they are "most like" in order to fully engage in the network.

Online interaction via the website forms the basis for the majority of mentoring facilitated by the ESWN, though in-person events often solidify the mentoring experience. Women often post questions to get advice on both professional and personal issues. In a 2009 survey of our membership, 95% of respondents said that they found the online interactions valuable (Archie and Laursen 2013). Interestingly, much of the mentoring occurs in a very passive way, with members reporting benefits from "listening in" on the online conversations. This is especially true when junior women can observe the peer-to-peer conversations of women in more advanced stages of their careers, allowing them to develop awareness of future issues they may face as well as already gaining insight into tools to address those same issues later in their careers. A significant percentage of the respondents report that participating in the network results in reduced isolation; one member commented, "ESWN gives me confidence in my abilities because I hear of others like me that are succeeding despite problems similar to mine. It provides a community and I feel I can address issues openly to get and give advice." Another member stated, "ESWN has built [her] confidence in reaching out to unofficial mentors for advice." In addition to seeking advice, women learn about professional workshops and meetings and organize informal events. In-person networking events have been organized at more than a dozen professional society meetings, reflecting both the diversity of disciplines within our membership and the utility of these types of events.

On the website, members are able to select the discussion groups they participate in, broadening the mentoring capabilities of ESWN. The majority of the 48 different hosted groups were created by members or in response to member requests. Members now define their interaction with the network by signing up for disciplinary groups such as "ESWN Dig It!" (for soil scientists); groups focused on specific challenges, such as "Lone Ranger" (for women who are the only or one of a few earth or environmental scientists at their institution) or "ESWN Moms" (for those interested in discussing the challenges of being a scientist and a parent); or location-specific groups, such as "ESWN on the Front Range" or "ESWN in the Twin Cities" to facilitate expanding their local professional and social network. By choosing their level of participation in the online discussions, members are able to tailor the information they receive and thus get more out of the network. The 2013 survey found that ESWN members who are more active in reading and sharing items online report higher gains than less active participants. Furthermore, women reported that the electronic network was the most important tool to them in gaining knowledge and understanding, in turn providing them with emotional support and reducing their feelings of isolation. One 2013 survey respondent commented that advice and a book recommendation she received from the listserv were "incredibly helpful" in helping her get her job: "I was given some feedback stating that I did a better job than other (female) candidates at delivering my work as assertive and showing my ownership over it."

The online community that ESWN has built is successful in part because it overcomes many of the mentoring challenges that women in the earth sciences face as minorities. While women may lack approachable and appropriate mentors in their home institution, the online community provides them with many mentoring options. The flexibility of online communication allows women in our network to fit mentoring into their personal schedule. This supports the findings of Muller (1997), who states that successful electronic communication leads to the development of strong online communities among people who have never met face-to-face.

The ESWN leadership board and its members also recognize the role of face-to-face interactions. In-person events provide opportunities for peer mentoring relationships to form, as well as a chance for participants to meet potential collaborators and future friends. Many of the leadership board–organized networking receptions are held at large scientific meetings. With similar goals as those promoted via online interactions, these networking events are designed to serve as a catalyst for future professional and social interactions. For example, since 2005 the ESWN leadership board has raised funding for and organized an annual networking reception on the first night of the annual American Geophysical Union (AGU) meeting, a conference that attracts over 20,000 geoscientists from around the world. The timing of the event is important: by placing it on the first night of a week-long conference, the reception serves as a jumping-off point for women to meet each other and forge collaborations and friendships that can be built upon over the subsequent days of the meeting. As a result, members' overall productivity at the meeting increases. In addition to these more formal networking receptions organized by the board, members regularly connect in person, often utilizing the website to facilitate group dinners at small conferences and get-togethers in local locations. Similar to the AGU networking receptions, these networking opportunities provide a venue for women to discuss everything from their latest research paper, to life as a scientist, to what they are missing in terms of mentoring.

It is important to note that when ESWN started, it was simply meant to be a way for six early-career women to support each other. There were no grand plans for a large international network. But the growth and success of ESWN shows that when you try to make the most of the connections you have already, great things can come from it. This is illustrated in the following anecdote from an ESWN member:

> When I first joined ESWN (~five years ago??), I introduced myself and said I was relocating and asked if anyone would like to have coffee.... That led to a connection with [another female scientist] who kindly invited me to give a talk at [a] global climate modeling center where there was a visiting scholar from China in the audience. He found my talk interesting/relevant to his work, and when he later went back to China he emailed me and asked if I would review a paper he was submitting. I helped with that and ended up co-authoring it. Our conversations continued, and he eventually got funds to invite me to China! I went, and we now have a paper in review on our work, and another project in process (with help from another ESWN member...)! Not only that, but another researcher at [a climate modeling center] saw my work at that talk and decided to use my data to validate a ... model. The validation was quite good, and was eventually published in [a well-respected journal in the field]. How great is that!?

**Taking Ownership of Your Mentoring**

In the traditional mentoring paradigm, people frequently focus on the reputations of their prospective mentors, rather than on what exactly they need from a mentor. We suggest an alternative approach: Focus on *what* you need, before thinking about *who* can meet that need. Receiving the best mentoring possible involves several steps. First, make sure you understand which areas of your life you need mentoring in (these might even be areas in which you already receive mentoring, but where the mentoring is not sufficient). Then, identify people who could provide mentoring for those areas. Lastly, figure out how to approach those people, how to stay in contact with them, and how to make the interaction mutually beneficial.

*Understanding and Meeting Your Mentoring Needs*

It is important to recognize that even the most effective advisors should not be expected to simultaneously be a sounding board for new ideas, a safe space, an emotional support, a sponsor, and an editor. Relying on any individual person for all of your needs can be overtaxing for your mentor, especially if you are a member of a minority group seeking mentoring from another member of the same group (for examples, see Rockquemore 2011). Instead, be strategic about whom you approach for support.

To strategically meet your mentoring needs it is important to first identify specific gaps in your support system. The following questions can help you identify your mentoring needs.

- What in your (work) life causes you the greatest frustration?
- What demands the most time or energy?
- Do you have adequate support to address those issues?
- How do you define success, personally and professionally?
- What do you need to fulfill that definition?

A helpful tool for taking inventory of your mentors in all different aspects of (work) life is the mentoring map (Figure 6.1). As young, female scientists we have benefited from this framework, especially in having a supportive and informative peer-mentoring network as part of our map. In many ways the foundation of ESWN's success is that it provides a positive and safe space where members feel comfortable sharing advice on both professional and personal issues that women in science face, with the value of the group driven by the participation and input of its membership.

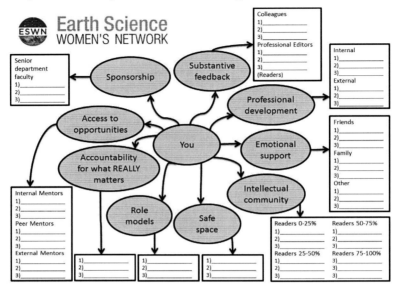

**FIGURE 6.1. ESWN mentoring map.** © National Center for Faculty Development and Diversity. Used with permission.

The mentoring map may not capture all the different needs you have, or might show categories that you think don't apply to you; we suggest you think about each category and whether you have people, organizations, or resources to meet each mentoring need. The framework we suggest is adaptable, and while we provide our interpretation below, what each mentoring domain entails is subjective. If needed, modify the categories to best suit your needs and build your interactions with people around this.

The most "classic" mentoring needs, those often associated with a graduate advisor, fall into the *substantive feedback* category. These needs range from very specific questions about what journal to submit to, to larger questions regarding the assessment of your career progression. Often these questions are best addressed by someone senior to you in the field. Examples include an academic advisor, the head of a research group, an editor of a journal, a department chair or team leader. However, unless you are a graduate student it is unlikely that you have to look "up" to find a mentor to meet these needs. Colleagues, professional editors, writing centers, or even external consulting firms can fulfill this need. In fact, many ESWN members report getting useful advice from peers they met via the network on tasks ranging from data interpretation methods to ideas on how to expand their current study.

In order to gain skills to use in your day-to-day life and improve yourself, you need to seek mentorship in the area of *professional development*. Whether the area for improvement involves time management skills, public speaking, writing, managing a research group, or conflict resolution techniques, this type of mentorship can be fulfilled in a variety of ways; many workplaces and professional organizations offer seminars or workshops addressing these needs. There are also a number of online resources (blogs, video series, and even online courses) for self-improvement. And do not overlook your peers as a part of your professional development: start or join a journal club or organize regular writing meetings with your colleagues as a way to improve different skills. One ESWN member cited Climatesnack.com as a useful tool for organizing a peer-mentoring writing group, whereby early career scientists work together on improving their writing skills while at the same time producing high-quality scientific content and building a supportive community. Because many professional development skills apply across careers and disciplines, think about outside resources that can help in this area. Organizations such as Toastmasters can provide opportunities to improve public speaking outside of academia, but the experience and mentors found in that sort of group can also positively impact your professional development within academia.

*Emotional support* is also a critical need for many of us, and having someone with whom you feel comfortable sharing your emotions, both positive and negative, is a part of your map. In many cases having emotional support can be as important as having "career support," and making this part of your mentoring framework from the outset, not just when crises arise, will result in greater success. Emotional support members are often family and friends, as well as trained professionals (e.g., therapists).

The people in your *intellectual community* are a sounding board for your work, assisting with study design, data analysis, and manuscript preparation. As manuscripts are the main product of academic work, it is important to have people from whom you can solicit feedback at each stage, from an initial idea to the finished product. We tend to hold on to our work without seeking feedback until it is almost finished, spending a lot of time on polishing a product that might have benefited from constructive criticism at an earlier stage.

In this sense, your intellectual community is built of people with whom you can share ideas at all stages, knowing that you will get honest feedback without having to fear that you will be ridiculed or that your ideas will be stolen. If you don't already have these people in your life, a good way to find intellectual community is to offer your support when someone else needs it. Of course, no one person will always be there, and it is often helpful to solicit feedback from multiple people. Building a large network will give you more options. If you are in the early stages of graduate school, offer to proofread someone's prospectus or thesis, or listen to a practice talk. As you advance in graduate school, ask your peers and/or advisor if you can help edit and proofread proposals or papers. This will help you find intellectually compatible people and forge relationships that provide mutual benefits.

While not mutually exclusive of the other mentoring categories, it is important to have people in your life whom you trust, people to whom you can express fears, concerns, and personal issues without needing to justify or explain yourself. These people fall into the *safe space* category. Here it is important to avoid conflicts of interest. For example, if someone is in the same field or research group, sharing your frustrations with your supervisor might put both of you in difficult positions. You want your safe space to always be trustworthy, so having people from different areas of your life—your sports team, your pottery group, your hometown, your profession— helps you maintain that.

It is important to have *role models*, people whose behavior we want to emulate in different aspects of our lives, such as work-life balance, work ethics, productivity, diplomacy, and professional recognition. No one role model has to be your ideal self; instead, you should keep in mind specific characteristics that you wish to cultivate. Be proactive in finding people you admire; if you know what your goals are, you can actively search out people who meet one or more of them, and when appropriate model your behavior on theirs. It is worthwhile to have role models at various career stages. While having a Nobel Prize–winning scientist as your role model might provide motivation and inspiration for your long-range career goals, this may not be helpful when you need to figure out a short-term strategy to reach a specific goal. Peer mentoring can be particularly helpful here. Having multiple role models who are one, two, or several career steps ahead of you gives you access to a variety of patterns to help you understand what leads to success or what is detrimental. Proximal role models can give advice from a perspective close to your own. They can also give ideas on more distant role models—that is, who are your role models' role models? Don't be afraid to "edit" your list of role models; if a role model ceases moving in your desired direction, don't hesitate to switch. The need for role models is apparent, for example, in the frequent requests on the ESWN website for contact with women who have left academia. Nonacademic career paths are often invisible from inside academia, and therefore connecting with individuals who have chosen different career paths (e.g., industry or nonprofit work) is beneficial.

Not only is it important to seek guidance and advice from others, we all need people who are willing to hold us accountable; such people establish an authority outside of yourself that will check on your progress with a given task. Being held accountable by someone other than yourself can help you get things done, and can help you get out of your own way when needed. You might look for help with *accountability* from a writing support group, a recreational circle, or the friend who helps you to evaluate your five-year plan. Accountability is an area of your network where peer mentoring can be exceptionally useful. It often works best if you can find an "accountability buddy"—someone with whom you can interact on a regular basis, whether it be online, in person, or over the phone. It is important that this be a reciprocal relationship, but your accountability buddy does not have to have the same goals as you. You might offer to help a friend be accountable for her fitness goals, and in return, you report at regular intervals on what you have accomplished with your current projects. However, if you do have common goals, you can also help each other develop realistic deliverables; for instance, you might both commit to writing a paragraph before an upcoming meeting, developing an exercise for a class, or generating some new material for a presentation. One example of an accountability buddy pairing that arose through ESWN formed at the 2012 ESWN professional development workshop in Madison (Glessmer, Wang, and Kontak 2012), where accountability only meant meeting up early in the morning for a swim before the workshop started for the day. But it developed into accountability to, for example, develop and submit job applications.

It is important to promote yourself within your network so that others can and will let you know about upcoming opportunities. Increasing your *access to opportunities*, be they workshops, summer schools, field opportunities, grant calls, job openings, speaking opportunities, media contacts, or research collaborations, can involve "real-life" connections as well as taking advantage of membership in organizations. Many organizations have newsletters with a section on upcoming conferences, workshops, field studies, and job opportunities; often you can receive this information via automated emails. You can also gain access to opportunities by forwarding information to others. When an opportunity comes across your desk that is not relevant to you, before deleting, think of someone it does pertain to and send the information her or his way. The more you do this for others, the more others will do the same for you. While more senior people are often well positioned to provide access to opportunities, they need to be aware of you. Being vocal about what your goals are and visible in what you are doing increases the likelihood that they will think of you when an opportunity comes across their desk. Recently on the ESWN website, several more senior members urged early career scientists to create and/or update their personal websites as a way to advertise themselves; this led to many members visiting each other's webpages and becoming aware of each other's skills, interests, and achievements.

It is important to have people who lobby for you behind closed doors; these are mentors that provide *sponsorship* to you by mentioning your name for promotions, suggesting you be given more responsibility in a project, or nominating you for an award. Identifying them can be a challenge, however. Think of ways to build relationships with people within your immediate work circle, and with those outside of your workplace but in your profession. After you have shown that you are good at what you do, you can ask people whether they would mind mentioning that in another context—for instance, at a faculty meeting or by nominating you for a fellowship. One ESWN member reported how she was personally asked by a journal editor to contribute yet another manuscript review because her reviews are always so thorough. She agreed to the review but also took the opportunity to mention to the editor the desirability of communicating her reputation with the journal to her department chair or one of her tenure committee members. The journal editor ended up nominating her for an award and writing her a personal letter (with a copy to her department chair) thanking her for her thorough, timely, and thoughtful reviews. In another case, a graduate student shared with her advisor a personal note she had received from one of the students in a course she was teaching, detailing several examples of her outstanding instruction. The advisor was inspired by the letter to nominate the graduate student for a teaching award, and found a great deal of support for the nomination in the department. A third example comes from an ESWN member who was interested in a scientific working group. Realizing that one of the members of the group was in ESWN, she emailed that member for more information; this inquiry led the working group member to remember and recommend her as an invited speaker at a later workshop. The key to this kind of mentoring relationship is that you need to give these individuals the information they need to lobby for you—that is, to keep them informed of the great things you are doing—and to make them recognize that you could use their support.

*Creating a Network of Mentoring Relationships*

Having identified people who can support you in specific areas, you will need to go about creating your network. But how do you actually do this? The easiest way to build a good network for yourself is to think about if and how you are fulfilling some of the functions on the mentoring map in someone else's network. Remember that networking is built on reciprocity. If you are, for example, a valuable part of someone's intellectual community, chances are the two of you will develop the kind of relationship in which he or she provides intellectual mentorship for you, too. The same holds for safe space, emotional support, and many of the other functions.

Mentoring relationships can grow organically. Approaching someone and asking, "will you be my mentor?" suggests that you want to rely on this one person for all of your mentoring needs, a responsibility and time commitment that many people will not want to take on (Rockquemore 2011). Instead, ask a specific question that can be answered quickly and easily. For example, instead of just saying "I wanted to introduce myself" to one of your scholarly idols, try "I recently read your paper on [X], and I am using a similar technique in my own research. Can I send you an email asking you about some of the details of your technique?" Then follow up with updates on how you used their advice and how it helped you succeed.

Given that you will never know whom you will one day want to communicate with, try to form a variety of connections by joining associations, networks, and working groups—and prove your own value to those networks. You can also reach out to alumni of your school, or to someone who has, for instance, received a scholarship or grant of the kind you are pursuing. It is important to think about your connection to that person if you are contacting them "out of the blue"; people are likely to be more receptive if you approach them asking about something specific (an accomplishment or scholarly finding) rather than due to a perceived similarity they have with you. In fact, if you contact prospective mentors for assistance or advice simply because they are part of the same minority group as you, you risk offending them and thus losing the chance to secure their help or service in the desired role. For example, one ESWN member reports actively seeking out a female committee member for her dissertation because she had not interacted on a regular basis with a female scientist since declaring her geology major as an undergraduate. While this woman proved to be extremely helpful scientifically, she did not act as a "role model" mentor in the way the member had hoped. She had incorrectly assumed that because this well-established scientist was female she would have better work-life balance than other faculty the member had interacted with. Your mentoring network is likely to be stronger if you build relationships based on shared connections and not perceived similarities.

Inviting peer or senior scholars in your field to give a seminar at your institution is a great way to build connections. From this standpoint, being on a committee organizing a seminar series can be a real advantage to you. The people invited become familiar with your name and associate you with being well connected and in a leading position, while at the same time you provide a service to your institution or organization. In addition to helping build your reputation, this kind of institutional service helps you to build your network, because you meet new people and get approached by other people hoping to secure a speaking slot for their guests. Organizing and chairing conference sessions can provide similar benefits and even greater visibility.

In addition to searching out mentors for the specific needs you identified, make use of mentoring programs at your institution, in your professional society, or online (such as the MentorNet site, http://mentornet.org). If you approach a person voluntarily associated with an established mentoring program with the goal of contributing to a single category on your mentoring map, you will have little chance of being disappointed or of expecting too much from that mentor. Another easy step is to sign up for email newsletters from professional organizations, funding agencies, and job sites. There are many organizations who compile these resources for you;

you don't necessarily have to do the legwork yourself. It is important to recognize that mentoring does not have to be top-down. Even relationships in which you would traditionally be perceived as "the mentor" might end up serving your own mentoring needs. Mentor and mentee feed off each other, so be open to connecting with people at all career stages.

*Maintaining Your Network*

Once you have made all those contacts, you need to sustain them. In a nutshell, make sure you are a person with whom many people want to correspond, so they feel that staying in touch with you is beneficial to them. Exactly what this entails varies from person to person, but we outline some strategies below.

We all have to choose how to spend our limited time, but it's important to maintain your relationships with those in your mentoring network. Be responsive when those people contact you, and make promises you can keep. If you are someone who is loyal and reliable, people will stay in contact with you and likely connect you with others.

Along the same lines, if you know many people and are *well informed*, more people will want to be connected to you and therefore more information will come to you. As previously noted, studies on mentoring show that mentors are more likely to engage in a mentoring relationship in which they see some benefit to themselves (Raggins and Cotton 1999). There are multiple ways to create this positive feedback loop, such as joining professional organizations, volunteering to organize get-togethers, and consistently passing along information to those for whom it might be relevant. If you are in the habit of thinking about who might be interested in a certain paper or job ad, you are also likelier to know who might have the information that you need when you need it. When and if that occurs, it is much easier for you to ask such people to return a favor, since you will have been sending information their way all along.

By connecting people, organizing local support networks or lecture series, and in general *acting as a hub*, you will ensure that people know who you are. These activities could be purely social as well, for instance organizing an interdepartmental happy hour for junior faculty or creating opportunities for overworked academics to meet people socially. Along the same lines, when you have the opportunity, *be a sponsor* to someone else. By being someone who recommends the perfect person for a job, a student to lead a field trip, or a senior colleague for a teaching or mentoring award, you will add value to your workplace. Your senior colleagues and peers will see you as someone who is *well connected* and thus someone with whom it is beneficial to cultivate a relationship. It is important to remember that mentoring is a two-way street. You need the feeling of community and belonging to stay motivated and productive, and so do your peers. Therefore, if you have benefited from workshops, informal get-togethers, or accountability groups, organize the next group meeting and invite new people to join, or inform other departments that these types of activities are beneficial and how to facilitate them. Empowering individuals within your network helps to sustain its value.

## Works Cited

Allen, T. D., M. L. Poteet, and S. M. Burroughs. 1997. "The Mentor's Perspective: A Qualitative Inquiry and Future Research Agenda." *Journal of Vocational Behavior* 51:70–89.

Archie, T., and S. Laursen. 2013. *Summative Report on the Earth Science Women's Network (ESWN) NSF ADVANCE PAID Collaborative Award (2009–2013)*. Report to ESWN. Boulder: CO: Ethnography & Evaluation Research. http://www.colorado.edu/eer/research/documents/ESWNfinalReportALL_2013.pdf.

Biernat, M., and C. B. Wortman. 1991. "Sharing of Home Responsibilities between Professionally Employed Women and Their Husbands." *Journal of Personality and Social Psychology* 60 (6): 844–60.

Chao, G. T., P. M. Waltz, and P. D. Gardner. 1992. "Formal and Informal Mentorships: A Comparison on Mentoring Functions and Contrast with Nonmentored Counterparts." *Personnel Psychology* 45 (3): 619–36. doi: 10.1111/j.1744-6570.1992.tb00863. x.

Chesler, N. C., and M. A. Chesler. 2002. "Gender-Informed Mentoring Strategies for Women Engineering Scholars: On Establishing a Caring Community." *Journal of Engineering Education* 91 (1): 49–55. doi: 10.1002/j.2168-9830.2002.tb00672. x.

Dreher, G. F., and R. A. Ash. 1990. "A Comparative Study of Mentoring among Men and Women in Managerial, Professional, and Technical Positions." *Journal of Applied* Psychology 75:538–46.

Etzkowitz, H., C. Kemelgor, M. Neuschatz, B. Uzzi, and J. Alonzo. 1994. "The Paradox of Critical Mass for Women in Science." *Science*, October 7, 51–54.

Fagenson, E. A. 1989. "The Mentor Advantage: Perceived Career/Job Experiences of Protégés versus Non-Protégés." *Journal of Organizational Behavior* 10:309–20. doi: 10.1002/job.4030100403.

Ginorio, A. 1996. "A Culture of Meaningful Community." In *Bridging the Gender Gap in Engineering and Science: The Challenge of Institutional Transformation*, 28–32. Pittsburgh, PA: Carnegie Mellon University.

Glessmer, M. S., Y. V. Wang, and R. Kontak. 2012. "Networking as a Tool for Earth Science Women to Build Community and Succeed." *Eos* 93 (41): 406–7. doi: 10.1029/ 2012EO410011.

Hansford, B. C., L. C. Ehrich, and L. Tennent. 2004. "Formal Mentoring Programs in Education and Other Professions: A Review of the Literature." *Educational Administration Quarterly* 40 (4): 518–40.

Holmes, M. A., and S. O'Connell. 2005. "Where Are the Women Geoscience Professors?" Report on the NSF/AWG workshop, "Where are the Women Geoscience Professors?" September 25–27, 2003, Washington, DC.

Kemelgor, C., and H. Etzkowitz. 2001. "Overcoming Isolation: Women's Dilemmas in American Academic Science." *Minerva* 39:239–57.

Kram, K. E. 1985. "Improving the Mentoring Process." *Training and Development Journal* 39:40–43.

Limbert, C. 1995. "Chrysalis, a Peer Mentoring Program for Faculty and Staff Women." *NWSA Journal* 7 (2): 86–99.

Mason, M. A., N. H. Wolfinger, and M. Goulden. 2013. *Do Babies Matter? Gender and Family in the Ivory Tower*. New Brunswick, NJ: Rutgers University Press.

Moss-Racusin, C. A., J. F. Dovidio, V. L. Brescoll, M. J. Graham, and J. Hendelsman. 2012. "Science Faculty's Subtle Gender Biases Favor Male Students." *Proceedings of the National Academy of Sciences* 109 (41): 16,474–79.

Muller, C. B. 1997. "The Potential of Industrial 'E-Mentoring' as a Retention Strategy for Women in Science and Engineering." In *Teaching and Learning in an Era of Change: Proceedings of the*

*27th Annual Frontiers in Education Conference*, vol. 2, 622–26. Champaign, IL: Stipes Publishing. doi: 10.1109/FIE.1997. 635880.

National Research Council. 2006. *To Recruit and Advance: Women Students and Faculty in Science and Engineering*. Washington, DC: National Academies Press.

Ragins, B. R. 1997. "Diversified Mentoring Relationships in Organizations: A Power Perspective." *Academy of Management Review* 22:482–521.

Ragins, B. R., and J. L. Cotton. 1999. "Mentoring Functions and Outcomes: A Comparison of Men and Women in Formal and Informal Mentoring Relationships." *Journal of Applied Psychology* 84:529–50.

Rockquemore, K. A. 2011. "Will You Be My Mentor?" *Inside Higher Ed*, November 11. http://www.insidehighered.com/advice/2011/ 11/14/essay-mentoring-and-minority-faculty-members.

Scandura, T. A. 1992. "Mentorship and Career Mobility: An Empirical Investigation." *Journal of Organizational Behavior* 13:169–74.

Tierney, W., and E. Bensimon. 1996. *Promotion and Tenure: Community and Socialization in Academe*. Albany: State University of New York Press.

# "Mentoring Up": Learning to Manage Your Mentoring Relationships

*Steven Paul Lee, Richard McGee, Christine Pfund, and Janet Branchaw*

R esearch mentoring relationships are critical for academic and professional success, yet vary considerably in their effectiveness.[1] This variability is often attributed to the ability of the research mentor to shape and guide the research experience for mentee(s). It is common to hear stories that range from inspiring mentors who help transform their mentees, to mentors who appear inaccessible and even sometimes a hindrance to their mentees' success. In this chapter we reframe the mentoring relationship as one in which there is shared responsibility and a continuous two-way conversation between mentor and mentee.

To highlight the mentee's role in this relationship, we advance the term "mentoring up" and offer specific strategies that mentees can use to consciously contribute to and guide the mentoring relationship. We also advocate for the importance of equipping mentees with the knowledge, skills, and confidence that will empower them to navigate through difficult situations, and to avoid passive patterns of behavior that may limit their own success.

Two case studies are presented to illustrate some of the common challenges that new mentees face as they learn to navigate their research mentoring relationships. In both cases new graduate students encounter challenges, which they address with varied methods and therefore obtain different results. These case studies are based upon real situations, with altered names to maintain confidentiality of the people involved, and are situated within contexts commonly encountered in STEMM (science, technology, engineering, math, and medicine) disciplines. While the authors' experience and

133

scholarly background is in these disciplines, we postulate that the skills needed to effectively "mentor up" are relevant and can be easily adapted across other disciplines.

## Case Study #1: Moving Target

Dan's start in graduate school has not been as auspicious as he had hoped. He applied to multiple top-tier research universities, but wasn't admitted into any of his favorite schools. He was finally admitted to his "safety school," his last resort, and was grateful for the opportunity. But even here he has struggled to find a research mentor. He spoke with many professors, but was disappointed when most turned him down. The faculty told him that tightened research budgets limited the number of students that they could accept. Things seemed to finally turn a corner when Dan met Professor Nevan, a new assistant professor who described many exciting projects and invited him into her research group.

Dan joined Professor Nevan's group and began working there. They planned his first project together, which seemed fascinating and suitable because it overlapped with his prior experiences and interests. Dan dove into the project, eager to impress his mentor and prove his worth. One month later, however, Professor Nevan approached him and strongly encouraged him to drop the original project and tackle a new research question. Dan was uncertain about the change, but Professor Nevan seemed excited about this new opportunity, so he followed accordingly. However, the same thing happened again two months later, when Professor Nevan came up with another entirely new research project and encouraged Dan to pursue it.

Dan is confused and frustrated, because he perceives that Professor Nevan is giving him a moving target. He also doesn't like that the process has been inefficient, taking more of his precious time and energy to wrap up the old project and begin a new direction. But he's also feeling trapped, because he doesn't have other faculty to consider, and doesn't know how to begin talking with his mentor about his frustrations without appearing ungrateful for being welcomed into the research group and unresponsive to his mentor's suggestions for research projects worth pursuing.

While Dr. Nevan's actions in the case study may frustrate Dan, they are understandable. As a new professor, she is learning how to mentor students, while struggling to find viable research projects that will help her and her students to succeed in a competitive funding environment. She may not be aware of the impact that the frequent changes in projects are having on Dan and may be receiving little or no guidance on how to be an effective mentor beyond her own experiences as a mentee. While there are many ways Dr. Nevan might have handled the situation differently, there are also many ways that Dan can address the challenges in his research mentoring relationship and play a more active role in improving it.

Traditional models of mentoring and training for mentoring relationships often focus on the mentor's responsibility to guide and direct the relationship. However, this de-emphasizes the importance of the mentee's responsibilities, opportunities for growth, and impact upon the relationship. For example, in the case study above, Dan has a tremendous opportunity and a responsibility to actively participate in the decision-making process when it comes to determining which project to focus on. Dan and Dr. Nevan *both* need to improve their communication so they better understand one another's reasoning, intentions, strengths, and weaknesses. Dan cannot react passively and expect Dr. Nevan to magically understand him and provide everything that he needs. He must actively engage in and share responsibility for making the relationship beneficial for himself and Dr. Nevan. He must "mentor up."

### "Mentoring Up"

"Mentoring up" is a concept that empowers mentees to be active participants in their mentoring relationships by shifting the emphasis from the mentors' responsibilities in the mentor-mentee relationship to equal emphasis on the mentees' contributions. "Mentoring up" is adapted from the concept of "managing up," introduced in Gabarro and Kotter's classic paper in the *Harvard Business Review* (1980). Gabarro and Kotter conducted field research on how business managers worked productively and discovered that effective managers not only managed their employees, but also managed their peers laterally and their supervisors upwardly. Their investigations led to the groundbreaking publication "Managing Your Boss," which provided case studies and strategic advice to managers on how to consciously work with their bosses for the benefit of their working relationship and the company. Despite criticism that they were promoting false flattery or political manipulation, Gabarro and Kotter's original ideas have persisted. The *Harvard Business Review* reprinted their paper twice (in 1993 and 2005) and their concept of managing up appears in multiple books and countless blogs directed at young managers.

Though Gabarro and Kotter's original audience consisted of managers in the corporate world, many of the principles and strategies they proposed can be applied in academic mentoring relationships. Their advice is based upon the understanding that the relationship with one's mentor involves *mutual dependence* between *fallible* persons. Thus, they stress the importance of assessing the mentor's and mentee's strengths, weaknesses, and preferences in working and communication. Most importantly, they stress the powerful role that mentees play when they proactively engage in the relationship: "Some superiors spell out their expectations very explicitly. But most do not. Ultimately, the burden falls on the subordinate to discover what the boss's expectations are" (Gabarro and Kotter 1980, 99). This means mentees must actively seek to understand their mentor's priorities and pressures, not passively assume that the mentor will be aware of and able to meet a mentee's needs. This does not mean the responsibility for an effective relationship lies solely with the mentee; rather, it points to the power mentees have to shape the relationship to meet their needs.

Adapting Gabarro and Kotter's concept, *we define* mentoring up *as the mentee's proactive engagement in the mentor-mentee relationship, so that both parties mutually benefit from the relationship and move forward towards an agreed-upon purpose or vision.* Mentoring up is a process in which the mentee continually learns about the relationship and develops skills to engage in it as the relationship evolves. Ultimately, learning the skills needed to proactively manage an evolving mentoring relationship will contribute significantly to the mentee's ability to effectively navigate and manage a career.

## Core Principles in Mentoring Relationships

Gabarro and Kotter provided a valuable approach to working effectively with one's boss; we believe a similar approach can be applied to mentoring relationships in higher education. Here we integrate their approach with core principles that have emerged from two evidence-based mentor and mentee training programs, *Entering Men-*

*toring* (Handelsman et al. 2005) and *Entering Research* (Branchaw, Pfund, and Rediske 2010), which have been shown to improve mentored research experiences and mentoring relationships. We place them into the "mentoring up" framework and show that the core principles upon which they are based align well with Gabarro and Kotter's original ideas and provide a framework for "mentoring up."

*Entering Mentoring* uses a process-based approach to research mentor training in which mentors working with mentees discuss and attempt to solve mentoring challenges across a range of core themes. Through these discussions, participants gain knowledge and skills needed to improve their mentoring practice. The *Entering Mentoring* curriculum was developed based on the experience of research mentors in the biological sciences; it draws on core principles in mentoring from a range of disciplines, including business. A combination of qualitative and quantitative data indicate that compared to untrained mentors, the mentors who participated in the *Entering Mentoring* training assess their mentees' skills and communicate with them more effectively. Moreover, undergraduate researchers indicated that they had a better experience with the trained, as compared to untrained, mentors (Pfund et al. 2006). One version of the *Entering Mentoring*–based curricula, targeting the faculty mentors of clinical and translational researchers, was tested in a randomized controlled trial conducted at 16 institutions with 283 mentor-mentee pairs. Mentors assigned to the training showed significantly higher skills gains compared with the control. This held true across career stage, institution, and gender. Mentors assigned to the training self-reported improvements in their mentoring behaviors, which were corroborated by their mentees (Pfund et al. 2014; Pfund et al. 2013).

*Entering Research* is a parallel curriculum for research mentees that brings undergraduate researchers together to discuss the challenges they face as novice researchers in learning to do research and in navigating their mentoring relationships. Like *Entering Mentoring*, it is a process-based curriculum in which the specific content of each session emerges from the mentees' experiences. The framework used to guide discussions in *Entering Research* was developed from the experience of undergraduate research program directors and the literature on undergraduate research experiences. Qualitative and quantitative data collected from undergraduate student mentees ($N = 64$) who participated in the *Entering Research* training showed significantly higher self-reported gains in research skills, knowledge, and confidence when compared to a control group of students ($N =$ 144) who also participated in undergraduate research experiences but not the *Entering Research* training. Of particular relevance were the *Entering Research* students' gains in "understanding the career paths of science faculty" and "what graduate school is like," which were significantly greater than those of the control students. In addition, 41% of *Entering Research* students reported that the training helped them learn how to effectively communicate and interact with their research mentors (Balster et al. 2010).

The principles described in *Entering Mentoring* and *Entering Research* form the foundation for effective mentoring relationships, and address various aspects of the relationship. Here we use these principles as a framework for applying the concept of "mentoring up" to mentors and mentees working in academic research settings. Below we present core principles that underlie these two evidence-based curricula. Each principle is accompanied by a short description adapted from the *Entering Mentoring* and *Entering Research* materials.

1. *Maintaining Effective Communication.* Good communication is a key element of any relationship and a mentoring relationship is no exception. It is critical that mentors and mentees seek to understand their own and the other's communication styles, and take time to practice communication skills.

2. *Aligning Expectations.* Another key element of effective mentor-mentee relationships is a shared understanding of what each person expects from the relationship. Problems and disappointment often arise from misunderstandings about expectations. Importantly, expectations change over time, so reflection, clear communication, and realignment of expectations are needed on a regular basis.

3. *Assessing Understanding.* Determining what you understand as well as if someone truly understands you is not easy, yet is critical to a productive mentor-mentee relationship. Developing strategies to self-assess and assess others' understanding is an important part of being an effective mentor and mentee.

4. *Addressing Equity and Inclusion.* Diversity along a range of dimensions offers both challenges and opportunities to any relationship. Learning to identify, reflect upon, learn

from, and engage with diverse perspectives is critical to forming and maintaining an effective mentoring relationship.

5. *Fostering Independence.* An important goal in any mentoring relationship is helping the mentee become independent; yet defining what an independent mentee knows and can do is not often articulated by either the mentor or the mentee. Identifying milestones towards independence and setting goals are key strategies to fostering independence in a mentoring relationship.

6. *Promoting Professional Development.* The ultimate goal of most mentoring situations is to enable the mentee to identify and achieve some academic and professional outcomes after the training period. It is the responsibility of both the mentor and mentee to identify and articulate these goals and to strive towards them together.

7. *Ethics.* Mentors and mentees must engage in and model ethical behavior, while openly discussing issues dealing with gray areas. Moreover, it can be important to acknowledge when a mentoring relationship includes an unequal power dynamic and any additional ethical considerations it raises.

The seven core principles above provide a foundation to understand the various aspects of an effective mentoring relationship that can mutually benefit the mentee and mentor. This chapter focuses specifically on the skills mentees need to develop to be effective, proactive, and successful partners in their mentoring relationships. However, we recognize that both the mentor and the mentee must gain mentoring knowledge and skills and intentionally engage in effective mentoring practices.

## Core Skills in Mentoring Up

The principles described above point to the need for mentees to effectively communicate across differences, align their own expectations with their mentors', assess their knowledge and understanding of concepts in the field, act in an ethical manner, and ultimately achieve independence in their professional career. One critical skill underlying all of these principles is the ability of mentees to understand themselves and the mentors with whom they are working.

Gabarro and Kotter discussed *the importance of understanding oneself and one's superior* in their original paper (1980, 94). The ability to self-assess is a critical aspect of mentoring up that impacts all of the core principles described above. For example, if mentees have inaccurate assessments of their communication skills or academic achievements, it will be more difficult to align their expectations with their mentors'. Therefore, before mentees can effectively manage their mentoring relationships, they must accurately assess themselves and develop the metacognitive skills needed to understand their own skills, preferences, strengths, and weaknesses. Numerous tests and resources for self-assessment are available, such as the Myers-Briggs Type Indicator (MBTI) personality inventory, StrengthsFinder (Rath and Conchie 2008), and the myIDP website (http://myidp.sciencecareers.org). Additionally, self-reflection exercises such as writing one's "Seven Success Stories" and "Forty-Year Vision" (Bolles 2013) can provide orthogonal and more comprehensive perspectives on strengths and weakness, experiences, and preferences.

Studies have shown that many people are not aware of their own strengths and weaknesses, thus reinforcing the value of self-assessments (Kruger and Dunning 1999; Dunning et al. 2003). As shown in the case study above, lack of awareness of one's strengths and weaknesses can lead to difficult obstacles in academic and professional development. Dan had high hopes for his applications to top-tier graduate programs, but was not granted admission, suggesting that he may not have accurately assessed his strengths, and/or that he has difficulty communicating his strengths effectively. Furthermore, his problems finding a research advisor suggest that he may not be effectively marketing his strengths to the faculty. An accurate self-assessment with validated tests and tools could have given Dan a framework and vocabulary for understanding and communicating his strengths and preferences to others. Generally, increased understanding of human behavior empowers mentees to make accommodations for themselves and those they work with, enables them to observe and detect healthy and unhealthy patterns, and sharpens their own strengths.

Extending from this critical element of mentoring up are specific strategies based on the core principles that mentees can use to foster their mentor-mentee relationships. Below we list several strategies for each core principle. This is not meant to be a comprehensive list, but rather a sample of approaches in mentoring up that mentees can use to make their mentoring relationships more effective.

1. *Maintaining Effective Communication*
   A. Determine your mentor's preferred medium of communication (face-to-face, phone, or email) and acknowledge if it differs from your own personal preference.
   B. Schedule a regular time to meet or check in with your mentor.
   C. Keep track and share progress toward project and professional goals, both verbally and in writing.
   D. Identify challenges and request your mentor's advice/ intervention when appropriate.
   E. Prepare for meetings with your mentor by articulating specifically what you want to get out of the meeting and how you will follow up after the meeting.

2. *Aligning Expectations*
   A. Ask your mentor for his or her expectations regarding
      i. mentees at your stage of career generally.
      ii. you as an individual scholar.
      iii. the research project.
   B. Share your expectations regarding
      i. your career as a scholar and professional.
      ii. the research project.
   C. Ask others in the research group, who know your mentor better, about the mentor's explicit and implicit expectations.
   D. Write down the expectations you agree to and revisit them often with your mentor. Use a mentor-mentee contract to formalize the expectations.

3. *Assessing Understanding*
   A. Ask questions when you do not understand something. If you are afraid to ask your mentor directly, start by asking your peers.
   B. Talk and write about your project, asking peers and mentors who know the field for feedback.
   C. Ask peers and mentors to share their perspectives on

your work and its meaning in the context of the field more broadly.

D. Explain your project to someone who is new to the field and help them to understand your project and its significance.

4. *Addressing Equity and Inclusion*

A. Be open to seeking out and valuing different perspectives.

B. Engage in honest conversation about individual differences with your mentor and co-workers.

C. Contribute positively to shared understandings and solutions to problems.

D. Talk to peers and mentors when you feel conflicted about the ways in which your personal identity intersects with your academic identity.

5. *Fostering Independence*

A. With your mentor, define what it takes to do independent work in your field.

B. Define a series of milestones to independence with your mentor and set goals for meeting these milestones as part of your research plan.

C. Ask peers and mentors to share with you their strategies for achieving independence.

6. *Promoting Professional Development*

A. Create an Individual Development Plan (IDP) to set goals and guide your professional development, using resources such as Science Career's myIDP website (http://myidp.sciencecareers.org).

B. Seek out and engage multiple mentors to help you achieve your professional goals.

C. Ask peers and mentors to discuss with you the fears and reservations you may have about pursuing a certain career path.

7. *Ethics*

A. Take responsibility for your own behavior.

B. Seek out formal and informal ways to understand the accepted norms of practice in your field.

C. Learn about ethical issues associated with your work

and proactively address them.
  D.  Learn about your university's policies for dealing with
      unethical behavior.

Returning to the case study, we can see how some of these strategies may have helped Dan in overcoming challenges he is facing in his mentoring relationship. The case suggests that Dan needs stability in this relationship—understandably, because he faced much uncertainty as he struggled to find a graduate program that would admit him, and then a research mentor who would accept him into a research group. Thus, Dan must learn how to request stability from his mentor, particularly in this critical, early stage of their relationship. Perhaps Dan could request a meeting with Professor Nevan to investigate some of the root principles of their discipline, so that he could work on learning some basic techniques or skills that would be valuable for multiple directions of their research. Thus, if the research question changed again, this initial training would still be valuable, and also provide some initial stability for Dan in the early stages of working under Professor Nevan. Alternatively, Dan could ask for Professor Nevan's long-term goals for their research projects. Dan perceives these research questions as dramatically different from each other, but perhaps for Professor Nevan they are simply different approaches that address the same, ultimate research question.

Dan might also consider how effective communication requires acknowledging the difference between intention and impact. In personal interactions, there are often unspoken intentions that have an impact on the other person. In Dan's mentoring relationship with Professor Nevan, he is experiencing the impact of a constantly moving target. If he does not communicate this impact to Professor Nevan, she may not be aware of it. She may genuinely intend to find a suitable research project for Dan and plan to adjust the project to fit Dan's interests and experiences, but if he does not communicate his need for stability and the impact of constantly changing projects, she may assume that he accepts and perhaps even welcomes these changes.

It is also critical for mentees to learn their responsibilities in the mentoring relationship. As Gabarro and Kotter wisely point out, most mentors do not explicitly spell out their expectations for the mentee, leaving the mentee to discover those expectations and responsibilities on their own (1980, 99). Thus, a primary responsibility for the mentee is to identify the spoken and unspoken responsibilities for their working relationship. For example, Dan has a responsibility to communicate the impact of the changing research projects on his level of stress and commitment to the projects, and to propose reasonable solutions to his problem.

The concept of mentoring up aims to empower mentees in what may appear to be powerless situations. However, mentees have enormous power and influence in their mentoring relationships. To exert their power effectively, it is critical that mentees are able to accurately self-assess, thereby allowing them to proactively reposition themselves in the relationship as it evolves. At the same time, effective and mutually beneficial mentoring relationships involve the mentee respectfully listening to mentors and engaging them in dialogue. Just as mentees need to develop skills in leadership, they also need to allow themselves to be "mentorable." They must exhibit respect, humility, patience, and flexibility in the relationship. Effective mentees learn to seek a balance between deferring to a mentor's greater experience, challenging the mentor with new ideas, and advocating for their own needs. Effective mentees also realize that this balance changes over time as mentees gain experience and achieve greater independence of thought and approach.

To reveal how these skills might be practiced, consider the case study on the facing page, which, in contrast to the first case study, provides a positive example of mentoring up. This is also based upon a real situation, with names altered to maintain confidentiality.

This second case study illustrates a sticky situation in which a mentee faces challenges not only with her faculty mentor, but also with the postdoc who functions as another informal mentor in her research group. Heather appears to be stuck between the interests of her research professor and the postdoc. Following the mentoring-up principles, Heather first attempts to assess her *understanding* of the project, asking questions when she does not understand and the protocols are not working. Unfortunately, her attempts to understand are brushed aside by the postdoc. Importantly, Heather does not jump to the assumption that she is doing something wrong. Rather she sensitively considers reasons that might be contributing to the postdoc's response.

To improve the situation, Heather attempts to improve *communication* among the parties involved, wisely requesting a joint meeting with the postdoc and the professor. Having everyone together in person allows all to be able to speak and listen carefully,

## Case Study #2: Navigating Between Two Mentors

Heather is a new grad student and has recently joined a research group with Professor Roman as her primary mentor. She was given multiple projects, including one started by a postdoctoral scholar in the group. She assumed that the postdoc would help her with the project, serving as an informal mentor.

Heather began working in the lab by following instructions that were written by the postdoc, but noticed problems with the results. When she asked the postdoc to confirm the instructions, he brushed her off with quick answers, and said that he didn't follow the written instructions exactly and that it contained errors. Heather was confused by his behavior, and began to suspect that the project had been taken from him and that he resented her work on it.

To better understand her project and resolve problems with her results, she asked for a joint meeting with both of her mentors: Professor Roman and the postdoc. In the joint meeting, she made sure that the postdoc was given an opportunity to speak openly and confirm that he approved handing the project over to Heather. However, after the meeting Heather continued to have problems with the instructions, and the postdoc continued to brush her off with quick and cryptic responses. Heather still suspected that the postdoc only agreed to hand over the project to her because he was afraid to disagree with Professor Roman. Heather is frustrated, because her progress depends on the past work and experiments that were started by the postdoc, so she is unable to proceed at a sufficient pace. The postdoc has not been helpful and seems to behave passive-aggressively towards her questions and requests for help.

Furthermore, the postdoc has asked that he be given first authorship if a paper were to be published, which Heather believes is acceptable since he started the project. But he has also started insisting that he be given first authorship on a second paper, even though Heather would have done most of the experimental work and writing of the paper. As Heather considered her various options, she discussed her multiple projects with Professor Roman and began to shift her energy towards other projects.

and forge a common understanding of the situation. Thus Heather understands the importance of clear and effective communication. In contrast, if Heather had tried to approach this sticky situation by email, or by communicating with her professor and the postdoc separately, the chances of miscommunication would have greatly increased. In the meeting Heather considers the *expectations* of both the mentor and the postdoc and allows the postdoc to express his feelings about Heather's role in the project, thus providing an opportunity for expectations to be verbalized for her and Dr. Roman.

However, after the joint meeting Heather suspects that the postdoc did not speak candidly, and continues to struggle with experimental problems from faulty instructions. She begins to think about the *ethical* considerations of authorship as well as her need to establish an *independent* research project with her as a first author. Heather must think about her own *professional development* needs as well as a solution that is *equitable* for everyone involved.

As the situation worsens, and in light of the postdoc's unreasonable demands, she realizes that she has alternatives that still allow her to progress. Heather is proactive and displays many of the critical skills involved in mentoring up, but also realizes that she has come to an impasse. By adapting with grace and wisdom, she sidesteps the impasse by refocusing on her other projects. The next step in this situation would be for Heather to tactfully inform her mentor and the postdoc that she is pursuing alternate interests, so that the postdoc can return to his project if he desires and the research group can complete that original direction of investigation.

### Mentoring Up at Different Career Stages

The case studies presented above involve two graduate students at the beginning and middle stages of their academic development. However, with a little imagination, one can consider very similar scenarios along the entire continuum in higher education: from undergraduate to graduate students to postdoctoral scholars and even junior faculty. From the beginning to later stages of professional development there will be colleagues who serve as subordinates, peers, and superiors—and even colleagues with unclear roles and responsibilities. Thus, the seven core principles of mentoring relationships are relevant and valuable across the spectrum. This section considers how these skills in mentoring up evolve across academic stages in the STEMM disciplines.

For *undergraduate students,* who likely have limited experiences with mentoring relationships, simply learning how to seek mentors in ways that are relevant and expected within their academic discipline and context is the starting point. Given their limited experience, self-assessment with respect to the field may be difficult. However, general self-assessment tools like the MBTI can still be effective at this stage in their careers if used with strong interpretative guidance. Undergraduate students can observe and record how they react to various styles of mentorship and guidance. Comparing notes with other students within a facilitated conversation can be very revealing. If the discipline involves research group meetings with a mentor and other group members, as is common in the sciences and engineering, being able to attend the research group meetings will allow the undergraduate mentee to observe how the mentor interacts with students and staff. They should also take advantage of opportunities to tutor, serve as a teaching assistant, or take on other leadership roles as ways to develop their leadership and mentorship styles. These types of experiences will help them to develop professional skills in communication, assess their own understanding, align their goals and expectations with those of others, and address diverse cultures and working styles.

*Graduate students* will likely have sharpened communication and leadership skills, but will need to continue seeking growth opportunities. They often are asked to select a research advisor among multiple options, and so will need to evaluate whether a potential partnership will meet their needs. They should reflect on current and past mentoring relationships, and evaluate how these relationships have impacted their academic and professional progress. Self-assessment tests can reveal preferred decision-making processes (for example, T- or F-types in the MBTI) and sharpen decision-making skills. Resources such as the myIDP website can help in the assessment of interests and strengths, and provide a framework for creating a plan to reach their academic and professional goals. If the discipline involves research rotations, as is common in biomedical research programs, these brief research experiences provide invaluable information as to whether or not a relationship might become productive and mutually beneficial for both the mentee and mentor. Graduate students should actively seek multiple mentors—formal, informal, and even peer mentors—who will create a community of support and provide multiple perspectives (Light and Micari 2013; Hunter, Laursen, and Seymour 2007). Lastly, graduate school can provide a valuable opportunity to begin developing one's mentorship skills simultaneously as a mentee and mentor. Graduate students will be able to see both sides of the relationship and begin testing new skills in mentoring and mentoring up.

*Postdoctoral scholars* (postdocs) should focus on deepening and broadening their skills in communication and leadership. As they expand their experiences in new contexts, they will foster their own independence through the creation and pursuit of novel research directions, yet still be in a position to benefit from the guidance of a research mentor. Postdocs should focus on increasing their network of connections, which will enable further development of their community of formal and informal mentors, peers, and mentees, who can support their professional development.

*Junior faculty* will likely focus much of their attention on mentoring students and postdocs, and they will likely have a lot of experience and skill development in mentoring from personal experiences and from participating in formal training for mentors. However, it is also important at this stage in one's career to continue to seek formal and informal mentors. In an academy that highly values independence, one runs the risk of becoming isolated. As junior faculty achieve greater success, it is still valuable to use networks for support and encouragement. These support networks can be essential as junior faculty try to manage increasing demands on their time (Sorcinelli and Yun 2007).

Awareness of one's strengths and styles is critical in all mentor-mentee relationships and at all career stages. The principles for fostering strong relationships outlined in this chapter can serve to anchor and guide one's continuous development of skills needed on both sides of the relationship and across all stages of one's career.

## Our Experiences in Training Mentees to Mentor Up

As described above, *Entering Research* provides a curriculum focused on mentoring-up principles for undergraduate researchers. Author Janet Branchaw serves as the course director of the *Entering Research* seminar for beginning undergraduate researchers at the University of Wisconsin–Madison. Similarly, author Christine Pfund directs the *Entering Mentoring* seminars for the pre-faculty and faculty mentors of these undergraduate students at the University of Wisconsin–Madison. Most recently, an adapted version of the *Entering Mentoring* curriculum was developed to train senior undergraduate students to transition from their role as a mentee to that of a peer research mentor. In this chapter we have described efforts undertaken for training graduate student mentees. The authors' perspectives, drawn from our collective experiences in the STEMM disciplines, may help readers determine which aspects are most relevant and valuable for their needs as a mentee or mentor, or in training others in mentoring relationships.

Author Rick McGee serves as the program director, and author Steve Lee recently served as the assistant director, of an NIH-funded initiative to enhance the scientific development of PhD students in the biosciences at Northwestern University. This program, called CLIMB (Collaborative Learning and Integrated Mentoring in the Biosciences), is partially supported by an NIH IMSD (Initiative to Maximize Student Development) award. Although the NIH funding supports underrepresented minority students, program activities are open to all bioscience PhD students. The training focuses on the first two years of the students' PhD programs, in order to address many of the transitional issues that incoming students encounter in their graduate programs. We provide frequent workshops on a wide variety of topics, such as choosing a research mentor, self-assessment, adapting to graduate-level courses, oral presentation skills, written communication skills, career planning, and (in a four-part series) mentoring up.

After an introduction to foundational principles of mentoring, this workshop series on mentoring up focuses on four specific areas: communication, aligning goals and expectations, diversity and unconscious assumptions, and fostering independence. These workshops have largely been based on training materials from the University of Wisconsin—that is, from *Entering Research*. Student feedback has been positive, but we are continuing to improve and adjust the workshops. As an example, during a workshop on aligning expectations, one student shared a communication struggle she was having with her mentor. The following week, based on the workshop and discussions, she initiated a more direct conversation with her mentor about her needs, which led to an immediate and dramatic improvement in communication between them.

These mentoring-up concepts have been warmly welcomed by faculty and program directors, who have experienced firsthand the need to train incoming graduate students in how to communicate effectively with their research advisers as they work together. During recent discussions with PhD program directors, the idea of teaching mentoring up to graduate students was met with unanimous and enthusiastic support; program directors were universally looking for ways to encourage students to take more active roles in their own mentoring. Even though we have started explicitly using the term mentoring up only recently, we have been using many of these concepts in our training for the past six years of our program's existence. Much of our training actually involves using case studies of the kind presented here to help the students consider how to navigate through and avoid difficult situations that they might encounter in their relationships with mentors. The feedback from students has been largely positive. Over the past six years, 81% of CLIMB students have agreed or strongly agreed that the program "made a positive impact upon my start to graduate school."[2]

In the academic world and beyond, mentoring and networking relationships play a key role in career satisfaction, productivity, and advancement. This is especially true for those in early stages of their academic and professional careers, such as graduate students, post-doctoral fellows, and junior faculty. To engage in the academic community, new mentees need to learn to participate in a full and intentional manner. But as young mentees are learning how to navigate within their academic disciplines, it can be incredibly challenging to quickly learn the unwritten (and often unclear) rules, adapt to new situations, and discern which options and people will help them become successful.

These challenges can be faced by learning to mentor up, just as Heather did in the second case study. In teaching the principles and skills of mentoring up, our goal is to equip, empower, and encourage new entrants to position themselves to become confident and contributing members of the academy. The authors have developed interventions that teach the skills of mentoring up and believe that these skills will not only empower mentees to be effective and proactive contributors to their mentoring relationships, but also effective and proactive mentors of the next generation of scholars.

## Notes

1. Representative publications in this area include Bland et al. 2009; Cho, Ramanan, and Feldman 2011; Feldman et al. 2010;

Garman, Wingard, and Reznik 2001; Palepu et al. 1998; Raggins and Kram 2007; Ramanan et al. 2002; Sambunjak, Straus, and Marusic 2010; Shea et al. 2011; Steiner et al. 2004; Keyser et al. 2008; and Silet, Asquith, and Fleming 2010.

2. Furthermore, the concept of mentoring up was presented by Lee in October 2013 at the national Society for Advancement of Chicanos and Native Americans in Science (SACNAS) conference. Afterwards, the evaluation revealed that 85% of respondents ($N =$ 41) indicated that the ideas/resources they will use from the workshop were either very good (41%) or excellent (44%). He will be providing similar workshops at his new institution, the University of California, Davis. Additionally, researchers at UW-Madison have collected resources on their website (https://mentoringresources.ictr. wisc.edu/MentoringResources) to help mentees proactively navigate their relationships, including questions to consider when choosing a new mentor and tips on effectively communicating with a mentor.

## Works Cited

Balster, N. J., C. Pfund, R. Rediske, and J. L. Branchaw. 2010. "*Entering Research:* A Course That Creates Community and Structure for Beginning Undergraduate Researchers in the STEM Disciplines." *CBE Life Sciences Education* 9 (2): 108–18.

Bland, C. J., A. L. Taylor, S. L. Shollen, A. M. Weber-Main, and P. A. Mulcahy. 2009. *Faculty Success through Mentoring: A Guide for Mentors, Mentees, and Leaders.* Lanham, MD: Rowman & Littlefield Education.

Bolles, Richard. 2013. *What Color Is Your Parachute? 2013: A Practical Manual for Job-Hunters and Career-Changers.* New York: Ten Speed.

Branchaw, Janet, Christine Pfund, and Raelyn Rediske. 2010. *Entering Research: A Facilitator's Manual.* New York: W. H. Freeman.

Cho, C. S., R. A. Ramanan, and M. D. Feldman. 2011. "Defining the Ideal Qualities of Mentorship: A Qualitative Analysis of the Characteristics of Outstanding Mentors." *American Journal of Medicine* 124 (5): 453–58.

Dunning, David, Kerri Johnson, Joyce Ehrlinger, and Justin Kruger. 2003. "Why People Fail to Recognize Their Own Incompetence." *Current Directions in Psychological Science* 12 (3):

83–87.

Feldman, M. D., P. A. Arean, S. J. Marshall, M. Lovett, and P. O'Sullivan. 2010. "Does Mentoring Matter: Results from a Survey of Faculty Mentees at a Large Health Sciences University." *Medical Education Online* 15:5063. doi: 10.3402/meo.v15i0.5063.

Gabarro, John, and John P. Kotter. 1980. "Managing Your Boss." *Harvard Business Review* 58 (1): 92–100.

Garman, K. A., D. L. Wingard, and V. Reznik. 2001. "Development of Junior Faculty's Self-efficacy: Outcomes of a National Center of Leadership in Academic Medicine." *Academic Medicine* 76 (10): S74–76.

Handelsman, Jo, Christine Pfund, Sarah Lauffer, and Christine Pribbenow. 2005. *Entering Mentoring: A Seminar to Train a New Generation of Scientists.* Madison: University of Wisconsin Press.

Hunter, Anne-Barrie, Sandra Laursen, and Elaine Seymour. 2007. "Becoming a Scientist: The Role of Undergraduate Research in Students' Cognitive, Personal, and Professional Development." *Science Education* 91:36–74.

Keyser, D. J., J. M. Lakoski, S. Lara-Cinisomo, D. J. Schultz, V. L. Williams, D. F. Zellers, and H. A. Pincus. 2008. "Advancing Institutional Efforts to Support Research Mentorship: A Conceptual Framework and Self-assessment Tool." *Academic Medicine* 83 (3): 217–25.

Kruger, Justin, and David Dunning. 1999. "Unskilled and Unaware of It: How Difficulties in Recognizing One's Own Incompetence Lead to Inflated Self-assessments." *Journal of Personality and Social Psychology* 77 (6): 1121–34. doi: 10.1037/0022-3514.77.6.1121.

Light, Gregory, and Marina Micari. 2013. *Making Scientists: Six Principles for Effective College Teaching.* Cambridge, MA: Harvard University Press.

Palepu, A., R. H. Friedman, R. C. Barnett, P. L. Carr, A. S. Ash, L. Szalacha, and M. A. Moskowitz. 1998. "Junior Faculty Members' Mentoring Relationships and Their Professional Development in U.S. Medical Schools." *Academic Medicine* 73 (3): 318–23.

Pfund, C., S. House, P. Asquith, M. Fleming, K. Buhr, E. Burnham, J. Eichenberger Gilmore, et al. 2014. "Training Mentors of Clinical and Translational Research Scholars: A Randomized

Controlled Trial." *Academic Medicine* 89 (5): 774–82. doi: 10.1097/ACM.0000000000000218.

Pfund, C., S. House, K. Spencer, P. Asquith, P. Carney, K. Masters, R. McGee, J. Shanedling, S. Vecchiarelli, and M. Fleming. 2013. "A Research Mentor Training Curriculum for Clinical and Translational Researchers." *Clinical and Translational Science* 6 (1): 26–33. doi: 10.1111/cts.12009.

Pfund, Christine, Christine Pribbenow, Janet Branchaw, Miller Lauffer, and Jo Handelsman. 2006. "The Merits of Training Mentors." *Science*, January 27, 473–74.

Raggins, B., and K. Kram. 2007. *The Handbook of Mentoring at Work: Theory, Research, and Practice.* Thousand Oaks, CA: SAGE.

Ramanan, R. A., R. S. Phillips, R. B. Davis, W. Silen, and J. Y. Reede. 2002. "Mentoring in Medicine: Keys to Satisfaction." *American Journal of Medicine* 112 (4): 336–41.

Rath, Tom, and Barry Conchie. 2008. *Strengths-Based Leadership: Great Leaders, Teams, and Why People Follow.* New York: Gallup Press.

Sambunjak, D., S. E. Straus, and A. Marusic. 2010. "A Systematic Review of Qualitative Research on the Meaning and Characteristics of Mentoring in Academic Medicine." *Journal of General Internal Medicine* 25 (1): 72–78.

Sorcinelli, Mary Deane, and Jung Yun. 2007. "From Mentor to Mentoring Networks: Mentoring in the New Academy." *Change*, November/December, 58–61.

Shea, J. A., D. T. Stern, P. E. Klotman, C. P. Clayton, J. L. O'Hara, M. D. Feldman, K. K. Griendling, M. Moss, S. E. Straus, and R. Jagsi. 2011. "Career Development of Physician Scientists: A Survey of Leaders in Academic Medicine." *American Journal of Medicine* 124 (8): 779–87.

Steiner, J. F., P. Curtis, B. P. Lanphear, K. O. Vu, and D. S. Main. 2004. "Assessing the Role of Influential Mentors in the Research Development of Primary Care Fellows." *Academic Medicine* 79 (9): 865–72.

Silet, K. A., P. Asquith, and M. F. Fleming. 2010. "A National Survey of Mentoring Programs for KL2 Scholars." *Clinical and Translational Science* 3 (6): 299–304. doi: 10.1111/j.1752-8062.2010.00237.x

# Shifting Vision: Mentoring as Faculty Development for All Levels of Experience

*Jennifer W. Shewmaker and Phyllis Bolin*

Mentoring is difficult to define but is characterized by the reciprocal relationship between mentor and mentee and the successful transformations of identity by each member of the pair (Zeind et al. 2005). In the mentoring environment, both mentor and mentee benefit from the experiences. Benefits are transformative and provide learning and growth for the pair. Businesses in the United States have long recognized the importance of mentoring new employees in order to encourage development and retention within the workplace. While businesses have been developing mentoring relationships for the last 30 years, mentoring of new faculty in academe has been slower in its formalization (Zellers, Howard, and Barcic 2008). More recently, mentoring of new faculty has been recognized as a strong component of both faculty development and retention and achievement of academic and institutional goals.

Newcomers to academe arrive unprepared and uncertain as to what to expect in their new surroundings. Many have concerns about not knowing enough, about how to deal with students and student issues, and how to navigate the murky waters of teaching and life outside the campus environment. The literature on mentoring has described many best practices and positive outcomes associated with evidence-based programs. We will examine the origin and development of a long-term, evidence-based faculty mentoring program at our institution, Abilene Christian University. This program provides a unique example of a mentoring initiative that began with a focus on one-to-one hierarchical mentoring relationships and evolved into a mentoring mosaic structure that provides opportunities for growth for all faculty members involved.

Abilene Christian University (ACU) was founded in 1906 to provide a Christian education for students in West Texas. More than 100 years later, ACU is among the premier universities for the education of Christ-centered global leaders, enrolling about 4,600 students annually from nearly every state and 43 countries. ACU is a private, comprehensive university located in Abilene, Texas (pop. 117,000), about 150 miles west of the Dallas/Fort Worth area. The university offers 71 baccalaureate majors in more than 125 areas of undergraduate study, in addition to its graduate programs. As an educational center for a large region, Abilene provides cultural, entertainment, and support programs and services normally associated with cities twice its size (Bolin 2011, 2).

This chapter offers insights and ideas for universities as they consider the development of faculty mentoring programs. We hope to provide historical context for the evolution of such programs and add to the existing literature on the effective structuring of faculty mentoring programs.

### Historical Background of ACU's Mentoring Program

In 1992, ACU opened the Adams Center for Teaching and Learning. The Adams Center exists to promote the lifelong learning of ACU's faculty as they strive to integrate their faith and their roles as teachers and scholars in higher education. It serves as a gathering place for faculty to share insights, raise questions, and develop skills in a hospitable, supportive context that allows faculty to experiment with new ways of teaching, learning, and conducting research. Faculty gather several times each week for lunch and conversations led by their colleagues. The Adams Center also holds week-long teaching institutes twice a year, and provides programming that supports scholarship and service. A faculty development committee was established to provide the Adams Center and its director of faculty enrichment with guidance regarding faculty development needs. The committee represents each college across campus and is made up of tenured professors committed to increasing faculty development opportunities across the university.

In the spring of 1997, the Adams Center performed an analysis of the needs of junior faculty. Information analyzed came from three sources: evaluations of New Faculty Orientations between 1994 and 1996, feedback from focus group meetings of new faculty cohorts, and feedback from academic leaders. Five needs were identified in this process and were addressed through a proposal for funding submitted to the Lilly Fellows Program. The proposal was authored by Mel Hailey, a faculty member, and Raye Lakey, a staff member in the Adams Center. It addressed the following needs:

1. consistency in departments' preparation and assimilation of their new faculty members
2. social networks to lend support for junior faculty across the university (i.e., outside the faculty member's home department)
3. rapid acculturation of junior faculty and their families in the campus community, local community, and region (acculturation being especially problematic for single faculty and female faculty)
4. guidance for junior faculty in how to integrate service learning, faith and learning, international perspectives, and other aspects of the university's mission into course content and teaching methods.
5. equipping junior faculty with survival skills for the classroom, including managing the course load at a teaching institution and becoming a role model and mentor to students.

The Lilly Foundation grant was successful, and in 1998 the New Faculty Mentoring Program was launched. Implemented by the director of faculty mentoring (a senior faculty member) and the director of faculty development (also a faculty member) in the Adams Center, the program provided a one-year, one-to-one mentoring experience for new faculty members with experienced faculty from outside their home department. It funded social events for experienced faculty and their junior faculty mentees, as well as monthly informational lunch meetings for all new faculty and mentors. The information sessions focused on increasing new faculty members' knowledge of on-campus resources for students (such as counseling and tutoring services) and of campus rules and regulations (entering grades, dealing with approved absences, and so forth). As funds from the Lilly Foundation grant were expended, the Office of the Provost took over funding for the program, ensuring continued resources for the mentoring program.

## Program Goals

Three goals originally established for the mentoring program remain a part of the effort today: professional development mentoring, social mentoring, and missional mentoring. *Professional development mentoring* provides assistance in improvement of teaching practices, growth of time management skills, development of quality relationships with students, and implementation of research-based practices in the classroom. *Social mentoring* develops social relationships outside of the new faculty member's department and promotes acculturation within the campus community, local community, and region. *Missional mentoring* gives guidance in the integration of faith and learning, including knowledge and understanding of the mission of the university.

*Mentoring for Mission* (Simon et al. 2003) describes the importance of communicating information about the culture and traditions of the university. As a Christian university affiliated with a particular church, the Churches of Christ, the environment at ACU is unique, and may present challenges to new faculty members. The university's mission is to educate students for Christian service and leadership throughout the world, and new faculty members may struggle with how this mission impacts the way they structure their classroom, provide feedback to students, and are themselves evaluated. New faculty need to understand and appreciate the historical background and priorities of the institution to feel connected. Simon uses the term "demographics of ownership" to describe the faculty member's degree of investment in the institutional mission. Consideration needs to be given to how mentoring programs can best foster a broad ownership of the mission of the university. ACU attempts to heed Simon and colleagues' advice that faculty mentoring programs at missional institutions be sensitive to "local faculty culture. They share common goals of inviting every new faculty member to become fully committed to the college's mission and aiding every new faculty member in becoming an effective contributor to the mission" (2003, 46). As the mentoring program at ACU has evolved, missional mentoring has become more important due to the distinctive aspects of working within a mission-focused university. While there are many resources for mentoring faculty in teaching and social areas, there are fewer for missional mentoring. An evaluation of our mentoring practices demonstrated less structured opportunities for missional mentoring. Given the unique setting in which ACU faculty operate and the mission of the university, teaching and mentoring of students is very mission oriented. Helping new faculty members understand this contextual expectation and coaching them on how to best integrate Christian practices into their own teaching in a way that is congruent with their own teaching style has become an important component of the New Faculty Mentoring Program.

The three goals require teamwork and training in a "user-friendly" environment, awareness of time constraints on new and current faculty, and flexibility and adaptability with respect to the changing needs of new and former faculty. With these considerations in mind, the program has been designed as a voluntary aid to new faculty rather than a series of compulsory events.

**Evolution of ACU's Program**

The program has evolved over the years but remains a successful and important part of the university's support for new faculty. While the formal mentoring relationship is scheduled for a one-year period, some pairs develop a bond that lasts for many years. At the end of each academic year, questionnaires distributed to new faculty and to mentors assess the program's success at reaching the goals set forth, collect feedback and advice for changes and adaptations to the program, and examine the involvement records of new faculty and mentors. This feedback loop provides an evidence-based plan for the program and adapts it to fit the changing demands and needs of the faculty. Strong points for the program include the following:

*New Faculty Orientation.* A new faculty orientation hosted by the director of faculty enrichment before the start of university meetings in late summer provides useful information for the start of the academic year, an introduction to other new faculty (to start the social networking early), an introduction to the faculty mentoring program and its schedule of monthly meetings, and an introduction to the culture and mission of the campus.

*Working with mentors.* One important component for those who serve as mentors is training before the mentoring process begins. Cross-department pairing provides new faculty with a confidant with whom they can feel comfortable talking and expressing their concerns, weaknesses, and fears. The pairs are able to discuss questions without fear of negative consequences for retention, tenure, or promotion.

*Regular meetings.* It is vital to schedule monthly meetings for new faculty and their mentors. The ACU New Faculty Mentoring Program invites guest speakers to discuss pertinent topics that match the goals of the program. Thus, some meetings focus on professional development topics, while others spotlight social or missional aspects of the work of new faculty members. The meetings are conducted during lunchtime, which is generally a convenient time for faculty. To encourage faculty attendance, the program provides lunch as well as small gifts with university logos and images.

*Unscheduled outings for mentoring pairs.* Shared activities are encouraged through funds allocated for tickets to plays, musicals, and cultural events on campus or in the city of Abilene. Family trips to the zoo, dinner outings, or other recreational activities serve to help the new faculty member and family feel welcomed and included in the new environment.

*Incentives.* Coupons for meals in the school cafeteria or coffee on campus provide a shared social networking experience for new faculty, mentors, and other invited faculty. The sharing of a meal or coffee break allows new faculty to meet and get to know other people working on campus and counters feelings of isolation in a new workplace.

**Perceived Needs**

As new faculty grew in experience, many began to express a desire to continue more formal mentoring relationships beyond the initial year of the program. Many departments and colleges perceived no need for purposefully planned mentoring efforts beyond the first year, and provisions of support drastically dropped. While some new faculty indeed developed informal mentoring networks of their own, such connections were unfortunately lacking for many others. Moreover, formal mentoring support was lacking in two areas in which faculty members are expected to grow in order to achieve tenure and promotion: teaching and scholarship. Inconsistency of mentoring at the department level also meant that unless faculty members were invited to participate as a mentor in the New Faculty Mentoring Program, there were few formal options to serve as a mentor to a colleague.

The lack of formal mentoring and support programs in these key areas left many faculty members with a perceived lack of support. While the Adams Center for Teaching and Learning had provided instruction in teaching through the aforementioned daily lunch workshops and regularly scheduled summer teaching institutes, there was little formal support for scholarship and few opportunities for mentoring a colleague or group of colleagues in producing strong creative and scholarly products. Thus, both new and more experienced faculty who had the ability to nurture their colleagues, or who were in need of guidance, struggled to connect with one another through informal channels.

Over the course of several years, faculty began to express their desire for more organized systems to support one another in teaching and scholarship. Informal conversations at lunch sessions and feedback obtained from faculty who participated in formal teaching or publication institutes through the Adams Center made it clear that faculty were longing for opportunities to connect with one another, learn from one another, and grow together. While the culture at ACU is one that tends to foster community, those efforts had generally been focused around social events or book groups of broad interest, rather than opportunities tailored to promote growth and relationships among faculty in the areas of teaching and scholarship.

In the late 1990s and early 2000s, a renewed focus by the provost on scholarship requirements for tenure and promotion brought added pressure on faculty members to publish and present their scholarship at professional conferences. These new requirements ignited faculty interest in mentoring in the areas of scholarship and publication. They also created opportunities for newer faculty, who had recently completed graduate programs with a strong focus on scholarship, to provide their colleagues with cutting-edge information and strategies for enhancing their scholarship and publication records.

The questions that emerged during this period of shifting vision for mentoring focused around the meaning and purpose of mentoring. Who was the appropriate mentor? Who was the appropriate mentee? What types of mentoring experiences do experienced faculty members need? What types of mentoring experiences do new faculty members need? Are there areas where the needs of all faculty members overlap? If so, how might a formal mentoring program be structured to provide support for faculty members throughout their academic careers?

### Seeking Faculty Feedback

In order to answer these questions, the director of faculty enrichment used several approaches to seek faculty feedback. The first approach involved a "question of the day" routine that was implemented in lunchtime sessions offered at the Adams Center. Sometimes the question of the day would be proposed to the faculty at large, allowing time for discussion with the entire group. At other times the question would be asked by Adams Center staff sitting at tables with faculty members conversing in groups of four or five. This allowed the Adams Center staff and the Director of Faculty Enrichment to informally obtain feedback from faculty in both large- and small-group settings.

The second approach focused on utilization of the already-established faculty development committee to work as a focus group. The members of the faculty development committee completed surveys providing their perspective on the needs and opportunities for mentoring at ACU. They were then asked to participate in small focus groups in which they expanded on the information in the survey.

The last approach used faculty involvement in different Adams Center sessions to form interest groups, and then those interest groups were called upon to serve as focus groups providing input on the mentoring needs in their particular area of interest. For example, faculty members who had participated in an Adams Center lunch session on qualitative research were asked to join focus groups in order to share their perceived needs in the area of scholarship and their interest in serving as both mentors and mentees. Thus, the information-gathering process included faculty at all levels of experience, ensuring broadly representative feedback.

As the information gathered from faculty was compiled, several themes emerged. First, it became clear that both new and more experienced faculty felt the need for an organized system of mentoring in the areas of teaching and scholarship. Second, faculty at all stages of their academic career indicated the need for mentoring in a variety of areas. Lastly, faculty at all levels of experience stated their willingness to provide mentoring to their colleagues in the areas of teaching and scholarship. This process clarified the needs and interests of faculty and provided the Adams Center with direction in shifting the paradigm for mentoring across the campus.

### Rethinking Mentoring

As the Adams Center went through the process of identifying the strengths, needs, and opportunities for mentoring programs for faculty, it became clear that the vision for mentoring needed to be reexamined. While a development program for new faculty existed, continuing opportunities for structured mentoring were inconsistent. While the Adams Center sponsored biannual week-long institutes focused on teaching or scholarship, these had little connection to ongoing development opportunities. Faculty feedback elucidated the need for consistent and connected programming that purposefully provided mentoring opportunities for faculty throughout their careers. It also established that faculty considered mentoring a more nuanced relationship than could be achieved by simply pairing a new and a more experienced faculty member. Whereas the original mentoring plan consistently put new faculty in the position of learner and more experienced faculty in the role of guide, feedback clarified that faculty at all levels of experience were interested in taking the role of mentor and mentee in different areas. As noted above, many of the new faculty at ACU bring with them knowledge of innovative research techniques and an up-to-date understanding of the demands of publication. These new faculty indicated their willingness to share that knowledge with their colleagues, and more experienced faculty showed an inclination for learning from their newer co-workers.

## Building Connectedness and Mutuality

One of the greatest needs indicated by faculty was that of more structured opportunities for developing mentoring relationships with colleagues across disciplines. However, the nature of the university and college system made developing these collaborations difficult without support from the Adams Center. In rethinking the concept of mentoring, we began to consider the model proposed by Mullen and Fletcher (2012), in which mentoring is a journey that is developmental, intentional, and generative for both mentor and mentee—at times focused not on a dyad, but on a community. In fact, Mullen (2009) introduces the concept of mentoring mosaics, which provide mentees with the opportunity to connect with a variety of other professionals across a wide range of areas. The mentoring mosaic model focuses on building cooperative, collegial cultures of support (Rath 2012). Within the ACU setting, this concept was familiar; learning communities for faculty at ACU were well established, having begun in the mid-1990s. These communities provided opportunities for faculty members with similar interests to gather on a regular basis in the Adams Center facility, where they were provided with lunch or refreshments, as well as support in purchasing books or other materials. The need for structured opportunities to develop mentoring relationships dovetailed with one of the established strengths of learning communities. Thus, we began to shift our vision of mentoring away from the dyad of a single mentee and mentor toward one that provided faculty with the chance to serve at various times in both roles, and to interact with a variety of colleagues in a mosaic that emphasized building alliances, networking, and a dispersion of responsibility (Kanuka and Marini 2004).

This more fluid understanding of mentoring relationships opened up new possibilities for both junior and senior faculty members. Rather than being locked in a particular role with only one other colleague, the mosaic model allowed for the emergence of leadership from a wider range of faculty members, each exercising a different skill set and sharing their particular knowledge with their co-workers throughout their careers. One of the benefits of this model is that it provides more experienced faculty members with structured opportunities to build their skills and knowledge base with support from their colleagues. Instead of being isolated in their search for emerging skills, they are supported and coached throughout the process. This provides newer faculty members with the opportunity to share the cutting-edge knowledge they obtained in graduate school for the benefit the university as a whole.

## Development of Mentoring Communities

One of the key considerations in the promotion of mentoring communities has been to ensure that we are providing faculty with opportunities that match their areas of interest. We realized that, rather than planning programs in a vacuum and hoping that faculty would attend, it was important to solicit faculty input regarding the mentoring communities. Focus groups were conducted with new and experienced faculty to determine which types of mentoring communities were most needed. We learned that faculty felt they needed most support in teaching, scholarship, and writing. In particular, faculty indicated a need for opportunities to meet with others who were conducting similar research projects in order to brainstorm, discuss optimal approaches to projects, and receive feedback on project planning in qualitative research programs. Across the board, faculty stated that they felt pressure to publish, but since we work in a university with a strong teaching focus, they often felt unable to find the time to devote to writing. In reference to teaching, even experienced faculty members reported that they viewed themselves as content experts, but not necessarily as experts in the field of teaching and learning. Professors at all levels of experience noted a need for support, innovative ideas, and connection with other teachers.

These three areas formed the foundation for the launch of ACU's faculty mentoring communities in the fall of 2012. Communities were formed by both a general invitation to faculty at large and via personal invitations to faculty members who had attended sessions or expressed interest in a particular topic. People who indicated a strong interest were asked to facilitate the interaction of the group for a semester. The Adams Center provided meeting space, lunch, and an introduction to the concept of mentoring communities during the first session. After that, members of the communities were responsible for developing a plan for regular meetings and for their content. Most communities decided to meet once per month during the lunch hour.

Each group ended up choosing a format whereby one group member would present on a topic relevant to the entire community for the first 15 minutes of the meeting. After discussion, one or two members of the group would bring a specific question or project to share with the group in order to obtain feedback.

Several enduring mentoring communities originated in this way. Among these were a *qualitative research community* consisting of 8–10 faculty members from a variety of disciplines, including biblical studies, human communication, sociology, marriage and family therapy, and education. In a given meeting, this mentoring community might start with a 15-minute presentation and brief question-and-answer time focused on how to interview subjects in a qualitative study. After that, one member of the community might describe a project currently being developed and ask the group for feedback on the best way to design the study. In this way, the faculty member could develop a much stronger research plan than she would have been able to devise on her own. As an outgrowth of this community, two faculty members who facilitated the meetings developed a three-day workshop, offered to the faculty at large, bringing the work that has been done in the community to a wider audience and expanding opportunities for other faculty members to grow in their knowledge and skills in this area. In end-of-the-year surveys, faculty involved in this community reported satisfaction with the program in terms of growth in knowledge and development of new relationships with other faculty members across the university.

ACU also implemented a *teaching community*, made up of 10–12 faculty members from a wide variety of disciplines (including education, social work, psychology, business administration and finance, biology, biochemistry, and family studies), focused on pedagogy and teaching techniques. This community developed a "show and tell" practice whereby members brought in specific teaching practices, discussed the empirical evidence for the effectiveness of the practice, and then demonstrated it for the group. Members learned new techniques, discussed the challenges and benefits of particular strategies, and reported back to one another about how the practice worked in particular disciplines and types of classes. Time was reserved during each community meeting for group members to share a particular challenge that they were having in their own classes. This practice allowed each faculty member to solicit suggestions from colleagues with a wide variety of experience and knowledge. A side benefit was that newer faculty members were able to see that all teachers face difficulties in the classroom, whether related to behavior management, incorporating technology, or finding an effective approach to presenting difficult material.

An end-of-the-year survey indicated that members of the teaching community were highly satisfied with the development of new skills and new relationships with colleagues, and found the community useful in developing their teaching. They indicated that their teaching practices had changed due to their involvement with the community, as they implemented new strategies in the classroom. Due to the positive response that faculty had to this community, the Adams Center has developed and piloted a Master Teacher Program with six faculty members from four different departments and exhibiting a range of teaching experience. This program, based on the mosaic mentoring model, provides structured support for teaching to faculty members of varied backgrounds. Faculty expressed great satisfaction with the program and noted specific changes in their practices, just as faculty involved with the primary mentoring community did. The success of both programs has led to the decision to pilot a teaching mentoring community, composed of 16 faculty members with differing levels of experience, and to add the Master Teacher Program as a year-long required component of the New Faculty Orientation.

Finally, ACU established a *scholarly writing community* comprised six to eight faculty members from fields such as computer science, language and literature, library science, education and psychology. Dr. Cole Bennett, director of the ACU Writing Center, agreed to lead this group, which focused on accountability, productivity, and a mutual provision of feedback on scholarly writing projects. Given his experience with writing groups, Dr. Bennett felt that a monthly face-to-face meeting would establish an ideal rhythm. He provided structure and accountability by encouraging members to develop specific writing goals that were shared with the group. This was important in allowing members to increase their writing productivity. One of the concerns that faculty had expressed was a lack of opportunity to obtain structured feedback on their writing from other professionals. In writing community meetings, one member would share a piece of writing and receive reactions and comments from colleagues. This allowed members to hone their work before sharing it with a more critical audience, and increased the quality of their writing. Some members used the community as an aid in revising journal articles, while others found in it an opportunity to complete work on their dissertations or creative writing projects. A focus group conducted with this community indicated that members found it valuable in increasing their productivity.

ACU has a strong tradition of providing mentoring services to new faculty. As the Adams Center listened to the expressed needs of the more experienced faculty members, it became clear that our programming needed to reflect the nuanced and complex nature of faculty mentoring. The shift in vision from a model that focused primarily on new faculty to one that considers the mentoring needs of faculty at all levels of experience has afforded a richer practice for all faculty members. Over the last two years, the old model of cross-departmental mentoring pairs has continued alongside the newly established mentoring communities. This has provided new faculty with different avenues to network and develop relationships with a wide variety of more experienced faculty. In reflecting on the experience of new faculty members, the Adams Center has seen value in both types of mentoring. However, due to the success of the mentoring communities, mentoring pairs are now engaged in group activities, such as reading groups, to foster community and connections more widely across the university. In keeping with the New Faculty Mentoring mosaic model, a *missional teaching community* has been established to allow cross-departmental pairs to focus on the practical implications of integrating faith and Christian practices with teaching. With increased systematic support in the areas of teaching and scholarship, all faculty have enhanced opportunities to grow and learn with one another. Most importantly, the new vision allows all faculty to flourish as they serve at various times in their careers as both mentors and mentees.

## Works Cited

Bolin, Phyllis. 2011. "Pursuit: A Journey of Research and Creative Expression." Quality Enhancement Plan. Abilene, TX: Abilene Christian University.

Kanuka, H., and A. Marini. 2004. "Empowering Untenured Faculty Through Mosaic Mentoring." *Canadian Journal of University Continuing Education* 30 (2): 11–38.

Mullen, Carol A. 2009. "Re-Imagining the Human Dimension of Mentoring: A Framework for Research Administration and the Academy." *Journal of Research Administration* 40 (1): 10–31.

Mullen, Carol A., and Sarah J. Fletcher, eds. 2012. *The SAGE Handbook of Mentoring and Coaching in Education*. London: SAGE.

Rath, Jean. 2012. "Research Mentoring in Higher Education." In *The SAGE Handbook of Mentoring and Coaching in Education*, edited by Carol A. Mullen and Sarah J. Fletcher, 506–19. London: SAGE.

Simon, Caroline J., Laura Bloxham, Denise Doyle, Mel Hailey, Jane Hokanson Hawks, Kathleen Light, Dominic P. Scibilia, and Ernest Simmons. 2003. *Mentoring for Mission: Nurturing New Faculty at Church-Related Colleges*. Grand Rapids, MI: William B. Eerdmans.

Zeind, Caroline S., Martin Zdanowicz, Kathleen MacDonald, Christine Parkhurst, Cynthia King, and Phillip Wizwer. 2005. "Developing a Sustainable Faculty Mentoring Program." *American Journal of Pharmaceutical Education* 69 (5): 1–13.

Zellers, Darlene, Valerie M. Howard, and Maureen A. Barcic. 2008. "Faculty Mentoring Programs: Reenvisioning Rather Than Reinventing the Wheel." *Review of Educational Research* 78:552–88.

# Building a Culture of Mentoring via a
# Faculty Mentoring Portal

*Julie Welch, Krista Hoffman-Longtin,
Miriam Cohen Dell, Jon Eynon, Daniel Rusyniak,
and Mary Dankoski*

Although academic institutions vary widely in how they approach faculty mentoring, the literature clearly emphasizes the critical importance of mentoring for the career success, satisfaction, and productivity of faculty members (Sambunjak, Straus, and Marusic 2006, 2010).[1] An institution's approach to faculty mentoring depends upon numerous factors—most importantly, the academic culture and commitment to mentoring. Additional factors may include size of the institution, the structure and interconnectedness of the departments or units, administrative infrastructure, resource allocation, and faculty composition. All of these factors influenced our approach and decision-making in the creation of a comprehensive mentoring website at the Indiana University School of Medicine (IUSM).

IUSM is the second largest medical school in the U.S., with a total student body of over 2,000, more than 1,100 fellows and resident physicians, and more than 2,000 full- and part-time faculty members across nine campuses. Due to the size, heterogeneity, and geographical spread of our faculty, a centralized faculty mentoring program and oversight is not feasible. According to the IUSM State of the Faculty Report (Dankoski et al. 2012), 92% of the 2,068 faculty members are full time, 36.5% are women, and 7% are underrepresented minorities. While the absolute number of tenure-track faculty members has remained flat over the past ten years, the number of clinical- (non-tenure-) track members continues to increase. For example, in 2001–02, tenure-track faculty comprised 61% of the total IUSM faculty community, while clinical-track faculty comprised 29%. In 2011–12, the percentages equalized, with clinical-track and tenure-track faculty each comprising 45% of the total faculty community; the remaining 10% comprised lecturers and non-tenure-track researchers.

169

Faculty members are distributed across nine campuses and 26 departments, which vary considerably in size and may be subdivided into divisions, sections, or research centers. In addition, the research, educational, and clinical activities of faculty members are individualized even within departments. The complex organizational structure and vast heterogeneity of our faculty underscore the importance of tailored mentoring for specific faculty groups. As such, faculty mentoring at IUSM has traditionally been rooted within departments, divisions, or research centers. At this level, mentoring practices vary widely, from structured formal mentoring programs to informal or ad hoc mentoring relationships. Despite this diversity, many components of effective mentoring and professional development represent needs common to most academic faculty members.

The need to address faculty mentoring at IUSM was identified through efforts of the Office of Faculty Affairs and Professional Development (OFAPD). In 2006, the OFAPD developed the Faculty Vitality Survey© to assess faculty satisfaction, productivity, engagement, career and life management, and perceptions of the institutional climate and leadership. Results from the 2009 survey revealed a high need for faculty mentoring. While 40% of faculty strongly agreed that mentoring is highly important to their academic vitality, nearly one quarter reported a lack of mentorship. In response, the OFAPD convened a mentoring task force composed of key faculty members with decades of professional experience and commitment to the mission of the School of Medicine. Their charge was to offer recommendations for improving the current state of academic mentoring within the school. The task force concluded, "IUSM could better serve the needs of mentors and mentored-faculty [sic] through Institutional (centralized) initiatives that would complement Departmental (local) efforts" (IUSM 2009, 4). Recommendations included the public endorse-ment of the value of mentoring by institutional leaders, central investment to support mentoring leadership roles, public recognition for mentoring excellence, and the creation of a repository for mentoring material and resources (IUSM 2009; Buchanan and Callahan 2011). Specifically, the task force recommended allocating resources to "develop a menu or tool-kit of mentoring materials and resources that could be adopted at a program level based on needs and interests of individual programs" (IUSM 2009, 21). In response, the OFAPD strategized to fund a Faculty Fellowship in Mentoring. This position (held by author Julie Welch) was charged with reviewing and implementing selected recommendations from the task force reports, including the creation of a website of faculty mentoring resources.

## Why a Web Portal?

Choosing web-based platforms to deliver information and instruction can beneficially supplement traditional education and faculty mentoring efforts. The use of web-based instruction is widely established in U.S. higher education institutions (Brooks 2011; Robin et al. 2011) and can overcome "barriers to learning such as time and distance, individualize instruction, and manage information" (Robin et al. 2011, 437). Additionally, web-based platforms meet the expectations of today's tech-savvy generation by offering the ease of asynchronous learning and individualized adaptability of resources.

As our mentoring task force emphasized, successful implementation of new technology depends not only upon the vision and content expertise of the project leader, but upon a shared vision, recognition, and support from the institutional leadership. In 2010, an international working group of medical educators put forth recommendations for supporting faculty in the use of new technology in education (Robin et al. 2011). Among their recommendations was that institutions consider allocating resources to (1) provide teams of technology specialists to support faculty, (2) train faculty to learn and use new technologies, (3) recognize new forms of academic scholarship, and (4) foster an online community that would collaborate to develop and share tools (Robin et al. 2011). While it takes time, money, personnel, and recognition to implement new technologies, these resources are imperative for faculty members' success.

In this chapter we describe the development, implementation, and evaluation of the IUSM Faculty Mentoring Portal, a centralized mentoring website designed to provide toolkits and resources to support local mentoring efforts at IUSM. Additionally, we outline in detail the design and content of the resource at the time of this volume's publication, recognizing that all online content is fluid and adaptable.

**Mentoring Portal Development Process**

The entire project was, and continues to be, an iterative process, which gains increased clarity after each cycle of information integration. The project was guided by the purpose of offering tangible, accessible resources to enhance both individual and departmental mentoring practices and programs.

Figure 9.1 offers a depiction of the Mentoring Portal's expert-guided development and evaluation cycles. The Faculty Fellow in Mentoring led the project through these iterative cycles in collaboration with the mentoring task force, the OFAPD, and the Faculty Development and Coordinating Committee (FDCC), a standing committee within IUSM comprised of broad faculty representation. In 2011, a Mentoring Task Force report reviewed the websites of 51 academic mentoring programs (Buchanan and Callahan 2011). In 2012, a team of faculty from the FDCC revisited selected websites and extracted key design elements and content that pertained to mentees, mentors, and academic mentoring in general. The Faculty Fellow synthesized all of these data into categories and augmented the content with relevant updates from the current mentoring literature. Periodic reports to the OFAPD and FDCC were presented; subsequent feedback and editing was used to further clarify and guide development of the mentoring

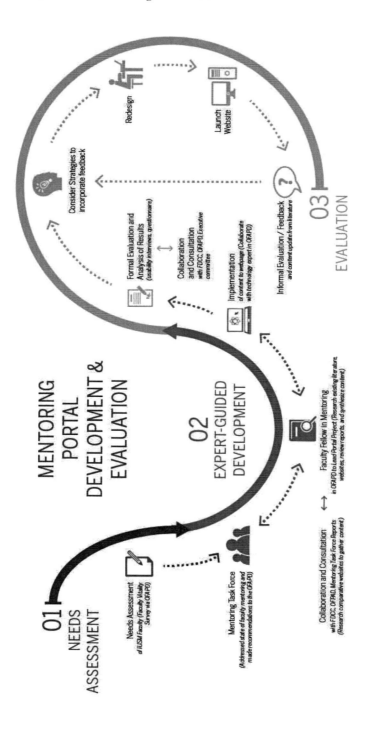

**FIGURE 9.1. Mentoring portal development and evaluation cycle.** *Source:* **Lauren Hernandez, IUSM OFAPD**

portal content. The implementation from paper to portal was a collaborative effort between the Faculty Fellow and members of the OFAPD, including a web designer. By soliciting faculty feedback throughout the process, we ensured that the portal was meeting the needs of faculty at large, while creating broad buy-in for the resource.

## Mentoring Portal Content

The IUSM Faculty Mentoring Portal is housed on the IUSM OFAPD home page under the Faculty Development tab; the direct address is http://faculty.medicine.iu.edu/mentoring. Each page and resource of the mentoring portal offers quotes, diagrams, and/or photos to enhance the user's experience. The design of the portal follows the standard requirements of our institution in terms of layout, navigation bar placement, and color selection. Primary navigation of the site occurs along the right-hand side of the page and includes tabs for the five major sections of the site: (1) Home, (2) Welcome from the Dean, (3) Mentoring Matters, (4) Mentoring Toolkit, and (5) Mentoring Awards. Each section includes subsections and additional resources as detailed in Figure 9.2.

### Home Page

The portal's home page highlights the institutional commitment to mentoring, the purpose of the site, and links to the IUSM Mentoring Task Force reports. Photos of leaders from the office are included, with quotes about their mentoring philosophies. The home page also includes a purpose statement:

> The goal of this centralized mentoring resource is to create an online portal to support local and departmental faculty mentoring programs. The mentoring menu and toolkit of resources are intended to facilitate individual and departmental mentoring practices and programs. Through this effort the OFAPD endorses the value of mentoring for sustaining a vital faculty and enhancing the academic enterprise of the institution.

### Welcome from the Dean

In response to a recommendation of the Mentoring Task Force, a dean's welcome page was included to provide an institutional endorsement of faculty mentoring. The dean's message focuses on the role of mentoring in faculty satisfaction and productivity, as well as the intrinsic benefits of mentoring relationships among faculty.

### Mentoring Matters

The "Mentoring Matters" section provides contextual background for those who are new to mentoring concepts, reviewing and defining (1) Models

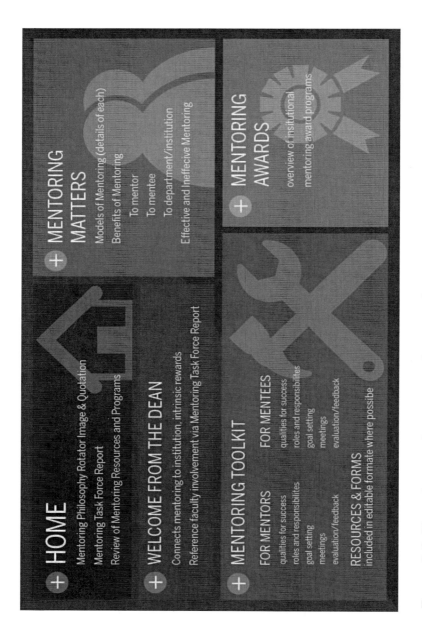

FIGURE 9. 2. Mentoring portal structure and content. *Source:* Lauren Hernandez, IUSM OFAPD

of Mentoring, (2) Benefits of Mentoring, and (3) Effective and Ineffective Mentoring practices. After reviewing the two dimensions of mentoring, career-advancement interventions and social-psychological support, the user can click on the links enumerated above for a self-tutorial. On each subsequent page, source material references are included (with links, if available) to give the reader more detailed information if desired. The "Models of Mentoring" page offers descriptions of various forms of mentoring including traditional one-on-one mentoring, mentoring panel or committee, functional mentoring, peer mentoring, group mentoring, and mosaic mentoring.

Next, the "Benefits of Mentoring" are outlined in detail, with specific emphasis on the benefits to the mentee, the mentor, and the department/institution. Our research on comparable websites and the current literature underscores the necessity in getting buy-in from all three parties in order to sustain successful mentoring practices and programs.

The third subsection, "Effective and Ineffective Mentoring," offers contrasting explanations for the successes and failures of mentoring relationships. One tab summarizes key habits and traits that serve to promote effective mentoring. The other tab itemizes potential pitfalls that can lead to "toxic" mentoring experiences.

### Mentoring Toolkit

The heart of the website is found under the "Mentoring Toolkit" link, with the vast majority of our content research and usability testing focused in this section. The stated purpose of the Mentoring Toolkit is "to assist mentors and mentees as they establish and maintain a productive mentoring relationship." Parallel toolkits were thoughtfully designed for the mentee and the mentor. The central navigation bar for each toolkit contains the same five tabs: Qualities for Success, Roles & Responsibilities, Goal Setting, Meetings, and Evaluation/Feedback. Each tab corresponds to one of five critical expectations for the mentoring relationship: (1) *Understand the qualities that lead to success* (What makes a great mentor and mentee? What are my skills and needs?); (2) *Clarify roles and responsibilities* (What does my mentor or mentee expect of me? Are the roles clear and responsibilities reasonable?); (3) *Set realistic goals and develop a plan* (Have we created an achievable plan and timeline?); (4) *Develop a schedule for meetings and have an agenda* (Is communication in person, by email, or by phone? Does each meeting have an agenda?) (5) *Establish evaluation and feedback plans*. The content and resources within each of these five tabs is similar, yet tailored to either the mentee or the mentor, as explained below (IUSM 2013).

*Mentee's Toolkit.* The Qualities for Success tab provides answers to the question, "What qualities should I look for in choosing a mentor?" Next, the mentee must turn an introspective eye and ask, "What qualities do I need as a mentee?" After a list of recommended qualities, a link to a comprehensive Mentee's Self-Assessment form is provided. This self-assessment has been left in an editable format (Microsoft Word) in order to allow the mentee or mentor to tailor the questions. Just as the activities of faculty members are diverse, so are their professional development and mentoring needs.

The Roles and Responsibilities tab opens with a statement: "A mentee who wants to get the most out of the mentoring relationship will actively employ 'MANAGING UP.' This concept means that the mentee takes ownership of and directs the relationship by being motivated to manage the work of the relationship in many of the following ways." The page then systematically describes a four-step process: (1) prepare for the mentoring relationship, (2) initiate and cultivate the mentoring relationship, (3) assist your mentor in giving relevant advice and counsel, and (4) follow through on assigned tasks and opportunities provided by the mentor. Included in this section are links to resources for establishing roles and responsibilities, including the Mentee's Self-Assessment form and an "Opportunity Is Knocking" planning worksheet designed to help the mentee prepare for and seize new opportunities as they arise (also provided in an editable format).

The next tab pertains to Goal Setting, and states, "[o]ne of the critical responsibilities for a mentoring relationship is to aid the mentee in setting and achieving career goals for short and long term aspirations, as well as, periodically evaluating new opportunities that arise. In addition, framing these career goals with respect to personal life ambitions and commitments is often necessary." Critical resources are provided to assist in goal setting, including an Individual Development Plan (IDP), the "Opportunity Is Knocking" planning worksheet, and a link to a tool for assessing the viability of the IDP, entitled, "Is it SMART?" Clicking on this link opens an interactive pop-out diagram that works through the questions involved in the SMART goal assessment, designed to ensure that goals are Specific, Measurable, Attainable, Results-oriented, and Time-limited.

The fourth tab, "Meetings," offers a printable version of a meeting checklist, which deals with how to prepare for the first meeting with your mentor, how to run the meeting, and what to do after the meeting. A "partnership agreement" form is recommended in order to set the expectations of confidentiality and no-fault termination. In addition, a "meeting agenda" resource is provided to structure the meeting flow, prioritize items, and record action plans for follow-up.

Finally, the Mentee Toolkit offers an "Evaluation/Feedback" tab, emphasizing that "[m]entees require honest, candid, time sensitive feedback from their mentor. Reciprocal and on-going feedback between the mentor and mentee is vital to the mentoring partnership." Clicking on the associated feedback diagram offers a schematic representation of the reciprocal nature of the mentoring relationship and highlights the key responsibilities of both the mentee and mentor in giving and receiving feedback. To assist in the evaluation process, forms are provided for the mentee and the mentor to evaluate one another.

*Mentor's Toolkit.* As noted, the central navigation toolbar parallels that of the Mentee's Toolkit. Although the content is similar, items are tailored specifically to mentors' potential needs. The "Qualities for Success" tab describes the characteristics of outstanding mentors as reported by Cho, Ramanan, and Feldman (2011) in a study analyzing nomination letters of esteemed mentors for a lifetime mentoring award. In addition, mentors are encouraged to assess whether they possess the skill set of successful mentors by taking a Mentor's Self-Assessment as provided in *"Nature's* Guide for Mentors"* (Lee, Dennis, and Campbell 2007). The "Roles and Responsibilities" section begins with the premise that "mentoring relationships are often tailored to the mentoring needs [of the mentee] in terms of providing career advancement interventions and psychosocial support. Mentors are encouraged to establish early on the expected roles and responsibilities of the relationship with their mentee." Following this, a systematic, three-step process is described: (1) prepare for the mentoring relationship, (2) cultivate the mentoring relationship, and (3) assist the mentee with career guidance and provide career advancement interventions. Accompanying resources include the Mentor's Self-Assessment form, an IDP, and the promotion and tenure criteria website for our institution. Additional citations offer further guidance on mentoring specific faculty groups (Baucher 2002; Detsky and Baerlocher 2007; Lee, Dennis, and Campbell 2007). The mentor's "Goal Setting" section provides resources that parallel the Mentee's Toolkit. A fourth tab addresses "Meetings" from the perspective of the mentor, with a printable checklist and agenda to ensure effective preparation, communication, and meeting pace. Finally, the "Evaluation/Feedback" tab is a mirror of that for mentees, as feedback is a reciprocal process (IUSM 2013).

*Resources/Forms.* The main navigation bar on the right-hand side of the web pages includes a wealth of information under the Resources/Forms link. This portion of the site consolidates in one place the resources found elsewhere on the IUSM Faculty Mentoring Portal. Additional examples of key resources from notable mentoring institutions augment these forms. Finally, a reference list of over 85 mentoring articles is provided for inquisitive readers.

### Mentoring Awards

The final section describes the purpose, criteria, and nomination process for the "Excellence in Faculty Mentoring Award," to be implemented in 2013–14. Although only IUSM faculty mentors are eligible for the awards, this page offers an example for other institutions to follow. The purpose of the award is

> to recognize the outstanding mentoring efforts of *one clinician and one basic scientist each year* who actively mentor other faculty members and learners. These prestigious awards acknowledge the time

sacrifice and dedication faculty mentors devote to foster the career development and academic success of colleagues and learners in the areas of research, education, service and clinical practice.

From an institutional perspective, these awards demonstrate the leadership's commitment to mentoring and "allow the school of medicine to honor and celebrate the valuable efforts of faculty mentors who embody the spirit of mentoring."

## Portal Evaluation

We employed a modified usability test (Nielsen 2012) to evaluate the IUSM Faculty Mentoring Portal. The goal of usability testing is to under-stand how users interact with the portal and to enhance the functionality and content of the site. Guidelines for usability testing hold that five to ten participants are necessary to ensure the reliability of responses (Faulkner 2003). Faculty volunteers for the testing were recruited from the IUSM Faculty Development and Coordinating Committee (FDCC) and the Academy of Teaching Scholars (ATS), a program to enhance the development of faculty as educators. A member of the OFAPD team conducted usability interviews to assess the portal's content, design, and efficiency. Per traditional usability testing guidelines (Nielsen 2012), a series of tasks were generated for participants to complete. The protocol for creating tasks was based on content identified as important by the IUSM Mentoring Task Force report (Buchanan and Callahan 2009). By closely following the movements of each tester and asking them to "talk through" their thought process in the portal, we sought to ensure that both the content and design felt appropriate and seamless for each faculty member. Sample tasks included accessing the Mentor's Self-Assessment form, finding a suggested agenda guide for meeting with a mentee, and locating information about why senior faculty should become mentors. The interviewer observed and videotaped each user's comments and ability to navigate through the website. Participants were asked to discuss their response to the overall design and layout of the portal in terms of accessibility and clarity of information presented. Additional questions assessed participants' perceptions of the purpose, relevance, and objectivity of the content. After each question, participants provided open-ended feedback about the portal. Results were compiled and coded by type and theme. Based on the results of the usability testing, strategies were considered to incorporate faculty members' content and design recommendations into the redesign of the portal.

The usability testing interviews were conducted with 11 faculty members recruited voluntarily from the IUSM FDCC and ATS. The faculty ranged from 4 to 32 years of service at IUSM, with a median of 14. Four of the participants (36%) were on the tenure track, while seven (64%) were on the clinical track. By rank, the faculty included two full professors (18%), five associate professors (45%) and four assistant professors (36%). The mean age was 48.5 years.

The results of the usability interviews were generally positive, but identified several needed changes for the IUSM Faculty Mentoring Portal. In terms of navigating the site, the participants were able to locate specific resources with relative ease. However, a few dead links to resources required correction. The perceptions of the participants regarding the overall design were mostly positive, and suggestions for improvement included clarification of headings, adding resources to the toolkits, linking back to the home page, and hyperlinking to mentoring articles. Several specific suggestions to improve the content have already been adopted: (1) to make the purpose clearer, (2) to add the welcome letter from the dean, and (3) to update the description of the mentoring awards.

Additional recommendations from the usability testing to improve the design and content of the website include (1) creating a "Mentoring Spotlight" page to highlight outstanding mentors, with photos and narrative comments from mentees; (2) adding a "how to use this site" page; (3) reformatting the resources page; (4) modifying content so as to address specific faculty groups; and (5) offering mentoring consultations for career and/or promotion and tenure advice. The final interview question asked the participants how they foresee faculty using the website. Four themes emerged: (1) faculty will go straight to the toolkits and resources; (2) mentors may use the toolkits with their mentees to have a more coordinated approach to the mentoring relationship; (3) departments could incorporate the toolkits and resources to enhance their own programs; (4) OFAPD should advertise the site at faculty orientations, as a resource for departments and mentoring panels, and as a recruitment tool for IUSM.

**Discussion and Challenges to Consider**

Mentoring among faculty in institutions of higher learning is a crucial element in sustaining a vital faculty community, promoting faculty development, and increasing faculty engagement and productivity (Felten, et al. 2013; Sambunjak, Straus, and Marusic 2006). Targeting mentoring initiatives to the needs of faculty, as well as considering the organizational culture, is critical if the goal is to create intergenerational collegiality among all members of the institution.

At IUSM, the goal of the Faculty Mentoring Portal is to offer centralized mentoring resources, while acknowledging the institutional reality of a heterogeneous faculty and localized programs. Each section of the portal is designed to adapt to the user. By focusing the sections of the site around user roles and needs, we offer our academic units flexibility. Departments without mentoring programs can begin with the end in mind, focusing on the goals of faculty success and implementing the tools broadly. Alternatively, for units with robust mentoring programs already in place, the content of the site offers much-needed tools for making mentoring a part of everyday work.

In developing and testing the project, we sought to shape the IUSM culture and build a collective commitment to the mentoring portal by using focused, deliberate language in our marketing efforts. Creating persuasive messages for multiple audiences can be challenging. Writing web content for large-scale use by a heterogeneous faculty meant the faculty fellow had to synthesize and convey maximum information in a concise manner. Strategic communication planning to the faculty about the mentoring portal effort became an active, iterative process, similar to the development of the mentoring portal itself. Messages to the faculty (including emails, newsletter stories, closed-circuit TV messages, and web banners) about this new mentoring portal were designed to reflect a purpose and provide a map to achieve a specific outcome. The goals of initial advertising messages were to underscore the institution's commitment to faculty mentoring, increase awareness of the importance of faculty mentoring, and announce the rollout of the mentoring portal. We launched this communication effort through multiple media channels, including a broadly circulated article in the IUSM weekly email newsletter, announcements in the biweekly OFAPD newsletter, the closed-circuit TV system used for broadcasting announcements at various locations on the medical school campus, and targeted email blasts to faculty and unit leaders. The website was also demonstrated at a meeting of the IUSM Faculty Steering Committee (similar to a faculty senate). Additionally, the faculty fellow and OFAPD sponsored educational sessions on mentoring at IUSM and IUPUI campuses, highlighting the mentoring portal resources and framework for developing a positive mentoring relationship. Our goal was to create a communication plan that targeted each faculty group engaged in the mentoring process. As others plan for a portal such as this, it is important to consider what motivates each segment of the faculty audience and craft messages around those motivations. For example, senior faculty might respond to a message about helping the next generation or leaving a legacy, while pre-tenure faculty might be motivated by messages about the promotion process.

Continuous research, measurement, and incorporation of findings are necessary to build a successful product and enhance a mentoring culture. While maintaining a focus on the theme of mentorship, we carefully framed our messages and further demonstrated the value of mentoring and the commitment to this endeavor by the institution's leaders. This process of building a comprehensive communication plan is both an asset and a limitation. It provides direction to achieve the goal of promoting mentoring, but at the same time requires constant attention and upkeep.

One of the key strengths of this approach is "basing strategic decisions on careful listening to the wants that are expressed by representative members of potential adopters" (Dearing, Maibach, and Buller 2006, 20). For this project the "potential adopters" are our faculty members.

Although reaching our target audience within IUSM is challenging, primarily due to the size of the school, we have attempted to improve our range by planning carefully and engaging a diverse pool of faculty. Incorporating faculty members into every step of the process is essential. From answering the recommendations of the faculty Mentoring Task Force, to developing the framework and content of the portal, to testing and incorporating feedback, faculty members were purposefully engaged. Effective engagement of faculty not only improves the product, but potentially increases buy-in, creates a shared vision, and enhances faculty development.

Soliciting faculty involvement throughout the process has presented both opportunities and drawbacks. For example, the inclusion of faculty throughout the process meant that a traditional "pilot test" approach was unnecessary. Instead, soliciting ongoing faculty feedback via the FDCC and conducting usability testing created an iterative cycle in which testing and revisions occurred almost simultaneously. The limitations to usability testing in this context include faculty unfamiliarity with the portal development and variations in how the tester might interact with the site in the presence of an interviewer.

There are two important factors institutions must consider before implementing a project of this scale: time and money. Realistically, OFAPD faculty and staff spent approximately 600 hours gathering the content, designing the structure of the portal, conducting usability testing and focus groups, and developing and implementing the communication plan. That estimate does not include the time faculty members volunteered to participate in testing and focus groups. Hiring a dedicated Faculty Fellow in Mentoring and paying for the OFAPD faculty and staff's time on this project were considerable expenses for the office. Expenses were kept manageable by using existing staff and student resources where appropriate. Specific personnel expenses included: 10% of a faculty member's time to write and manage the content of the portal; approximately 120 hours' labor by a graduate student in Communication to manage and implement the usability testing and marketing plan; 120 hours by an instructional technology specialist to develop the site; and 40 hours by a program manager to supervise the project.

Ongoing attention and expenses will be required to keep the portal updated and relevant. Although an endeavor of this size should not be taken lightly, the return on our investment could be significant. Our portal has the potential to serve 1,400 full-time and 800 part-time and volunteer faculty. Our reach could expand to learners as well; both our medical student affairs office and graduate programs have expressed interest in using the mentoring tools for their trainees. Further, the site is not limited to members of the IUSM community, and thus is available for use by other members on the campus, other institutions, and the general public.

While the Faculty Mentoring Portal answered an institutional need, measuring its impact on our faculty is a less straightforward process.

Anecdotal evidence about the use of the portal indicates that it is perceived as a useful, practical resource and is fulfilling a need. The website and its tools are highlighted every year in the IUSM New Faculty Welcome event and are enthusiastically received. Additionally, OFAPD offers a year-long professional development program for junior faculty that includes a session on finding a mentor and maximize mentoring relationships. This session has been augmented and improved by use of the tools on the Faculty Mentoring Portal. Further, several departments and divisions have used the tools in local mentoring programs and events, including Emergency Medicine, Family Medicine, Psychiatry, Anatomy, Neonatology, and Pulmonary/Critical Care. Additionally, offices that serve the campus at large have used resources from the portal in their programs and events, including the campus academic affairs and research affairs offices, as well as the campus office for women and the Clinical and Translational and Sciences Institute (CTSI).

There are additional indicators of a more positive culture of mentoring across the institution. These indicators include IUSM's newly revised standardized CV format for promotion and tenure, which includes for the first time a heading for mentoring, and a similar space to report mentoring in the annual faculty effort report. While we do not claim that these changes were a direct result of the development of the Faculty Mentoring Portal, they were adopted in the same time frame. The fact that faculty could report on their mentoring activity in the annual report and CV sent another message that the institution values mentoring as a critical aspect of faculty life.

Future research is needed to determine the most appropriate and practical methods by which to measure the effectiveness of technology in supporting and influencing transformative mentorship. Tracking the number of site users and resource downloads gives a quantitative measure. The site has had over 5,500 hits in its first 24 months, with the Mentoring Toolkits and Resources/Forms pages receiving the highest number of views. One can infer that if the number of hits on the site is sustained over time, it is providing a needed resource. A mechanism to track how site use breaks down by trainee, faculty, departments, mentoring programs, and/or training programs could guide future iterations of the portal, improving the content and tailoring it to specific needs. In addition, studying the difference between faculty relationships where mentoring resources are in place, and where they are not, would be valuable in understanding their impact on the mentoring relationship.

The pressures facing faculty in higher education today are unprecedented, and the support and guidance of a good mentor can greatly influence a faculty member's career satisfaction, productivity, and academic advancement. Indeed, mentoring can be considered part of the "lifeblood" of the faculty experience. The give-and-take of mentoring requires commitment, time, and preparation. However, as senior faculty face pressure to be ever more productive, mentoring can unfortunately become a low-priority activity. Institutions must find cost-effective and practical, yet high-impact ways to communicate the value of mentoring and the expectation that mentoring is everyone's job. Further, institutions must find ways to make mentoring easier and more successful. Creating a centralized Faculty Mentoring Portal as described in this chapter can provide concrete tools both to support mentoring and to communicate an institutional commitment to a culture of mentoring.

### Note

1. The authors wish to acknowledge the contributions to this chapter by the faculty and staff of the Indiana University School of Medicine: Megan Palmer, PhD; Randy Brutkiewicz, PhD; Emily Walvoord, MD; Lauren Hernandez, MBA; Kurt Kroenke, MD; Cherri Hobgood, MD; and Stephen Bogdewic, PhD.

### Works Cited

Bauchner H. 2002. "Mentoring Clinical Researchers." *Archives of Disease in Childhood* 87:82–84.

Brooks, C. F. 2010. "Toward 'Hybridised' Faculty Development for the Twenty-First Century: Blending Online Communities of Practice and Face-To-Face Meetings in Instructional and Professional Support Programmes." *Innovations in Education and Teaching International* 47 (3): 261–70. doi: 10.1080/14703297.2010.498177

Buchanan, N. C., and C. Callahan. 2011. "Review of Local and National Mentoring Resources and Programs." Indiana University School of Medicine. http://faculty.medicine.iu.edu/wp-content/uploads/2013/10/IUSM-Review-of-Mentoring-Resources-2011.pdf.

Cho, C. S., R. A. Ramanan, and M. D. Feldman. 2011. "Defining the Ideal Qualities of Mentorship: A Qualitative Analysis of the Characteristics of Outstanding Mentors." *American Journal of Medicine* 124:453–58.

Dankoski, M. E., K. Hoffmann-Longtin, L. H. Wakefield, M. M. Palmer, R. R. Brutkiewicz, E. E. Walvoord, S. P. Bogdewic, E. Park, and M. Ziskin. 2012. "*State of the Faculty Report*. Indiana University School of Medicine." Indiana University School of Medicine. http://faculty.medicine.iu.edu/about-us/annual-reports.

Dearing, J. W., E. W. Maibach, and D. B. Buller. 2006. "A Convergent Diffusion and Social Marketing Approach for Disseminating Proven Approaches to Physical Activity Promotion." *American Journal of Preventive Medicine* 31:S11–23.

Detsky, A. S., and M. O. Baerlocher. 2007. "Academic Mentoring—How to Give It and How to Get It." *Journal of the American Medical*

*Association* 297:2134–36.

Faulkner, L. 2003. "Beyond the Five-User Assumption: Benefits of Increased Sample Sizes in Usability Testing." *Behavior Research Methods, Instruments, and Computers* 35:379–83.

Felten, P., H. L. Bauman, A. Kheriaty, and E. Taylor. 2013. *Transformative Conversations: A Guide to Mentoring Communities Among Colleagues in Higher Education*. Jossey-Bass: San Francisco.

Indiana University School of Medicine. 2009. "Report of the Indiana University School of Medicine Mentoring Task Force." Indiana University School of Medicine. http://faculty.medicine.iu.edu/wp-content/uploads/2013/10/IUSM-Mentoring-TF-Report-2009.pdf.

Lee, A., C. Dennis, and P. Campbell. 2007. "*Nature's* Guide for Mentors." *Nature* 447:791–97.

Nielsen, J. 2012. "Usability 101: Introduction to Usability." Nielsen Norman Group. http://www.nngroup.com/articles/usability-101-introduction-to-usability.

Office of Faculty Affairs and Professional Development, Indiana University School of Medicine. 2013. "Faculty Mentoring Portal." Indiana University School of Medicine. http://faculty.medicine.iu.edu/mentoring.

Robin, B. R., S. G. McNeil, D. A. Cook, K. L. Agarwal, and G. R. Singhal. 2011. "Preparing for the Changing Role of Instructional Technologies in Medical Education." *Academic Medicine* 86:435–39.

Sambunjak, D., S. E. Straus, and A. Marusic. 2006. "Mentoring in Academic Medicine: A Systematic Review." *Journal of the American Medical Association* 296:1103–15.

Sambunjak, D., S. E. Straus, and A. Marusic. 2010. "A Systematic Review of Qualitative Research on the Meaning and Characteristics of Mentoring in Academic Medicine." *Journal of General Internal Medicine* 25:72–78.

PART THREE

# DIALOGUES AND REFLECTIONS

# Graduate Student Peer-Mentoring Programs: Benefiting Students, Faculty, and Academic Programs

## Beth A. Boehm and Amy J. Lueck

Peer mentoring—students mentoring other students—is an area of increasing interest for scholars and administrators of graduate education. The range of activities that constitute peer mentoring is vast, but includes providing insights into the departmental culture, guidance through major program milestones, psychosocial support, and friendship (Kram and Isabella 1985; Grant-Vallone and Ensher 2000). While most students are assigned a faculty advisor or mentor, the perspectives of peer mentors who may be only a year or two ahead of the mentee are valuable in different but powerful ways (Kram and Isabella 1985). While it is most common to talk about peer mentors helping new students adapt to a graduate program, peer mentees and mentors both can benefit from the mentoring relationship by co-presenting at conferences, forming study groups, or co-authoring articles. These other models of co-mentoring and group support are increasingly recognized alongside one-on-one peer mentoring as supportive of student retention, satisfaction, and success in graduate studies (Allen, McManus, and Russell 1999; McGuire and Reger 2003).

In this chapter, we will draw on our diverse experiences with peer mentoring programs, Beth from the perspective of an English faculty program advisor and administrator and Amy as a graduate student mentor/mentee at our institution, the University of Louisville. What unites our experiences is the programming we have developed to support peer mentoring programs across the disciplines through the School of Interdisciplinary and Graduate Studies (SIGS), where Amy works as a research assistant to Beth, who now serves as the Vice Provost for Graduate Studies and Dean of SIGS at the University of Louisville. Through the following dialogue,[1] we will

187

address the benefits of peer mentoring to various constituencies involved in graduate education and describe our own institutional attempts to foster peer mentoring across the disciplines.

While peer mentoring has always occurred informally through advice-seeking and collegial relationships among students, facilitating peer mentoring formally through departmental and university-wide programming is important for ensuring that all students have access to the benefits of peer mentoring and for maximizing the benefits of peer mentoring for faculty and programs. Some students do not seek out or secure fruitful peer-mentoring relationships on their own, and informal mentoring does not help faculty and programs in their work with graduate students. We argue that formal peer-mentoring programs support faculty by relieving the full burden of mentoring from the primary mentor and benefit graduate programs by dispersing the efforts of recruitment, orientation, and acculturation of incoming students. We describe the various forms of peer mentoring that we have supported and participated in—from one-on-one mentor pairings to intergenerational writing groups and interdisciplinary support groups—focusing throughout on the specific benefits to faculty and programs as well as students. By demonstrating the varied benefits of formalized peer-mentoring programs, we hope to increase the faculty and departmental support necessary for the success of such programs.

Peer-mentoring programs provide ways for students to take control of their own learning and professional development process, but these efforts need to be supported. Formalizing peer-mentoring programs provides that support, and a well-functioning peer-mentoring program subsequently releases crucial faculty time and resources, which can be allocated to more focused and effective forms of student support. Though some research suggests that informal mentoring is perceived by protégés as more effective than formal mentoring (Chao, Walz, and Gardner 1992; Allen, McManus, and Russell 1999), especially on career-related functions such as sponsorship, coaching, exposure, and visibility, these two models certainly need not be mutually exclusive. Instead, assigned peer mentors represent just one node in what should be a network of formal and informal mentoring relationships for graduate students.

**Beginnings**

AMY: Arriving in Louisville on a cold March day in 2010, I was greeted at the airport by a warm and energetic Nepalese man named

Shyam. I was coming to Louisville at that time for a visitation day that welcomed newly accepted PhD applicants to the program, and though I hadn't accepted my position in the program yet, Shyam had been assigned as my peer mentor. He had already contacted me prior to visitation day to extend his welcome to the program, answer any questions I might have, and, yes, offer to cart me around Louisville during my first visit. As a third-year student, Shyam had successfully navigated the transition to Louisville and the first years of coursework and exams. As Beth would say, he had been vetted as a student who could represent the program well and guide others through. He had first-hand knowledge of the program that he was willing to share, and wasn't too far removed from the experience himself to remember how difficult it can be to find one's way through the first days, months, and years of graduate study at a new university.

Coming from Pittsburgh, with no local network or friends in Kentucky, I was comforted to have someone to help show me the ropes. From my first call home to Pittsburgh that night from the bed-and-breakfast, Shyam's was the first name my family would know, and one they would hear again and again throughout my first years at the University of Louisville, as he moved from being a mentor, to being a colleague, to being a friend.

*BETH: The idea to begin a "peer mentoring" program at the University of Louisville was born of necessity. I was in my second or third year as the director of graduate studies (DGS) in English (in 1998 or 1999), making my annual calls to doctoral students, letting them know that we had chosen them for a spot in our program. I gave a standard spiel about the strengths of our program: that we hosted the then-still-new biennial Watson Conference on Rhetoric and Composition and in the off years had a prestigious visiting professor in the discipline, and that it was an extremely collegial program, where collaboration between doctoral students was valued far more than competition, and where students frequently presented together at conferences and co-authored articles. I bragged about how this collaborative spirit made our program unique. I always ended my recruitment phone calls by asking what questions they had for me, and the questions were usually quite basic, about timelines, teaching loads, and so on.*

*But this year, students asked questions that I really couldn't answer. "What is the social life like for graduate students? Is there a Louisville music scene? How do graduate students meet each other outside of class?"*

*As the mother of two children under the age of three at the time, whose music scene consisted of The Wiggles and Raffi, I laughed out loud: I had no idea what the music scene was like, and while I knew graduate students quite well from the courses I taught and from sitting with them in my office, I really had no idea what most of them did outside of class. A question from the very next student I called was similar, in that she asked what kind of lifestyle she could maintain in Louisville on the stipend, how much an average one-bedroom apartment in areas where students wanted to live would cost, and how safe people felt walking in areas close to campus. I realized that while I knew what rents were ten years before when I had first moved to Louisville, I hadn't bothered to keep up since buying my own home, and as a faculty member, I had parking on campus and did not walk in the neighborhood after dark. My inability to honestly answer these questions led me to ask several of the graduate students who I knew were friendly, smart, and helpful folks to call not only these students, but all the students we had given admittance to that year, so that they could answer the recruits' questions about what it was really like to live and learn in Louisville, and all of them leapt at the opportunity to help recruit the next cohort.*

*I didn't conceive of these initial phone calls as part of a peer mentoring program or even as part of a recruitment program, but every potential student who was called and every current student who made a call thanked me for putting them in touch with one another. That first year, we had a 100% acceptance rate, and thus the practice was established as a regular part of the recruitment process. The next year, most of those first-year students who had received a call from a student further along in the program volunteered to call a student we were hoping to recruit. Over the years, as each successive DGS modified and further formalized the program, it has become stronger and more useful to both departmental administrators and students. It allows the work of recruitment to be distributed among many, and it also encourages a cross-cohort engagement of students with one another. What began simply as a way for me to find answers to prospective students' questions has become a program that has strengthened the collaborative culture of the doctoral program and of the department as a whole.*

## Recruitment

AMY: Having applied to several doctoral programs, I had not decided whether to attend the University of Louisville by the time of my visit in March 2010. With Louisville's early notification, I was still waiting to hear from two other prestigious programs in my field. However, with the personalized attention afforded me through my peer mentor and the overall collegial and welcoming atmosphere of the program, my mind was all but made up by the time I left Louisville that weekend. Other programs were difficult to contact, and the information I received from administrative assistants often felt rehearsed. At Louisville, communicating with my peer mentor made me feel as though I was already a part of the community, and provided a personal touch to the decision process that was nothing if not persuasive.

As a peer mentor myself now, I have built a network of contacts both through students who have matriculated to our program and even some of those who decided to go elsewhere. I now serve as coordinator of our department's peer-mentoring program, and I encourage all of our peer mentors to make early connections with prospective students and to attend as many of the visitation day activities as possible. But this effort involves more than salesmanship. As my relationships with my peer mentor Shyam and my peer mentees Meghan and Jamila attest, structured peer-mentoring assignments can greatly aid in the transition of new students into the program, and can establish a collegial connection that benefits both mentor and mentee throughout their time in the program. Of course, not all peer-mentoring matches will result in meaningful personal and professional connections. However, my experience has been that providing this opportunity to students is particularly useful early on. After they matriculate into the program, students may certainly develop other, perhaps more successful mentoring relationships and friendships. But they also may not. Those students who are shy or who don't want to seem like they "need help" may particularly benefit from the assignment of a peer mentor early on.

Asking peer mentors to participate in recruitment activities also builds the mentor's connection to and interaction with the department. The PhD can feel like a lonely journey, and student engagement among graduate students tends to be low due to their research obligations and their difference from the undergraduate students who are the emphasis of most Student Affairs efforts (Kern-Bowen and Gardner 2010). But as they help with the recruitment activities, students also interact with other peer mentors and faculty members, gaining valuable personal and professional networking opportunities.

**Transitioning to the Program**

AMY: The importance of formalized peer mentoring to me lies in the fact that students transitioning to graduate school often don't understand how graduate school is different from their undergraduate experience, what the expectations are for coursework or other departmental activities, etc.—but they don't always know that they don't know these things. I am always drawn to the idea of what learning theorists call "unconscious incompetence." This is identified with the first of four stages of development towards skill acquisition (also applicable to cultural acclimation and proficiency), when the inductees don't even know what questions they should be asking—they don't know what they don't know. This concept resonates with me because it perfectly describes my own experience in my master's program. In my first semester of coursework, I was assigned what I now understand to be a staple genre of graduate education: a seminar paper. I knew this term was new to me but, like so many new students, didn't want to ask what seemed like a stupid question. Everyone else clearly knew what a seminar paper was, so I used my experience as an undergrad to arrive at my own definition. I was wrong. Instead of producing an original, researched argument, I simply reported on the sources I located. To be honest, it may not have even been a very strong undergraduate paper, but the archival research methods we were using in the class were so unfamiliar to me, this was all I could imagine producing from them.

I try not to blame my past self for not asking for more guidance from my professor, but I also believe that this situation could have been addressed quite easily if I had had a peer mentor to discuss my progress with. In the conversation I imagine, a peer mentor might ask what the argument of my paper was going to be, and I might then realize that an original researched argument was what was expected. Even if this conversation would not have occurred with my imagined mentor, I nonetheless draw on this memory to shape my own interactions with my mentees, and share this example with others to help them consider what knowledge their mentees might be assuming—to uncover and address their unconscious incompetencies.

New graduate students also do not know the departmental culture they are entering. If there are tensions or politics within the department, a new graduate student may not know they are there until they trigger them. Academic advisors and faculty mentors are not usually in a position to discuss their colleagues with incoming students, but fellow graduate students certainly are. This "gossip" is not just senseless chatter, but important to understanding and successfully navigating the discourse community of the department. While the students will pick up on much of this culture through their experience, it is helpful to have a guide who can provide insider knowledge and a "safe space" for asking sticky questions. In my own department, it was my peers who thought to clue me in to the fact that certain faculty members were actually married to one another, which helped me avoid any *faux pas* in my conversations with them.

The safe space afforded by peer interactions is an important psychosocial support mechanism that faculty often cannot provide. Because of the clear power differential between graduate students and faculty, I am more likely to experience "imposter syndrome" in my relations with faculty, afraid to ask questions that may reveal my own ignorance. With peers, I have a greater sense of trust, confident in the expectation that they may have quite recently asked the same questions and faced the same uncertainties.

*BETH: Amy clearly articulates why official peer mentoring programs are useful to students as they transition to graduate school. As her own story illustrates, the differences in expectations between undergraduate work and graduate work are not always transparent, and faculty often fail to explicitly define the skills they hope to see demonstrated in graduate work. Whether in the classroom or the lab, more experienced graduate students can help guide new students in learning the skills they will need to survive in that particular environment. And when the relationship between experienced and inexperienced students is formalized by the program as a peer-mentoring relationship, the experienced student can take pride in the mentee's successes, rather than feeling threatened by them. Additionally, if all students are provided a peer mentor, then no student need feel embarrassed to ask for one or "remediated" if encouraged to seek one out: students who don't know what they don't know (and thus won't seek out a mentor on their own through informal processes) won't be left out if a formal mentoring program is in place for all students.*

*Perhaps even more important to new students is the vital role peer mentors play as explicators of the unwritten rules of department culture regarding things such as whether students are expected to attend departmental talks and receptions, whether to call faculty by title or first name, whether there are departmental politics (or partnerships) that might make it awkward to ask some faculty members to be on the same committee, and so on. A colleague once jokingly told me to stop encouraging graduate students to talk to one another: "It's like the telephone game. What begins as a simple statement winds up as a full-blown drama." Of course, there's some truth to the claim that student anxieties can escalate in a culture of gossip, but peer mentoring programs can actually work toward limiting those anxieties and runaway gossip by giving students a mentor from whom they can expect accurate, professional advice. When peer mentors are properly trained and understand their roles as both helping the program (by improving its recruitment and retention of students) AND supporting new students in their transition from undergraduate work to graduate work, most will be professional AND supportive. Peer mentors occupy a space between representing the program and university and being a friend to the new student. Training in how to manage this space is terrific preparation for assuming a faculty position, which is likewise suspended between the sometimes competing interests of institution, programs, colleagues, and students.*

## Ongoing Co-Mentoring

AMY: While the role of my peer mentor, Shyam, was central to my matriculation and transition into the program, it is our later collegial engagements that I found the most valuable. Once I found my footing in the program, the peer-mentoring relationship Shyam and I had developed morphed into a collegial co-mentoring that helped us both to meet our professional goals (McGuire and Reger 2003). During my first summer as a PhD student, Shyam and I organized a writing "partnership." We each selected a seminar paper that we wanted to develop into a publishable article, and met twice each month to share and comment on each other's drafts. These meetings made us accountable to continue to write over the unstructured summer months, and resulted in conference papers as well as a collaboratively designed essay that was published in 2013 (Lueck and Sharma 2013).

In addition, Shyam invited me co-present with him at our field's largest national conference. The content we presented was not in my area of expertise, but Shyam recognized both that I had useful contributions to offer and that I would benefit from the experience. Never having presented at this conference, I was what Jean Lave and Etienne Wenger (1991) have termed a "legitimate peripheral participant." Nonetheless, the experience was invaluable in my transition towards full scholarly participation at conferences in my field. As a way to describe and theorize the process by which a newcomer is invited to learn through participating alongside the experts in a "community of practice," I find Lave and Wenger's concept of legitimate peripheral participation to be particularly useful for understanding the affordances of peer mentoring relationships where students learn through collaboration.

But I was not the only one who benefited from these collaborative endeavors with Shyam. Of course, Shyam stood to benefit from the writing accountability group and from sharing the burden of the conference presentation. In addition, though, when it came time for Shyam to go on the job market, I was there to help proofread application documents. He got an editor; I got early and valuable insight into the process of applying for academic jobs. Though I'm not the only person Shyam sought feedback from on these documents, I was probably one of the only ones whom he could email in the middle of the night and ask for an immediate turnaround. And he knew I would be glad to do it, because of our professional and "official" commitment to one another's progress as peers and co-mentors. In other words, he knew he wouldn't be putting me out, as he might if asking a friend; as a peer-mentoring pair, we both saw it as "our job" to help one another, and did so willingly. I think this is one of the particular benefits of a strong peer-mentoring program—making it "official" that we have someone to rely on, and even to impose on if necessary.

As a mentor myself, I draw on my experience with Shyam to try to develop effective mentoring relationships. Though I quickly learned that I couldn't replicate the experience I had with Shyam for my own mentees, I've learned some important insights over my last three years as a peer mentor.

*Every mentee is different, so my strategies as a mentor have to be different too.* Though I really benefited from Shyam's direct and structured approach to our peer mentoring relationship, other students may not be as receptive to this mentoring style, which can seem overbearing or simply too clinical. When I was assigned my first mentee, my initial instinct was to set up a writing group and to talk about collaborating on a project. But I found that she wasn't necessarily interested in this kind of experience, or wasn't interested in pursuing it with me. Either way, that strategy was not going to work in this relationship. And each subsequent mentee has brought out a different kind of mentor in me, as I respond to their personalities and styles. Sometimes, the mentoring pair might just not be right regardless of my approach, and that's okay too. Formalizing peer mentoring runs that risk, but it also opens possibilities for relationships that wouldn't evolve on their own. This has led me to the next realization, which is...

*My mentee might not need me in the ways I expected.* Since the first mentee that I was assigned was a student who had come through our university's master's program and had been in Louisville longer than I had, I had a hard time imagining how I could be useful to her. I was prepared to introduce someone to the city, to give insider's knowledge about the department and program, to help someone meet new friends—but what did I have to offer to a student who didn't need these things? What did *I* know? This was quite difficult for me, as it required me to more actively acknowledge my own expertise, as well as my own limitations. As it turns out, there was one thing the new student definitely did not know yet: what it was like to be a PhD student. In particular, I could share my experiences and provide guidance as my mentee navigated program require-ments. In fact, I have come to recognize that...

*Peer mentors are invaluable as guides through program milestones.* Many program benchmarks and milestones—passing qualifying exams, writing dissertation proposals, etc.—are isolated genre per-formances that students have never before and will never again be asked to practice. There is little reliable information on the Web, because the expectations vary across departments and programs. But peer mentors are uniquely valuable in helping students navigate program milestones because they have just recently navigated them themselves. They know what it's *really* like and how to be successful. And, having already passed through themselves, they are minimally defensive and competitive, like peers in one's cohort might be.

*My mentoring relationship is inflected by my informal, social relationship with my mentee.* As Kathy Kram noted in her germinal work on mentoring (1985), mentors perform both career and psycho-social functions for their mentees. In other words, mentors provide more than professional advice; they also provide confirmation, acceptance, role modeling and friendship. In peer-mentoring rela-tionships, this may be particularly true. I have found that when I am good friends with my mentee, I sometimes have a hard time per-forming my role as "mentor" in the same way. I may be less prone to give advice, as asking to meet over coffee simply as a way to check in seems artificial. Though it sometimes feels difficult to strike a balance between my role as friend and role as mentor in these cases, I have less anxiety about it than I used to now that I have begun to think more about "networked mentoring."

*Peer mentors are never a student's sole mentor, but can be an important node in a network of mentors.* As Kerry Ann Rockquemore notes in a recent article in *Inside Higher Ed* (2013), mentees have a wide range of needs. These will not be met by one person—the "guru mentor," as she calls it—but instead will be addressed by a network of mentors at different levels. In focusing on the diverse needs of mentees, Rockquemore's networked approach proposes a different role for mentors: "Instead of YOU meeting all those needs, the network model suggests you initiate the conversation, ask powerful questions, validate needs, help brainstorm solutions, make connections, and confirm next steps" (n.p.). Though she is discussing the mentoring of new faculty by senior faculty, her comments apply just as well to peer mentors at the graduate level, if not better. As most new peer mentors fear, they indeed *don't* know all of the answers, and don't always have the best advice. What they do have, though, is the knowledge and experience to point newer students in the right direction, and they can encourage, validate, and follow up with the student.

## Utilizing Peer Mentoring to Improve Faculty Mentoring

BETH: *After serving as a director of graduate studies in English for almost ten years, I was asked to take on an associate dean's position in the School of Interdisciplinary and Graduate Studies (SIGS) at the University of Louisville in late 2008; I was charged with advocating for graduate student welfare and professional development in the newly formed unit (prior to the summer of 2008, the unit was called the Graduate School). After a stint as interim dean when the previous holder of that office left for another position in the university, I was chosen to lead the unit as the dean and vice provost for graduate studies. With Amy as my assistant, we designated 2012–2013 the "Year of the Mentor" and developed a year-long series of workshops designed to increase awareness of the importance of faculty mentors to graduate students, and to improve the quality of mentoring at the university. We launched the year with a half-day program that included a graduate student improv troupe from the Department of Theatre Arts performing a series of vignettes, written by graduate students, that illustrated mentoring moments gone wrong; faculty and students were invited to step in as each vignette was performed a second time, to offer different perspectives and different ways of handling the same mentoring moments. The event also included a panel session with four of the first six winners* of the *SIGS Faculty Mentor Award*, which has been given since 2009. The mentors who spoke were some of the university's most rigorous, most successful (in terms of number of students who had earned their doctorates), and most beloved. Since the improvised vignettes mostly depicted mentors as non-caring, selfish, or inadequate (remember, they were written from the students' perspective!), the panel in many ways served as an antidote; these expert faculty mentors spoke persuasively and passionately about the importance of mentoring and on the rewards of mentoring well.

What is most relevant about that panel conversation to this discussion, however, is the way these very successful faculty mentors used informal peer mentoring to improve their own efficiency. One, a highly funded and very productive diabetes researcher, talked about his lab, and how he brings together postdocs, graduate students at different stages of their work, and undergraduates, all of whom are working on individual projects that are part of his research. Each student is expected to mentor a student who is junior, so that even new graduate students begin immediately mentoring undergraduates. This informal peer mentoring, which the faculty member oversees to make sure no one is left "unmentored," encourages all the students in the lab to be problem solvers who seek to help each other when experiments do not work out as planned. This arrangement also saves the faculty member from having to answer every new student's questions and reading every draft of every student's papers. Having trained the first two or three students to mentor other students well, he effectively trains the entire lab, and while he holds weekly lab meetings with the entire group, this method allows him to mentor a higher number of students than he could possibly train one-by-one. While this peer-mentoring system clearly helps the faculty member both maintain his research productivity and mentor many students, his students also feel they benefit from the system: many of his former students wrote about him as part of his nomination, particularly praising him for giving them that early opportunity to mentor others. Just as *Amy* learned so much from being mentored by *Shyam* and by mentoring the new students who were assigned to her, I am willing to bet that the students who leave his lab begin their careers as stronger mentors than most new faculty.

While scientists often work in teams in the lab and rely upon supervised peer mentoring, such arrangements are much less common in the humanities. Yet faculty in library-based disciplines can also create peer-mentoring groups that benefit themselves and their students. Another of our "Outstanding Mentors," a professor of English, spoke about the *reading group she has established for her doctoral students. All students who have asked her to direct their dissertations meet regularly as a group to discuss their progress, to share drafts, to comment on each other's work, and to suggest possible avenues for revision or further exploration. While the faculty member oversees the group meetings and continues to meet individually with students, the group cuts her workload and individual meetings almost in half, she said, by distributing responsibility for leading the discussion of drafts and by providing feedback that keeps students writing between individual meetings. Because the students who work under this professor share a common methodology and theoretical perspective, they are able to offer substantial advice to each other, despite their sometimes very different dissertation topics. I am not suggesting that such writing groups and lab teams are equivalent to a "formal peer-mentoring program," but like those programs, these faculty-organized groups help to create a sense of community, provide examples of others who are struggling and succeeding in similar ways, and help future faculty learn how to respond to colleagues' and students' presentations in productive ways.*

*Another benefit of bringing small groups of students together to discuss their work with a faculty mentor is that the conventions of dissertation work (or experimental design) become more transparent: as one student's lab tragedy or badly written chapter is discussed by the group, the others learn how the work could be done "better." When one student learns to survive a failed experiment or having to start a chapter over, the entire group learns that failure is indeed part of the process. They also learn the importance of resiliency. When the group is composed of students at different stages of their work, students who are just beginning their programs learn what a dissertation "proposal" or a "literature review" looks like before they have to produce one. And frankly, all mentors—but particularly new faculty mentors—benefit from being forced to articulate those conventions and life skills in a more explicit fashion than they might if they were working one-on-one with students.*

## Taking It on the Road: Programs to Support Peer Mentoring

Since Beth began the peer-mentoring program in our English department, it has continued to grow and become more formalized each year as we become more strategic about drawing on the benefits we've witnessed. This last year, Amy advocated for and eventually established an MA peer-mentoring program, and we've begun to see the effects of this effort in the increased involvement of both funded and unfunded MA students in department activities. In addition, students revived an English Graduate Organization Facebook page to connect students to one another and support a networked approach to peer mentoring. This has been a very effective strategy, whereby common questions can be answered just once, for the benefit of all, rather than individually by each mentor. The answers provided in this forum are generally more thorough and more accurate than those that one peer mentor could provide, further extending the initial informational function Beth sought from peer mentoring in the beginning.

Because we have had such a positive experience with a formal peer-mentoring program in our English department, we have worked centrally at the School of Interdisciplinary and Graduate Studies to help spread such programs to other departments to benefit the recruitment, retention, and success of their students, and to build a culture of mentoring on our campus.

Our effort to foster peer mentoring on campus began with several workshops for graduate students, introducing them to the idea of peer mentoring and sharing some of the research on how it can help students and programs. From those workshops, we found that there was really a low level of knowledge and engagement around the topic of mentoring on our campus, with many students understanding mentorship quite narrowly as pertaining only to their dissertation director or lab advisor. Without knowledge about alternative forms of mentoring, many students expressed dissatisfaction with their mentoring experiences but seemed to have no strategies for taking responsibility and improving their situations. We came to see peer mentoring as part of a larger conversation about mentoring on our campus, and organized the half-day workshop described above to initiate a campus-wide conversation about the role of mentoring in graduate education at our university. This "Mentoring Kick-Off" was a great success, and generated energy and interest among faculty and students to think more purposefully about both faculty- and peer-mentoring practices.

Out of that Kick-Off, we developed more workshops dealing with different aspects of peer mentoring for students, including sessions on how to start a peer-mentoring program in one's department, strategies for effective peer mentoring, and models for networked mentoring and co-mentoring for students in later stages of graduate study. We present these workshops to graduate students from across the departments through SIGS' program for graduate student professional development, called the PLAN (Professional development, Life skills, Academic development, and Networking). The many activities and workshops that SIGS sponsors to improve the graduate student experience are organized under the PLAN umbrella.[2] In addition, we offer targeted workshops for individual departments or programs, such as the peer-mentoring orientation we recently organized and presented for the College of Education.

In addition to these more pragmatic workshops, we organized reading groups and learning communities targeted at both graduate students and faculty. In these contexts we read research on mentoring and discussed the implications of mentoring—both peer and faculty—as a praxis. These discussions were productive as a means both to share strategies and to consider mentoring and changes to graduate education in the twenty-first century more theoretically.

Finally, we developed the MentorCenter, an online repository of resources and FAQ-style information about faculty and peer mentoring. Included on that site is a MentorConnect portal, which provides faculty and graduate students an outlet for asking their own mentoring questions in a more anonymous interdisciplinary forum. The questions are forwarded to our Mentoring Advisory Board, which is comprised of faculty recipients of the Outstanding Mentor Award. We are continuing to build this site and develop digital resources to support mentoring across the departments, including a series of video introductions to peer mentoring and program development.

From our centralized position at the School of Interdisciplinary and Graduate Studies, we can support formalized peer mentoring programs by providing information, trainings, and resources, and by fostering a culture of mentoring in which conversations about mentoring as a praxis are the norm. From there, it is up to students and faculty in each department to establish and support a peer-mentoring program of their own. The work of this chapter, we hope, is to use our own experiences to make clear the affordances of such a program not only to students, but also to faculty mentors, program directors, and perhaps even graduate education as a whole.

### Notes

1. We introduce our respective sections by name. Additionally, Amy's sections appear in roman type, Beth's in italics.

2. See our website at http://louisville.edu/graduate/plan.

## Works Cited

Allen, Tammy D., Stacy E. McManus, and Joyce E. A. Russell. 1999. "Newcomer Socialization and Stress: Formal Peer Relationships as a Source of Support." *Journal of Vocational Behavior* 54:453–70. doi: 10.1006/jvbe.1998.1674.

Chao, Georgia T., Patm Walz, and Philip D. Gardner. 1992. "Formal and Informal Mentorships: A Comparison on Mentoring Functions and Contrast with Nonmentored Counterparts." *Personnel Psychology* 45 (3): 619–36. doi: 10.1111/j.1744-6570.1992.tb00863.x.

Grant-Vallone, Elisa J., and Ellen A. Ensher. 2000. "Effects of Peer Mentoring on Types of Mentor Support, Program Satisfaction and Graduate Student Stress: A Dyadic Perspective." *Journal of College Student Development* 41 (6): 637–42.

Kern-Bowen, Jodie, and Rick Gardner. 2010. "Creating Campus Community for Graduate Students through Programs, Services, and Facilities." *The Bulletin of the Association of College Unions International* 78 (2). http://www.acui.org/publications/bulletin/article.aspx?issue=22641&id=12132.

Kram, Kathy E. 1985. *Mentoring at Work*. Glenview, IL: Scott Foresman.

Kram, Kathy E., and Lynn A. Isabella. 1985. "Mentoring Alternatives: The Role of Peer Relationships in Career Development." *Academy of Management Journal* 28 (1): 110–32. doi: 10.2307/256064.

Lave, Jean, and Etienne Wenger. 1991. *Situated Learning: Legitimate Peripheral Participation*. New York: Cambridge University Press.

Lueck, Amy, and Shyam Sharma. 2013. "Writing a Translingual Script: Closed Captions in the English Multilingual Hearing Classroom." *Kairos* 17 (3). http://kairos.technorhetoric.net/17.3/praxis/lueck/index.html.

McGuire, Gail M., and Jo Reger. 2003. "Feminist Co-Mentoring: A Model for Academic Professional Development." *NWSA Journal* 15 (1): 54–72. http://www.jstor.org/stable/4316944.

Rockquemore, Kerry Ann. 2013. "A New Model of Mentoring." *Inside Higher Ed*, July 22. http://www.insidehighered.com/advice/2013/07/22/essay-calling-senior-faculty-embrace-new-style-mentoring.

# The Family Plan:
# A Dialogue about Graduate Students,
# Babies, and the Unique Demands of the
# Advisor-Student Relation

## *Leonard Cassuto and Jane Van Slembrouck*

What's so special about the tie between graduate students and their advisors? One way to answer such a vast question is to break it down and approach it through its particulars. The following dialogue concerns one of those particulars: the decision by graduate students to become parents. The following conversation developed from an exchange on that particular vexed topic with one of my dissertation advisees, Jane Van Slembrouck, who made the decision to have children during her graduate student years.

As we discovered together, the particular case of graduate students having children offers a way to discuss the workings of the graduate student–advisor connection more generally. A student's decision to become a parent—and how the advisor should respect that decision—becomes a prism that refracts the overall dynamic between graduate student and advisor, especially the professional-personal balance and the need to be realistic about the goals and prospects of PhD students during these difficult and changing times. Because the relationship between advisor and student should center on exchange, so does this essay.

*—Leonard Cassuto*

❖           ❖           ❖

JANE VAN SLEMBROUCK: Let's start with what got us started talking about this topic in the first place. Several months ago I read an article in *Slate* about female graduate students with children [Mason

2013], and I was struck especially by the stories in the article of women dealing with unsupportive mentors. I quickly emailed you the link and mentioned how happy I am that you've never made me feel like I should apologize for being both a parent and a student. Our brief email conversation that followed reminded me of another talk we'd had several years earlier, right after you become my dissertation director.

LEONARD CASSUTO: Yes. I recall. I told you that as a dissertation advisor, I consider that my job is to consult, not dictate. You'd be the CEO of your dissertation.

JVS: And you actually brought up the issue of children!

LC: Right. I mentioned that you might choose to start a family while you're in graduate school, or you might not. Whatever your decision, I said that my job would be to support you and help you reach your goals.

JVS: I have to say I was a bit taken a little aback by that, since I thought our discussion would only concern my dissertation. But as I thought about it afterward, I appreciated your raising the topic. And now, from where I stand eight years later, having seen how my PhD has tracked so many crucial years of my life—several moves, different jobs, and, yes, the births of two children—I realize that it absolutely makes sense to bring up personal decisions and how they might factor into the graduate school process.

LC: When I have those mentoring conversations, I have no idea if students are even planning to have families, but it's important to put it out there: whatever personal path you choose, I'll support you.

JVS: Starting out in graduate school, I knew I would probably start a family by the time I finished my degree. My friends with children had said to me that graduate school is a stage in life that offers some scheduling flexibility. I also began the PhD program in my late twenties, so it seemed realistic for that reason as well. On my initial campus visit, I had lunch with a few female grad students and made a point of asking whether the department seemed family-friendly. So parenthood was on my mind early on, and I actually think that their feedback about the university being family-friendly factored into my decision.

But I was still surprised that you would bring that up at our meeting. I suppose I just assumed that decisions about children are "personal," something to be silently or at best briefly acknowledged, mainly to assure an advisor that you're going to continue performing academically in spite of the new "distraction."

LC: There's a long tradition in academia of treating personal matters as peripheral to the "real" work of writing and career preparation. As you're suggesting, those divisions are artificial, but they persist.

JVS: In my experience, academic culture reinforces them. I've seen peers run into problems when they announce their pregnancies. A couple of them have had advisors who withdrew their support and others have encountered university policies that seem downright hostile to parents. When a friend at another university told her advisor that she was pregnant, the advisor dropped her head into her hands, said, "Oh, God," then lifted her head and said, "Congratulations!" Thankfully, she was able to change her advisor's attitude, and she is now seen by her department as a model for how to successfully combine academic work and parenting. But another friend learned that she'd have to give up a prestigious fellowship if she took a semester off school to have a baby. Her mentors were supportive of her, but they were blocked by administrators and rules that didn't account for the possibility that grad students might want to become parents. Someone even told her it was her fault for not planning to have her son over summer break. She went back to teaching just two weeks after giving birth!

LC: So much of this personal and institutional behavior stems from the academic ideal of the pure *cogito*, the disembodied thinker. You would think that with all of our studies of the body and the integrative views of being that we accept and subscribe to, that we would know better.

JVS: That would be nice, but also hard to imagine right now. I definitely felt pressure to separate my mind from my body as far back as my master's program. I remember once, when I was a new instructor working on my MA, a much older female faculty member came to evaluate the composition course I was teaching. In our conversation afterward, she praised my teaching. I confided to her that I still felt a lot of self-doubt and asked if she felt that her identity as a woman factored into her feelings about her teaching. I remember her reply very clearly because it was so odd: "Well, I try not to think of myself as a woman, just as a teacher, a scholar—a person."

For some reason, that description really appealed to me at the time, and I resolved to start thinking of myself that way too. *Just a person.* But as time passed, and especially as my two children entered my life—my whole life, not just my personal life—that mindset proved downright unrealistic. A *person* doesn't suffer from morning sickness that stops her from doing her academic work until it passes. A person, in the abstract, doesn't teach and create scholarship.

In fact, parenting has been the opposite of abstract for me, to the point that writing my dissertation will be forever linked in my mind to being the mother of very young children. My daughter, Bea, was born during my fifth year in the PhD program at Fordham. I was finishing a two-year appointment as the campus writing center director at the time. My tutoring staff gave me a card and a nice send-off, and a week later held my first child in my arms! At that point, I was just over a year into my dissertation, and it felt like a good time to have a baby. I took a semester off teaching and returned to writing when Bea was eight weeks old. I was able to get back to teaching soon after, thanks to my husband and our fantastic babysitter. Without them, I doubt I could have made much progress at all. Over the next few semesters, I researched, taught, drafted an article, served on a campus committee, and won a dissertation fellowship that allowed me to focus on my writing for a year. Our son, Johnny, arrived after that fellowship period ended, two years after Bea.

LC: My own particulars are a little different. I waited till after I got tenure to become a parent. I was fortunate to become an assistant professor in my late twenties, so the biological clock had an earlier setting for us. Even with our wait, my wife was still in her mid-thirties when our daughter was born in 1999. We've co-parented from the beginning. I did a stint as a stay-at-home dad, and through elementary school I was the contact parent, the one waiting outside the school for the little ones to be dismissed, and so on. I know what it feels like to have to wrap my professional schedule around a young child's. During the years when these duties were making the greatest demands on me, I always made a point of mentioning that it was childcare responsibilities that might keep me from this meeting or that one. I wanted to use my own security of tenure to assert that these scheduling limitations aren't just a "women's issue," and that they deserve respect.

JVS: They need to be brought out of the shadows.

LC: And that applies to academics who want to become parents in graduate school. As an advisor, I can't just bracket out your choices and say they're not my problem. The length of graduate school, coupled with where it falls in one's adult life, makes viewing a student's whole life a necessity. Average time to degree in the humanities stands at about nine years in the U.S. right now.[1] That's a staggering number and a profession-wide disgrace, but it's a reality. If someone starts graduate school right after college—which I don't recommend, by the way—then she'll finish in her thirties.[2] So people have important life decisions to make during that time, and it's artificial to pretend otherwise. The life decisions that you and other advisees face, including whether (or when) to have children, are your choices, not mine.

JVS: So you brought it up in that first meeting for the purpose of saying that it's none of your business!

LC: Exactly. I could have just said nothing. One might reasonably argue that keeping silent would have been the better choice, but I don't think so. Even though it's none of my business, I have to make it my business to tell you so. It's the great paradox of our professional relationship.

JVS: By putting it out there, you made it clear that where you're concerned, I'm free to live my life, and you'll be supportive.

LC: Just so. Your thesis—and your long preparation for the job market, including the decisions about what to publish and how to balance article and dissertation writing—take up a large chunk of your existence, and as your advisor, I'll be part of those professional decisions. So my actions affect your whole life. If I fail to acknowledge the way personal decisions are marbled together with professional ones (by saying nothing about family planning, for example), I'm not making those personal issues go away. I'm just avoiding discussing them.

JVS: Your silence would also be hard to interpret. If I didn't know the reason for it, I might worry that you were quietly disapproving of me if I did choose to have children.

LC: It's a sorry statement about the professional world of graduate school that I have to go out of my way to state something that should be obvious. Other professions in the United States are similarly unevolved. The only difference is that professors think they're more progressive than they actually are.

JVS: You and I have been reading the recent book *Do Babies Matter?* [Mason, Wolfinger, and Goulden 2013] in preparation for this conversation. It presents a disturbing picture of gender and family in the ivory tower. The authors found that women make up the majority of adjunct and other part-time faculty, and mothers of young children tend to remain locked in second-tier positions or leave academia altogether.

LC: It's a depressing scene. Fewer women than men occupy the tenure-track ranks, and women are less likely than male professors to be married and have children. Men get rewarded economically for having children, while women pay a price. Consequently, even though women make up a majority of the faculty in many fields (including ours), the implicit professorial stereotype continues to be a man with children and a wife at home to care for them.

JVS: Yes! All of which is to say that I'm not making my choices in a vacuum. My choices are mine, sure, but they aren't entirely mine. The tension reminds me of a literature seminar I recently taught about mythologies of success and failure in American literature. The course traced the roots of the "bootstraps" ideology of success—that very American belief that gritty self-determination guarantees wealth and happiness. We looked at counterexamples from both literature and life and noted some of the ways that race, class, gender, and ability shape a person's experience of achievement and success.

So in the classroom, I was critiquing dominant cultural notions of success, but I wasn't extending this analysis to my own life and seeing both my own privilege and the way my profession defines success.

LC: And autonomy along with it. Part of the problem is that academia idealizes autonomy, but parenting is all about abridged freedom.[3]

JVS: Yes, and that's true for other people too, not only for parents. People have all sorts of reasons why they can't perform solely as scholars. We're all dependent on other people for support, or else we have people who are dependent on us. That's a defining part of our lives, and it's nothing to be ashamed of. It reminds me of what Eva Kittay, a disability studies scholar, says, that a liberal political culture needs to factor in relationships of dependency in order to give everyone a real chance at citizenship [1999]. That applies to academia also—to creating a positive sense of academic citizenship.

LC: That's interesting about dependency. From an advisor's perspective, we have to be realistic about the ways students depend on us. A major part of "meeting our students where they are" is acknowledging that they have different goals.

We also need to admit the ways in which the profession is changing and think long and hard about how this should inform our advising. For one thing, the shape and contours of PhD education in the arts and sciences are inherently dishonest—they're disconnected from graduate students' reality. The requirements of seminars and dissertations are still modeled on program requirements from the 1960s, when anyone who could get a doctorate could also get a tenure-track professorship. The demand for professors during that one postwar generation of abundance meant that lots of PhD candidates got the degree in five years, and sometimes less. (Though commentators still judged it too high then—if they could see it now!) That time of plenty ended in the 1970s, but universities tried to coax it back into existence for longer than it actually was in existence.

JVS: Things are changing lately, and that absolutely needs to be part of the mentor-student discussion.

LC: No question. Advisors can hope that their students will become professors, but they must teach to the reality that many will not. There have been salutary movements in this direction lately—such as the 2014 Report of the MLA Task Force on Doctoral Study in Modern Language and Literature [http://www.mla.org/report_doctoral_study_2014]—but the structure of American doctoral education is still based on educating PhD students to follow their advisors into the kind of research university job that the advisor holds. That's inefficient at best; such a model of replication actively works against meeting students where they are. It's focused on imagining that graduate students are someplace else, but "where they are" is up against an academic job market whose cold numbers say that at least half of them will never get tenure-track jobs. Yet what happens in doctoral education—at every stage—doesn't reflect this fact.

If we want to meet students where they are, we need to acknowledge these facts and take into account students' individual goals. Not all grad students want to be professors. And some of those who do also want to become parents.

JVS: This brings us full circle back to our initial mentoring conversation about our plans for working together. There's plenty that advisors can do to help graduate students who decide to become parents. Telling them that it's okay to do so, however silly it may feel to say so, is one important step.

LC: Yes, it's a good first step. Advisors should also guide grad students in setting ambitious yet realistic deadlines. Parenting can result in academic pauses, gaps, and detours. A student—man or woman—whose family adds children during graduate school is probably going to need more time than one who remains childless during that time. The statistics used to tabulate time to the PhD degree don't take parental leaves into account; they're calculated by just subtracting one date from another. I seek no absolution for the industry here—time to degree is still embarrassingly long. But if the time-to-degree statistics are inflexible, it reflects the fact that graduate school education is likewise, and that's a global problem that needs much more attention than it receives.

JVS: Advisors can also alert students to any university benefits available to them, such as parental leave. Programs and the universities could do so much more to make students aware of such entitlements.[4]

LC: Oh yes. I've had grad students who weren't aware that maternity leave was even an option! What does this say about the culture of graduate education that students sometimes don't even *expect* such entitlements? Advisors who fail to acknowledge the personal aspects of their graduate students' lives—and help them integrate those aspects with their professional selves—are (and here's that paradox again) acting unprofessionally.

JVS: This brings us back to that contradiction we discussed about students' personal decisions not being your business but how you have to make them your business.

LC: Advisors need to confront that blend of the professional and the personal. It's pretty clear that administrative changes are badly needed, but they won't work unless they also change minds on the ground. One way that we can make graduate school more accommodating is by starting there, with the advisor-student relationship. So we need to remember that graduate students are grownups facing adult choices. Parents who raise their children to be just like them are usually making a mistake. So too with dissertation advisors. By acknowledging the unique role we play, we can best help them freely make those tough personal choices.[5]

JVS: We agree, then, that advisors have to deliberately dispel any sense of mystery about their values. Most grad students really want to please their mentors, and in the absence of clearly stated support, they can believe the worst. Advisors can short-circuit this concern by stating up front where they stand.

LC: Indeed.

JVS: I'd also add that advisors can strengthen their support by integrating their own lives into their public personas as scholars, just as you mentioned. You all risk little by being open about your personal responsibilities, which means you can help lift the stigma from those with less secure positions.

LC: I've made a conscious choice to do that. It seems to me that by visibly combining both their personal and professional lives, advisors can help foster a humane culture in which grad students aren't afraid to ask for support.

JVS: Let's not forget another way that advisors can help grad students knit their personal and professional lives: dinner parties! Every month you, I, and a half-dozen other graduate student dissertators of yours meet over a potluck to discuss our works in progress. My peers are my first readers, and the friendships that have developed in those meetings are so meaningful to me. Those meetings have been an education in academic writing, but they've also become an important part of my social life.

LC: I've been doing that for years now. It's a simple idea, really—get people together over a meal.

JVS: But the benefits are huge for the otherwise-solitary dissertator. I would go so far as to say that meeting that way over the years has helped me integrate my professional and personal identities. My peers support me as a scholar, but they're also interested in my life as a person. Interestingly, some of the discussion from those dinners has spilled over into the Web. Several of those real-life friends and I now have a Facebook discussion group where we discuss the challenges and joys of dissertating.

LC: Graduate students face so many different responsibilities and challenges on their way to the degree. That kind of interaction has got to help.

JVS: Yes, and I think you helped set the tone for those interactions by discouraging a sense of competition among your advisees and by communicating that you don't think those of us with children will fall behind just because we have major personal responsibilities. That's something advisors need to make a point of saying.

LC: Even if our students don't bring up the topic.

JVS: Maybe *especially* if they don't bring it up.

**Notes**

1. This data is widely available. A good graphical presentation is available in the "Higher Education" section of the website *Humanities Indicators*, sponsored by the American Academy of Arts and Sciences (http://www.humanitiesindicators.org/content/indicatordoc.aspx?i=9).

2. For Lenny's thoughts about why prospective students should not apply directly to graduate school, see Cassuto 2013.

3. Mason, Wolfinger, and Goulden (2013) show that awareness and enforcement are key. Graduate students are often unaware that if their institutional policies don't provide basic provisions and protections, they are entitled to unpaid leave and job protection under the provisions of Title IX (24). Likewise, faculty often don't know that entitlements such as family leave, teaching relief, and stopping the tenure clock are on the books at their institutions. At the very least, the Family and Medical Leave Act (FMLA) guarantees faculty at American colleges and universities a minimum of 12 weeks of unpaid leave. Department chairs, the ones who should promoting these provisions, are often ignorant themselves (111).

Somewhat surprisingly, there is also a notable gender disparity in available campus policies. Fifty-eight percent of colleges and universities offer at least six weeks' paid leave for faculty mothers, but only 16% offer one week of paid gender-neutral "parental" leave (Mason, Wolfinger, and Goulden 2013, 110). Yet even when such leave exists, fathers often pass on the chance to take time off out of fear that they'll be seen as not rigorous or serious enough. Faculty mothers are more likely to take leave, but the numbers suggest that many are also reluctant to briefly step away from the workforce; many don't take advantage of leave options available to them. If academia wants to gain a reputation as supportive of families, the authors suggest, administrators and department chairs need to strip bias from their family-related policies, communicate their existence, and go out of their way to encourage faculty to take advantage of them.

Mason, Wolfinger, and Goulden add that this family-friendliness needs to be nurtured in the graduate school years. Many people make decisions about family during their doctoral programs. The research shows that women (far more than men) often delay or forgo having children because, from the graduate student's vantage point, the academy doesn't seem a viable place to mix family and career. If female grad students do have children during or shortly after their doctoral degree programs, many will wind up with adjunct or other contingent employment. Universities can counter these trends by making on-campus childcare, family leave, and other basic entitlements available to working graduate students. Only 13% of universities offer grads six weeks of paid maternity leave and only 23% offer six weeks leave to postdocs (2013, 108). Such provisions, the authors note, would signal to emerging scholars that it is possible to integrate the roles of parent and professor in academia.

4. Mason, Wolfinger, and Goulden (2013) suggest that awareness is a major problem (24, 111). See note 3 above.

5. The connection between doctoral student and advisor has, from the earliest days of PhD education in the United States, evolved to do this. That's because it has, from the beginning, been imagined as a family relation. The idea of the guiding master originated in Germany, but in the United States that relation quickly translated into a deeply personal, almost cultish, tie of admiring loyalty. So powerful was this tie that the proposal was once considered to have the PhD carry the name of one's "master" rather than the university one attended (Veysey 1965, 156–57). The tie binds like family in the U.S., and genealogical metaphors for it abound. Some famous professors even become the trunk nodes of their own family tree diagrams. Veysey (1965) reports that the students of the legendary historian Frederick Jackson Turner used to refer to him as "my professional father," and that they would do so "in direct address" (157, n. 113).

## Works Cited

Cassuto, Leonard. 2013. "To Apply or Not to Apply." *The Chronicle of Higher Education*, June 3. http://chronicle.com/article/To-Apply-or-Not-to-Apply/139539.

Kittay, Eva. 1999. *Love's Labor: Essays on Women, Equality, and Dependency.* New York: Routledge.

Mason, Mary Ann. 2013. "In the Ivory Tower, Men Only." *Slate*, June 17. http://www.slate.com/articles/double_x/doublex/2013/06/female_academics_pay_a_heavy_baby_ penalty.html.

Mason, Mary Ann, Nicholas H. Wolfinger, and Marc Goulden. 2013. *Do Babies Matter? Gender and Family in the Ivory Tower.* New Brunswick, NJ, and London: Rutgers University Press.

Veysey, Lawrence. 1965. *The Emergence of the American University.* Chicago: University of Chicago Press.

# Cross-Race Faculty Mentoring

## *Christine A. Stanley and Yvonna S. Lincoln**

There are many synonyms for the word "mentor": coach, guide, role model, peer advisor, and sponsor, among others. The plethora of terms would suggest that we know something about this role, but most of the research on mentoring has been conducted in business and industry rather than in education. In fact, junior and senior faculty and administrators alike are often uncertain about how to foster effective mentoring relationships. This is especially true when faculty of color are recruited to predominantly white colleges and universities.

Attacks on affirmative action continue and have created a nationwide institutional paralysis when it comes to recruiting and retaining faculty of color. In comparison to majority faculty, the numbers of faculty of color in higher education remain disproportionately low. Mentoring is an important strategy for retaining these faculty members. There is nothing more isolating and alienating than to be the first or only person of one's race and/or ethnicity to be hired in a department, and a mentoring relationship is one way to escape from that isolation. But while it is especially important that faculty of color be mentored effectively, majority administrators and senior faculty are likely to be perplexed by the task, because they may have no previous experience with minority colleagues to draw upon.

Consequently, some authors have observed, majority faculty are reluctant to mentor new faculty of color; few overtures toward faculty of color are made; and minority scholars feel keenly the absence of warm, constructive mentoring relationships. It is almost always assumed that mentoring is more beneficial when mentor and protégé are of the same gender and race or ethnicity, are in the same discipline, and share similar

* This chapter was originally published in *Change: The Magazine of Higher Learning* 37.2 (2005): 44–50. The Suggested Readings have been updated and a postscript added. Reprinted material used with permission.

professional interests.

But while there are advantages to like-on-like mentoring, as D. J. Levinson et al. note, it is "the character of the relationship and the functions it serves" that makes a difference between successful mentoring and merely assuming an assignment (1978, 98). R. S. Cafarella defines mentoring as an "intense caring relationship in which persons with more experience work with less experienced persons to promote both professional and personal development" (1992, 38).

The successful mentoring relationship, in our experience, is characterized by trust, honesty, a willingness to learn about self and others, and the ability to share power and privilege. Mentors also must learn how to recognize their protégés' strengths and weaknesses, nurture their autonomy, treat them as individuals, capitalize on their skills, and create opportunities for challenge and growth.

Guided by insights drawn from the research, and more importantly from our experiences and from observing others, we describe here our relationship as mentor/protégé and share the lessons we have learned about how to establish and maintain meaningful cross-race mentoring relationships.

## Our Mentor/Protégé Journey

***Christine's narrative:*** I am a black woman who grew up in Jamaica, the West Indies, and emigrated to the United States in 1980. All my mentors in administration and the professoriate, except two, have been white women. I met Yvonna, my faculty mentor at Texas A&M University, in fall 1999, when I was recruited to join the faculty in the Department of Educational Administration in the College of Education and Human Development. All I knew about Yvonna before I met her was that she is regarded as "the queen of qualitative research," although she certainly would not characterize herself that way. In the first two years of our acquaintance, she was named distinguished professor and given the Ruth Harrington Chair in Educational Leadership, and I learned that she was a former department head.

Needless to say, these characteristics were quite intimidating to me, a younger junior faculty member and a woman of color. After all, how does one measure up to a woman of her stature? When I left Ohio State for Texas A&M, one colleague remarked, "You are going to be in the same department and the same research program area with *the* Yvonna Lincoln."

I'm not exactly sure how our mentoring relationship began, but being the extrovert that I am, I do recall seeking her out on several occasions when I had questions about the departmental culture, the *unwritten* rules about promotion and tenure, how to be a good citizen while maintaining a scholarly agenda, and diversity issues in the department and the college. I found her approachable, with plenty of southern charm—she'll greet you in the hallway or by the mailbox with, "Hi honey! How are you doing? Did you bring your lunch?"

I learned a lot about her, the department, the college, and the university during our occasional lunches. We had honest and open conversations about diversity and social justice in higher education. While we often had different opinions, I discovered that she is a strong ally for diversity. She is a white woman who *gets* it. This may be in part because for many years, she was the only woman in the department.

When I point out disparaging behaviors and attitudes that are racist, sexist, or xenophobic, for example, she has never once said, "You are being too sensitive" or "This has nothing to do with race at all." She listens keenly. She asks questions. She reflects. She tries to understand my perspective. She is not dismissive. She is also honest and open. Sometimes I receive feedback that I do not agree with, but I know that it is from a voice of experience and a place of caring.

I was the only black faculty member in my department until recently. I'm reminded of this fact every day—in faculty meetings, in class, when I am asked a question that assumes that I speak on behalf of all black people or Jamaicans, and when I remain silent during battles about diversity issues that I choose not to engage in that day. Needless to say, trust is paramount to me. I felt that I could trust as well as learn from Yvonna. Since I was one of "the only's" and untenured at the time, she became my voice at faculty meetings. I was ever mindful of the fact that as an untenured faculty member, my comments or gestures could be misunderstood, particularly when I spoke about issues concerning diversity and social justice. But when I did, Yvonna did not hesitate to support me.

Her support was crucial when I was preparing for promotion and tenure, a process which a colleague of mine likens to "academic hazing." I felt like I was under a microscope the entire year. Waiting for the decisions at every level of the process is enough to put anyone on Prozac. While I was preparing my dossier, Yvonna and I had several meetings off campus over a cup of coffee. During these meetings she explained not only the process but how I should prepare my dossier. She carefully reviewed my *vitae* as well, and gave me feedback on my written statements regarding teaching, research, and service. She took the time to read my research carefully and to solicit external reviewers who would, she felt, provide a fair assessment of my scholarship.

Yvonna has been my advocate. She was instrumental in writing a letter supporting my nomination and later successful application for the College of Education's "Outstanding New Faculty Award." I was promoted to associate professor and tenured in 2003 and later promoted to assistant dean of faculties. When the dean of faculties and associate provost asked her, in my presence, what she thought of the decision to promote me to assistant dean, Yvonna told her emphatically that she needed someone with my skills and experience in faculty development for that position. I felt empowered by her confidence and trust in me. In 2004, she recommended me to the editor of the book *Higher Education: Handbook of Theory and Research* to write a chapter on professional development. I'm not sure I would have had the invitation if she hadn't known about and valued my work in faculty development.

The mentoring relationship is reciprocal. I rely on her for advice, and I am humbled when she asks the same of me. I have come to value and expect Yvonna's, "Here is what you need to do...." When I look at her, I'm challenged and motivated to be a productive scholar.

**Yvonna's Narrative:** In some ways, I know how Christine has felt. This is my third appointment as a tenured or tenure-track faculty member in roughly 30 years. In two of the places where I worked, for some years I was the only woman—or the first and only woman—in the department. In my first department, I was told to ask the secretary for my mail. When I observed that all the other faculty had mailboxes and I didn't, the department secretary told me that since the department head had vowed that I "would be gone in a year," there was no need to redo the alphabetic label of mailboxes to fit me in. He had not wanted to hire a female, but the affirmative action officer at the institution had insisted that he diversify the department. So I became the only assistant professor who had to ask the department secretary for my mail. And picking it up after returning from a conference on the weekend was impossible; it remained locked in her desk until she returned.

Shortly after moving to another institution, I asked for the computer that the dean had promised me at the interview. The dean asked whether or not I "had that computer in writing." I went back to my appointment letter, and sure enough, I did not. It was then that I noticed that no woman in our department had a computer on her desk, although every male professor did, whether he used it or not.

So while I can never understand the "hidden injuries" of race, I understand full well about the hidden injuries of gender. Double that, triple that, and I begin to see the nature and extent of the trouble that faces a faculty member who is a woman of color.

When Christine first arrived in our department, I discovered a rare and marvelous combination: dignity combined with a rollicking wit and humor. I immediately knew we were going to be friends. She paid me the compliment of asking that I read her papers and played out ideas for future writing projects with me. I was delighted to read her proposed pieces, because she writes clearly and directly.

Furthermore, she obeys an old dictum that one should write not only from research, but also from experience. Consequently, whenever she takes on a new task, she thinks about what she learned and whether or not it might be valuable for someone else faced with a similar task. If so, she writes about it.

Christine was thoughtful about the dynamics at play in the department and the university, and I was happy to share with her my own insights. In an institution that was formerly an all-male, largely military academy and that has transformed itself in the past 30 to 40 years into a coed land-grant, space-grant, and sea-grant institution, clearly there were conflicting forces at work.

Sorting them out with someone else turned out to be less a mentoring experience than one that was simply fun and intellectually intriguing. Christine was always open to conversations about the power implications of race, ethnicity, and gender in this environment, and I believe it made our reflections on our working context sharper and clearer for both of us.

Mentoring, whether cross-race, cross-gender, or same race/gender, has always seemed to me to be an integral part of what senior scholars owe across the generations to their junior colleagues. I have personally heard senior scholars request "release time" for mentoring, as though it were a course from which one might be excused.

My own belief is that it is a part of the institutional citizenship responsibilities of every senior faculty member, not a form of "overload." Consequently, mentoring is a normal responsibility for me—although Christine made it more fun than I can ever remember it being.

Because she came with extensive administrative experience and was highly disciplined about her work, I needed to do little by way of nudging her to write. I found I could be useful, however, in helping her to organize a "scholarly" *vitae* (as opposed to an administrative one) and by supporting her opportunities both within and external to the institution. She has rapidly grown beyond a need for mentoring as she assumes her own leadership roles, but I find the intellectual challenges and the friendship remain intact—principally because that was a part of what we built together in the early years.

### Lessons Extracted from Our Experience

While the mentoring relationship is a highly individualized process, our experience suggests some general points about how to make it more effective. Here are ten lessons about cross-race mentoring that we have taken away:

1) *Cross-race mentoring requires extra sensitivity.* Faculty of color do not seek preferential treatment based on their race or ethnicity. But they want majority groups to understand that cross-race mentoring relationships require understanding that racial, cultural, and ethnic differences strongly influence how individuals view the world.

Interpersonal conflicts often occur with respect to guiding beliefs, values, epistemology, ontology, logic, concept of time, and concept of self. These potential points of difference cannot be overlooked when mentors and protégés want to know each other and learn from the perspective each brings to the mentoring relationship. For example, from one cultural point of view it might seem desirable to seek help. But from another perspective, saving face might be just as, if not more, important. Increasing one's awareness of these differences can only enhance the richness of the mentoring relationship.

2) *Cross-race mentoring takes some familiarity with research topics that are often taken up by scholars of color.* In the field of higher education, these may include contemporary and historical research on the effects of higher education on students of color, critical perspectives on race and ethnicity in the academy, affirmative action and its outcomes, and the like. Although these kinds of research are highly useful in furthering the goal of increasing diversity in higher education, they are not always rewarded in the academy. New faculty members are often told to refrain from engaging in these non-mainstream forms of research until they have achieved tenure.

Such advice, while possibly well meaning, serves an assimilationist agenda. To demand that a marginalized faculty group conform to conventional research agendas serves only to create the impression that non-mainstream research is without value, that diversity is respected only insofar as it conforms to majority interests, and that faculty of color are to some degree incapable of laying out research agendas of their own. Mentors can use their familiarity with and understanding of such research to influence decision making during faculty recruitment, performance assessments, promotion and tenure reviews, and department and college benchmarking.

3) *Cross-race mentoring may begin with an "assignment," but it is built on a relationship.* Faculty members are sometimes given the task of mentoring new members of their departments. But successful mentoring relationships require more than fulfilling an assignment—they are built on mutual respect and admiration. Like any relationship that is outside our comfort zone, there are periods of adjustment and growth during which individuals are learning about and from one another while valuing each other's differences. There is a higher probability of success, though, when there is a reciprocal level of trust, honesty, commitment to human development, and openness to providing and receiving constructive feedback.

Faculty of color are sensitive to being singled out and to assumptions being made about them based on their race or ethnicity. A cross-race mentoring relationship that is built on the deficit model—you need a mentor because you are a minority and minorities come to academia with scholarly deficits—will create an unwelcoming climate for faculty of color and ultimately an unsuccessful mentoring relationship.

4) *Cross-race mentoring requires work on both sides—including deep reflection on the meaning(s) of white privilege; the assumption of white seniority and "voice"; and departmental and college mores, traditions, and values.* Peggy McIntosh, associate director of the Wellesley Centers for Women, describes privilege as resulting from "invisible systems conferring dominance on your group." She goes on to say that "privilege is a favored state, whether earned or conferred by birth or luck. Some conditions work to overempower certain groups. Such privilege simply confers dominance because of one's race or

gender" (1988, 34).

For example, most white faculty can speak in a public setting without putting their race on trial, or they can take a job with an affirmative-action employer and not worry that their colleagues will think they got the job because of their race. Some white faculty do not think that racism affects them because they do not see whiteness as a racial identity or they have learned not to recognize their own privilege. But it is important for mentors and protégés in cross-race mentoring relationships to acknowledge that privilege.

Race and gender are not the only sources of advantage in academia. There are others related to age or seniority, ethnicity, physical ability, sexual orientation, nationality, and religion. Departments and colleges on a university campus have cultures, mores, and traditions of their own regarding who gets listened to at faculty meetings and social gatherings, as well as who is assigned which courses and committees, who mentors whom, who is nominated for awards, who is promoted, who advises students, and the like. It is important to be aware of these systems of privilege.

5) *Cross-race mentoring requires assuming some responsibility for the mentored individual.* For instance, when it is time for promotion and tenure, the mentor might need to volunteer for the promotion and tenure committee. Since the mentor may be the individual who best understands—and has read the largest portion of—the protégé's research and understands who might make the best external reviewers, the mentor is clearly better able than others to "represent" the dossier to the department, the college, and the university community. The same is true for the third-year review process, which is now often mandated to provide junior scholars with feedback on their progress toward promotion and tenure.

6) *Cross-race mentoring is a multifoliate activity, addressing needs expressed by the individual mentored but also those that the individual may not be aware of. This can lead to conflict when constructive feedback is not considered supportive by the protégé.* Mentors and protégés come to the relationship with certain goals and expectations. During the course of the relationship, new needs may arise, and they may involve conflict. Conflict exists even if only one person acknowledges the struggle. It can occur when faculty of color receive critical responses to their research, teaching, or service activities. But if managed well, conflict can lead to growth of understanding between mentor and protégé.

For example, a protégé might feel on track with respect to his or her scholarly agenda but receive feedback from the mentor that suggests otherwise. While this feedback might be hard to accept, if there is trust and respect in the relationship, the protégé should come to realize that such honest feedback is important for professional development.

This trust can be nurtured if feedback for improvement occurs at several agreed-upon intervals throughout the year. It can take the form of reviewing manuscripts for publication, observing classroom teaching, reviewing progress toward promotion and/or tenure, collaborating on grant proposals, buffering the call to serve on college and university-wide diversity committees, and helping the new faculty member carve out a research agenda.

7) *Cross-race mentoring may often mean expressing views that the scholar of color feels strongly about but may be afraid to raise in public meetings.* Many senior white administrators and faculty do not understand the fear felt by junior faculty who may want to speak up about certain issues but fail to do so because they suspect that such forthrightness might be used against them in personnel decisions.

For faculty of color who are present in small numbers or who are the only one of their racial and/or ethnic group in a department or college, this fear is sometimes paralyzing. Mentors can assure protégés that they should speak up because they will be supported, as well as educate other faculty that this fear is a pervasive problem. Furthermore, mentors can be strong allies for diversity and social justice when they publicly denounce any behaviors that have a paralyzing effect.

8) *Cross-race mentoring involves sharing opportunities for professional development and promotion, as well as pointing out landmines in the academic landscape.* The academy can be a very alien place for any new faculty member, but it is even more so when one looks around and sees few people like oneself represented in a variety of academic ranks and positions. With few role models, faculty of color often cannot determine how and where to seek opportunities for advancement or whom to trust for advice.

Cross-race mentoring provides a unique opportunity for mentors and protégés to be agents of change in helping to create a more inclusive academic community. Such mentoring is an opportunity for majority faculty to coach faculty of color who aspire to senior administrative positions or have talents and expertise that would serve the college or university community well. Many individuals in higher education advocate "growing your own" as a strategy for diversifying the faculty ranks; this strategy also works for the administrative ranks.

9) *Cross-race mentoring is not academic cloning. It is the giving of self, expertise, and experience to help others achieve their goals.* Many faculty want to see "more people like us" in the academy, whether the similarity is in how we see the world around us, the type of research we pursue, how we came to be academics, what it took for us to be successful, or what we view as normative and good.

But scholars of color do not wish to be white scholars. Rather, they desire to be themselves and to be valued for who they are and how they can enlarge the academy's vision by virtue of their different voices, research themes, and perspectives. It is the goals of the individual scholar that are important; it is the role of the mentor to assist in achieving those goals.

Faculty of color often experience what W. A. Smith (2003) calls "racial battle fatigue" resulting from experiences related to individual, cultural, and institutional oppression. In a cross-race mentoring relationship, these experiences have to be taken into account when working to guide someone through the academic ranks.

10) *Finally, cross-race mentoring requires the majority faculty member to become sensitive to issues that might have seemed unimportant in the past.* Faculty of color may serve the mentor, as well as the larger faculty group, as "tuning forks." That is, issues that seemed less than critical to a majority faculty member make take on new significance when seen through the eyes of faculty of color. Discussions regarding new hires, conversations about emerging lines of research, the framing of announcements for open positions—all may be freighted in ways previously not considered.

Majority mentors can learn much about the experiences of faculty of color if they routinely debrief their protégés about recent discussions. Faculty of color who trust their mentors will tell them what was good about a discussion and what they found disadvantaging. Such debriefing sessions serve to educate mentors in subtleties of which they might be unaware. Learning on both sides is possible, and indeed necessary, if the mentoring is to be effective. Many white mentors do not possess the requisite knowledge, understanding, or skills to mentor without some learning curve. Asking the protégé for help is one meaningful way to enter that curve.

Cross-race mentoring for diversity and faculty development is challenging for mentor and protégé alike. Individuals bring to the mentoring process a complex set of experiences, mental models, social and cultural identities, expertise, goals, expectations, values, and beliefs, all of which make for potential areas of conflict. But if managed well, these differences can lead to rich learning. Higher education cannot diversify the faculty ranks without paying close attention to those who are sitting on the margins of our institutions. We need deeper dialogues in order to learn, grow, and change as we extend a warm welcoming hand to individuals who aspire to join the professorial ranks.

### Postscript

Since the publication of this article in 2005, we have benefited greatly from the feedback received from colleagues over the past ten years about our journey, and the lessons extracted from our cross-race faculty mentoring relationship. Yvonna remains an internationally known scholar, and Christine has since been promoted to full professor and is now serving both as acting vice provost for academic affairs and as vice president and associate provost for diversity. While our mentor-protégé journey began from a relationship built across race, over the years, we have enjoyed an enduring friendship that has surpassed professorial rank, eminence, and power. In fact, we have come to a place where we can have deeper, difficult dialogues about issues that continue to plague higher education and the academy, including institutionalized racism and sexism. Our mentoring relationship is reciprocal. We challenge, support, and advocate for each other. We talk, listen, and talk and listen some more. Like most dialogues, when conflicts and challenges to perspective-taking occur, we remain committed to engaged dialogues and self-reflection about who we are as scholars and colleagues, and, more importantly, trusted friends.

## Works Cited

Cafarella, R. S. 1992. *Psychosocial Development of Women: Linkages to Teaching and Leadership in Adult Education*. Information Series 350. Columbus, OH: Center on Education and Training for Employment, The Ohio State University. ERIC, ED 354 386.

Levinson, D. J., C. N. Darrow, E. B. Klein, M. H. Levinson, and B. McKee. 1978. *The Seasons of a Man's Life*. New York: Random House.

McIntosh, P. 1988. *White Privilege and Male Privilege: A Personal Account of Coming to See Correspondences Through Work in Women's Studies*. Working Paper 189. Wellesley, MA: Wellesley Centers for Women.

Smith, W. A. 2003. "A Long Way to Go: Conversations about Race by African American Faculty and Graduate Students in Higher Education." Paper presented at the 28th annual conference of the Association for the Study of Higher Education (ASHE), Portland, OR.

## APPENDIX: Suggested Readings

Blackwood, J., and S. Brown-Welty. 2011. "Mentoring and Interim Positions: Pathways to Leadership for Women of Color." *Diversity in Higher Education* 10: 109–33.

Griffin, K.A., and R. J. Reddick. 2011. "Surveillance and Sacrifice: Gender Differences in the Mentoring Patterns of Black Professors at Predominantly White Research Universities." *American Educational Research Journal* 48 (5): 1032–57.

Turner, C. S., and J. C. Gonzalez. 2015. *Modeling Mentoring Across Race/ Ethnicity and Gender: Practices to Cultivate the Next Generation of Scholars*. Sterling, VA: Stylus.

Turner, C. S. V., J. C. Gonzalez, and J. L. Wood. 2008. "Faculty of Color in Academe: What 20 Years of Literature Tells Us." *Journal of Diversity in Higher Education* 1 (3): 139–68.

# Graduate Student ISO a Mentor: A Dialogue about Mentoring

*Jan Allen and Kevin Johnston*

*Talented History GA ISO a Mentor. Intelligent, hard-working doctoral student with teaching and research experience seeks interested History faculty for professional guidance. PhD in southern history preferred.* Sincere interest and honest care about the state of the profession, higher education, teaching, and research necessary. Some time commitment required, but experience guaranteed to benefit both.

We wrote this tongue-in-cheek (or was it?) personal ad 18 years ago when we started our first conversation about mentoring (Allen and Johnston 1997). The conversation developed over time into a dialogue, coupled with research, programming, and more writing about the many forms and functions of mentoring in higher education. With this opportunity, we share our ongoing conversation below.

We met on the day that Kevin began a PhD program in history at the University of Tennessee (UT). At that time, Jan had been a faculty member in human ecology for 16 years and had recently been appointed assistant dean in the Graduate School. Our conversations about mentoring for success in graduate school, begun at new student orientation and at TA Orientation that year, led to an invitation for Kevin to join a small team of three faculty (representing agricultural economics/rural sociology, education, and human ecology) and three graduate students (from education, marketing, and psychology) to develop and implement a campus-wide mentoring program. Later, Kevin was appointed as a graduate assistant in the Graduate School, and the conversations continued. In the 15 years since Kevin left UT, initially for Michigan State to work in TA development, we have maintained an ongoing exchange about mentoring, both its sustaining power and nuanced challenges.

Mentoring as a strategy for facilitating professional development and success has received increasing attention over the past several decades. In higher education, the faculty development movement in the 1970s, as well as efforts beginning in the 1980s to recruit and retain minority students, have focused much attention on mentoring of faculty—particularly of junior, female, and minority faculty—and on undergraduates, particularly at-risk freshmen. Although the focus on mentoring graduate students is more recent, a quick Google Scholar search shows over 150,000 publications on this topic.

A review of research on mentoring in higher education reveals that both individuals and institutions benefit from mentoring relationships (Espinoza-Herold and Gonzalez 2007; Fedynich and Bain 2011; Girves, Zepeda, and Gwathmey 2005; Johnson and Huwe 2003; Johnsrud 1990; Terrell and Hussell 1994; Wheeler and Schuster 1990). Graduate students in mentoring relationships report advantages in job placement, research skills, and collaborative publications with mentors (Hunt and Michael 1983). Mentors also reap benefits in the form of regeneration and revitalization (Blackburn, Chapman, and Cameron 1981; Busch 1985). And institutions benefit from the enhanced quality of learning and of the academic environment (Wunsch 1994). These benefits, as well as the challenges we encountered in mentoring and being mentored, were components of our mentoring dialogue over the years.

JAN: Mentoring as a model for training doctoral students is most evident in their role as researchers, and most of the literature on mentoring in higher education supports its benefits to research productivity—not teaching, service, or the numerous other roles and responsibilities expected of faculty. Twenty years ago, in the summer of 1994, my colleague Sky Huck and I hosted focus-group discussions with University of Tennessee graduate students representing schools and colleges university-wide. All of the 50 students we talked to believed they had a faculty member who functioned as a mentor for their professional development as a researcher. However, when we asked, "Do you have a faculty member who similarly serves as a mentor in your professional development as a teacher?" none reported a "teaching mentor." This singular focus on research Slevin [1993] has described as "the final irony." The work we are best preparing future faculty to do—research—often is not done well (or quickly enough for tenure review) because scholarly contributions are "delayed, sidetracked, or rushed" as teaching, advising, curriculum development, and department/university service (for which future faculty are often unprepared) become burdensome [Slevin 1993]. But as graduate training has responded to external pressures—especially from graduate students confronting, or confronted by, the challenges of the academic job market—graduate faculty and administrators are transforming graduate training to develop future faculty and future professionals for multiple careers paths, roles, and responsibilities.

KEVIN: I don't disagree. This singular focus on research in doctoral education was certainly true for your graduate training. But it's also the case that concern in the past few years—most urgently expressed by doctoral students among my cohort—about the increasingly bleak job market for future faculty has led some graduate schools and programs to expand their career focus to include preparation for careers beyond the faculty role.

JAN: Yes, this dialogue of the past decade has resulted in an expanded focus and new programming. For example, at Columbia University, starting in 2014, advanced doctoral students have had an opportunity to participate for five to ten hours a week in an administrative internship in one of 20 offices on campus, meeting for an hour every other week with an administrative mentor and attending a weekly workshop on issues in higher education administration. For several years at Cornell University, graduate students and postdoctoral fellows have participated in a Leadership Certificate Program, a semester-long series of seminars to help students develop personal leadership skills related to self-knowledge, cultural fluency, planning and problem solving, group dynamics and team building, and conflict and change management. The program is designed to help participants develop and market skills transferable to multiple career placements. Going back even further, during the early days of Preparing Future Faculty (PFF) programs—campus-wide programs designed to prepare doctoral students for the "new realities" of faculty work, including teaching and service at a variety of institutions [Gaff et al. 2000]—some graduate schools created a modified professional development model, Preparing Future Professionals (PFP). Expanding the scope of the PFF approach, PFP programs focused on helping graduate students identify alternate career paths and develop a broader skill set prior to seeking employment in publishing, consulting, and other fields. Notable programs continuing the PFP approach today include those at North Carolina State University, the University of Colorado, and Florida State University.

KEVIN: These programs, often offered centrally by graduate schools and teaching centers, allow us to serve dozens if not hundreds of students in various professional development activities—especially valuable insofar as some faculty or programs have been reluctant to advise students to consider roles other than that of faculty. Whether this hesitancy is due to lack of knowledge about non-faculty placements, reluctance to modify graduate curricula, or simply optimism about the job market in the long term, what these programs lack is the one-to-one apprentice model that has long characterized mentoring in graduate education.

JAN: As mentoring has been perhaps the best framework for acculturating future faculty, it can remain a model for preparing students for a broader array of positions. The mentoring relationship, like any successful relationship, must be defined by its participants in terms of its goals, processes, commitments, even duration. Several years ago I began offering a workshop for graduate students, entitled "Working with Mentors and Tormentors," focused on both desired functions and common dysfunctions in mentoring relationships. To prepare students to consider the various needs a mentor or mentoring relationship could meet for them, I gave students a list of 15 mentoring roles or functions.[1] It was compiled, for the most part, from numerous research studies that focused on one or more of these functions as independent variables, with successful outcomes or satisfaction with the mentoring relationship as dependent variables. I asked students to use the list and check which needs they had that could be met by a faculty mentor. I suggested they not check all 15 items; no one faculty member would have the time, skills, or inclination to engage in all the roles needed by graduate students. But it's essential that students assess and identify their needs and then discuss their expectations with potential mentors—and to do this regularly throughout the stages of their graduate programs: during coursework, through qualifying exams, and in the dissertation research and writing years. Graduate students, as they move from novice researchers and teachers to more independence as scholars, scientists, or artists, have evolving developmental needs.

For me as a mentor, mentoring is *exposure*. As a mentor, I want to *expose the academy and professoriate* as accessible to graduate students. I want to guide students to experience our academic and research culture as collaborators, co-investigators, and co-teachers. I also want to *expose my work* as valuable. And not just my research as a valuable activity and contribution, but my teaching and service as well. Further, I must *expose the challenges we face* in higher education—funding and budget crises, balancing and integrating so many roles and expectations that compete for our time and departmental resources, and valuing the Scholarship of Teaching and Learning (SoTL) at a research university. Returning to an earlier point, one of the most crucial challenges faced by faculty, graduate program directors, and administrators at all levels of the university is the need to train our graduate students for new placements. Career paths outside the professoriate are no longer be viewed as "alternative" placements for students; they have become the "new normal" for many fields. Graduate students must understand these issues so they can engage more fully in their graduate education and in the dialogue for its reform.

And finally, *I take a risk and expose myself*, both who I am as a person and why I have chosen this profession. It's what for me is the meaning of my humanity: a willingness to share what I have—my knowledge, my skills, myself—with my students.

KEVIN: "I think you have something important to say!" said a departmental professor to me during a conversation about my research and classwork early in my doctoral program. I do not think I fully knew the significance of the statement at the time, but the compliment has never left me. Subsequent conversations with him have brought that comment into fuller light, providing me with important confidence in my work. His interest, so precisely imparted, conveyed a trust in my abilities. His continuing counsel was some of the most important support I received during my doctoral work. By believing that I could produce something meaningful in the field and *telling me so*, this professor fulfilled what for me is the primary goal of a mentoring relationship: trusting that a subordinate can experience the mystery and possibility of an accomplished professional. I believe that at base, mentors *invite us* to experience by representing the results of the process and sincerely caring about us as students—but also by caring about the discipline and profession, about all the professional paths we might take over the course of our careers.

This experience and various other interactions with campus faculty during my graduate work sharpened my ideas about what it is that graduate students should expect from their faculty. Perhaps the only immutable conclusion I have reached is that very few students or faculty have thought about what it means to mentor or to be mentored. Ask ten people what they think of mentoring and you are likely to get ten different answers, although all respondents probably base their understanding of a proper mentoring relationship in a belief that someone "who has accomplished" in one way or another assists someone else "to accomplish." Words like "teacher," "guide," "parent," or "overseer" describe a relationship that is paternal, maternal, motivational, caring, sensitive, and tyrannical, all at the same time. Like good teaching, we are not always sure how to define it, but we claim to know it when we see it.

The *details* throw us, both as mentors and as their charges. Published works describe a wide range of mentoring methods, styles, and results, each suited to different environments, various temperaments, and desired outcomes. Certainly no singular model exists for defining the proper mentoring relationship, just as those involved vary greatly in personality, motivation, workloads, and expectations. (Nor are we sure exactly *when* we are mentoring and being mentored.) Yet graduate students and faculty often rest their professional hopes and dreams on poorly considered notions of mentoring, if they have thought about it at all.

Most students and faculty have only partially formed concepts of what should be expected from the relationship, and thus neither benefits fully from it. Higher learning suffers as a result. We live and work within an organic community based upon critical thinking, intellectualism, and interested communication; it's a community critically dependent on careful sharing. The mentoring relationship, too, is a shared, symbolic experience.

JAN: Often the most effective and sought-after mentors understand that being a role model of only a researcher, a scientist, or a scholar is limiting. Cornell Human Ecology professor Kathleen Rasmussen, who recently was recognized with a mentoring award voted by graduate students campus-wide, describes mentoring beyond subject matter. It's also mentoring by example in the way one treats people. It's mentoring for living your life while having a "compelling" (i.e., demanding) job. It's being open to unexpected mentoring, in both giving and receiving. For example, Kathleen attributes some of her mentoring success to her students, who share their expectations ("Give me praise before criticism.") and help her further develop skills in teaching, for example.

KEVIN: Yes, simply considering well the *details* of mentoring greatly enhances the educational/professional experience for everyone involved, including those we teach.

JAN: These details and the specific expectations of the mentoring relationship are critical. I often think about a graduate student I know in a business doctoral program. Her mentor was internationally respected, a prolific author, and highly sought-after as an advisor by graduate students in business and psychology for the chance to be associated with a well-known scholar. But he candidly told his prospective graduate students that he would not often be available to work with them. They could email their papers to him, and he would comment when and if he had time to do so. So this student invited all the professor's graduate students, her peers both new and advanced, to nightly work sessions, Monday through Thursday, in the departmental offices. From 6:00 to 10:00 PM, they talked through their research ideas, wrote funding and conference proposals, submitted IRB protocols for approval, emailed surveys to collect their data, analyzed data, and wrote papers, theses, and dissertations. By the time Veronica completed her doctoral degree (in less than five years), she had made 29 conference presentations and had published 11 papers.

Most compelling about this story is that the graduate students determined both what they needed from their mentor and what was possible given his ability and available time to meet those mentoring needs. Rather than seek a different mentor or find another graduate program or institution, they created a peer support group that was extremely effective for their purposes. By all measures, they were a very successful cohort of students.[2]

KEVIN: Our experience with peer mentoring at the University of

Tennessee was quite a discovery. The Developing Future Faculty as Teacher-Scholars program was initially designed as a mentoring program for master's and doctoral students who served as graduate teaching assistants at the university. Affectionately referred to as the Graduate TA (GTA) mentoring program, it supported graduate students in their instructional role and responsibilities with the goal of helping them be better and more efficient teachers. It also provided support for their many other roles—as students, researchers, scientists, collaborators, and citizens of the university. Students in teams of 12 (in the earlier years, and then later 6 to 8) were assigned to a faculty mentor, someone from a different department than the members of the team. Each year there were ten groups meeting roughly every two weeks throughout the year. Additional monthly events, primarily workshops and social gatherings, allowed all of the up to 120 students in each year's program to come together to hear speakers, discuss issues, and network across the different disciplines and departments represented in the mentoring program. As noted, there was a faculty mentor who guided and facilitated each group. But in the first year of the program, we discovered the power of peer mentoring.

JAN: Boy, did we ever! In our first year of the program, although we very thoughtfully and judiciously selected and invited our mentors for the program, one of the mentors turned out to have a very, shall we say, authoritarian style. Rather than facilitating her team's discussions and helping them to collaboratively construct their knowledge about the issues and challenges facing them as graduate students and teaching assistants, her style in each team meeting was to solicit students' questions and then to provide *her* answers. Boom, boom, boom. Their questions, her answers. Next question. Her answer. One of the graduate students in this team came to me, as one of the program coordinators, and reported that her "team dynamic didn't seem to be working the way it should," and she wanted to switch to another team. In our conversation, I asked her what she would do in a classroom where an authority figure (instructor or student) seemed to monopolize the discussion. We considered other, "real world," situations where one might not easily be able to switch teams or offices or faculty mentors. I'll never forget this student for several reasons, but one was her response to this situation. She returned for the next team meeting. And after the first question arose, and the faculty mentor offered her definitive answer, Anna interjected, "Does anyone else have another idea or solution or thought about this?" Her team members quickly took the opportunity to respond, offer suggestions, and move to a more collaborative, socially constructed discussion. From that meeting forward, peers became their own facilitators, guides, and mentors in the group. They *all* had something to offer. At the end of the year, by all formal and informal assessments, this was one of the most effective mentoring teams of all. We as coordinators moved the next year to incorporate more opportunities for peer support and mentoring in the program.

KEVIN: Faculty and graduate students both should consider what it is they want out of such a relationship, realizing that any opinions they first form will change and evolve with the relationship itself. Interested mentors can lead, cajole, criticize, and support. Thoughtful graduate students can learn that help may come from many places, and often in what are at first unrecognizable forms. The professor who told me "You have something important to say!" neither sat on my committee nor had any official advising role, yet he had more impact on me, and my confidence and persistence, as a doctoral student than any advisor. Mentoring takes effort from all parties involved, yet very few have considered what all that effort entails. Graduate students know they must ask. But we are also looking for honest queries. We seek faculty who ask and who listen. Faculty who ask us to share our goals, aspirations, and vulnerabilities. One of Jan's Cornell colleagues, Economics professor John Abowd, described it perfectly: "I try to see my graduate students as peers but with a little less experience." Ultimately, we are looking for possibilities. Of course, we must be interested in what we learn. Faculty interest in what we do certainly serves not only as quality control but as an important invitation to continue. I am not sure we graduate students can ask for any more than sincere concern from our mentors that we understand more about this process and relationship. Learning to be a good mentee is half the battle!

**Notes**

1. This list appears elsewhere in the volume as Table 2.1 (p. 27).

2. See chapter 2 for a more detailed discussion of the peer mentoring model and programs.

**Works Cited**

Allen, J., and K. Johnston. 1997. "Mentoring, Being Mentored." *Context*, February, 15.

Blackburn, R., D. Chapman, and S. Cameron. 1981. "Cloning in Academe: Mentoring and Academic Careers." *Research in Higher Education* 15 (4): 315–27.

Busch, J. W. 1985. "Mentoring in Graduate Schools of Education: Mentors' Perceptions." *American Education Research Journal* 22:257–65.

Espinoza-Herold, M., and V. Gonzalez. 2007. "The Voices of Senior Scholars on Mentoring Graduate Students and Junior Scholars." *Hispanic Journal of Behavioral Sciences* 29 (3): 313–35.

Fedynich, L., and S. Bain. 2011. "Mentoring the Successful Graduate Student of Tomorrow." *Research in Higher Education Journal* 12:1–7.

Gaff, J., A. Pruitt-Logan, R. Weibl, and Participants in the Preparing Future Faculty Program. 2000. *Building the Faculty We Need: Colleges and Universities Working Together*. Washington, DC: Association of American Colleges and Universities.

Girves, J., Y. Zepeda, and J. Gwathmey. 2005. "Mentoring in a Post–Affirmative Action World." *Journal of Social Issues* 61 (3): 449–79.

Hunt, D., and C. Michael. 1983. "A Career Training and Development Tool." *Academy of Management Review* 8 (3): 475–85.

Johnson, W. B., and J. M. Huwe. 2003. *Getting Mentored in Graduate School*. Washington, DC: American Psychological Association.

Johnsrud, L. 1990. "Mentor Relationships: Those That Help and Those That Hinder." *New Directions for Higher Education* 72:57–66.

Slevin, J. 1993. "Finding Voices in the Culture of Silence: Graduate Education for the Next Generation." *Liberal Education* 79 (2): 4–9.

Terrell, M., and R. Hussell. 1994. "Mentoring Undergraduate Minority Students: An Overview, Survey, and Model Program." *New Directions for Teaching and Learning* 55:35–46.

Wheeler, D. W., and J. H. Schuster. 1990. "Building Comprehensive Programs to Enhance Faculty Development." In *Enhancing Faculty Careers: Strategies for Development and Renewal*, edited by

J. H. Schuster et al., 275–97. San Francisco: Jossey-Bass.

Wunsch, M. 1994. "Developing Mentoring Programs: Major Themes and Issues." *New Directions for Teaching and Learning* 55:27–34.

# Growing into Mentoring, and into the Profession: A Reflection on Intentionally Cultivating Mentoring Communities

*Nina B. Namaste*

In graduate school at Indiana University I yearned for a dissertation director who was hands-on and directive, like I saw with a few colleagues' directors. In fact, I even defined mentorship in terms of top-down instruction from a successful faculty mentor, a "sage on the stage" who would impart the insider's "what to do" checklist of behaviors that an aspiring faculty member needed to abide by to be successful. Looking back, I had a narrow definition of mentorship: someone successful in the field imparting and sharing their knowledge on how to be successful. To my recollection I experienced only one instance of direct faculty mentorship during my time in graduate school. Upon completing my MA qualifying exams I confessed to a faculty member that I couldn't imagine writing a dissertation and therefore wasn't sure if I would be going on to a PhD. He told me the key to completing a dissertation was to pick a topic I was genuinely passionate about because, after two or more years of researching and writing, passion and determination would see me through. While this advice was a massive oversimplification, it did set me on the path towards continued graduate studies in Hispanic Literatures and towards a dissertation topic interesting enough to remain the focal point of my continued research agenda: the construction of identity via food imagery in contemporary Hispanic literature.

Curiously, even though in graduate school I always sought an expert-novice mentorship relationship that would somehow confer "insider" understanding, the real keys to my successful completion of an MA and PhD were the peer study groups and committed colleagues with whom I exchanged feedback. For months leading up to

my MA exams, I met with a colleague weekly to discuss our interpretations of the texts on our required reading list, to place those
texts in a sociocultural context, and to practice answering possible
exam questions. That same trusted colleague, as well as a few others,
read my early dissertation chapter drafts, so that when I submitted
them to my director they were better developed and framed versions.
Yet my limited "sage on the stage" definition of mentorship didn't
allow me to see either myself or those instrumental peers as mentors.
Thus I moved to the next stage of my career firmly attached to the
perspective that someone expert, someone else needed to teach me
how to navigate the complexities of work life.

After graduate school and in my first tenure-track job at Grand
Valley State University in Michigan, I even went so far as contacting
someone whose research I greatly admired and explicitly asking for
mentorship. While I am sure this approach works for some, resound-
ing silence was the only thing I received in return. After all, why
would a star in the field mentor a still-on-the-ground newbie like
myself? With no mentor in sight, I did what any other new faculty
member does—start working and figuring things out on my own. I
created umpteen new courses, planned interesting and thoughtful
classes, taught with dedication, pored over students' work to analyze
if I was effective in eliciting their learning, tried to find colleagues
with whom I could relate and talk about teaching and research, read
as much as I possibly could during the year and enormous amounts
during the summer, and wrote conference papers that I'd then
submit for consideration for publication (only to get rejected and
have to figure out what I wasn't understanding about the publishing
process), all the while trying to understand the student, faculty,
departmental, and institutional culture where I worked. It was
dizzying, exhausting work, and when I returned to my graduate
institution two years after graduating I asked a former professor,
"Why didn't you teach us at all about the profession?! I know how
to do research well, but hell if I know how to navigate all the
demands and complexities of the job!" She responded unequivocally,
"Because no one would go into the profession if we did!"

Understanding that mentoring was not going to come
spontaneously from someone else no matter how hard I tried to build
my professional network and connections at disciplinary conferences,

I set out to replicate the structures that had helped me succeed in graduate school: study groups and committed colleagues who exchanged feedback. Importantly, I turned my focus towards my local context of a mid-size state school. I tentatively started creating discussion groups around topics of interest, mainly teaching and the scholarship of teaching and learning, with colleagues at my institution. I applied for micro-grants from the university's center for teaching and learning to fund coffee and snacks for discussions centered around teaching. Once funded and with invitations sent to the entire university faculty, I positioned myself in the group as the meeting organizer—I certainly wasn't an expert on the topic I had proposed for discussion: how to develop students' critical thinking skills. In fact, none of us were experts. But we came together as a group of colleagues ready and willing to explore and learn together, regardless of rank or standing at the university. We each found articles discussing critical thinking in our field and shared them with the group. We debated whether and how critical thinking could be taught in lower-level courses, and we exchanged ideas on how to teach more effectively. We implemented changes directly related to critical thinking into our courses and shared with the group our successes and failures.

Unbeknownst to us, what we created was a learning community. Learning communities are groups of people who formulate, exchange, and even produce knowledge through shared discourse (Bonk, Wisher, and Nigrelli 2004). Even more important, for me, was attaining a level of agency in initiating discussions that were happening among a group of colleagues. If, as Knight and Trowler state, "socialization is created from the discourses and practices of the community within which one works" (1999, 23), what happens when you are the one to initiate discussion and engagement with one of those discourses? In my case, I derived intense satisfaction and affirmation from the impact I found I could have on my own and others' learning. Also, I discovered that there were many colleagues across the institution who were craving deeper intellectual discussions and connections. The only thing necessary was a willingness on my part to be the initiator of those discussions and extend an invitation. In effect, I discovered the ability to control my response to the demands and pressures of work life while also coming to a better understanding of faculty and university cultures, all the while furthering my intellectual and personal growth.

Due to life circumstances, namely a spouse completing his PhD and being on the job market, I took the opportunity to move to an institution that was more akin to my own highly influential and formative undergraduate alma mater, St. Olaf College in Minnesota—a small liberal arts institution that intentionally focused on and openly discussed (not just at special discussion group meetings) teaching and learning. I brought the experience of having a small group of people with whom to discuss issues of common interest with me to my second institution, Elon University in North Carolina. Again via the teaching and learning center on campus, I helped form a multi-disciplinary writing group and can definitively state that without the monthly group gatherings and sharing of our work I could not have been as productive in my disciplinary research as I have been, considering all the attention given to teaching and service at my institution. That said, I admittedly struggled to integrate into my new departmental culture. I came from GVSU with lots of experience related to assessment (university assessment committee, departmental assessment work, etc.) and I assumed that at a teaching institution like Elon, assessment would be integrated into all aspects of departmental work. Until I realized that core assumption and could better understand why my colleagues were perceiving my insistence on assessment of student learning as a threat, I remained on the margins, not being able to fully integrate into my department.

Again, trying to make sense of the fact that Elon's focus on and support of scholarly teaching fit me well, but that I was clearly remaining on the fringe with my disciplinary colleagues, I set out to investigate how new faculty integrate into departments at my institution and if there were structures in place that facilitated such integration. I collaborated with two other colleagues in my department and designed a Scholarship of Teaching and Learning (SoTL) study; we created a survey, conducted interviews, and looked over the results to see what patterns emerged. However, the most important learning came not from the study itself, but from the process of creating, collecting, researching, and analyzing the data with a group of colleagues in my department—again, knowing that I had initiated that learning process. I proved to myself that the same research methods practiced in my disciplinary field could be applied to other areas of my professional life: start with an intriguing idea or perplexing question, research and analyze what has been written about the topic, plan and execute a study or action informed by the research, analyze and reflect upon the results, and evaluate the effectiveness of that study or action. With these two successful ventures, the writing group and SoTL study, plus a core framework of collaborative exchange from which to work, I slowly started forming multiple groups related to teaching, research, and even service.

Significantly, the groups had core values and practices imbedded into them: action based on documented good practices and research in the field. My teaching-focused group researched pedagogical methods that addressed a pressing issue (critical thinking, writing, intercultural competency, etc.), crossing disciplinary boundaries. In my writing group, we circulated our (strictly discipline-based) papers among each other. While we viewed the works through entirely different disciplinary lenses, we focused feedback on clarity, substantiation and contextualization of argument, and style. To the extent that I could control it, service work too related to my interests. In committee work we researched topics from multiple perspectives and disciplines and acted based on a group integration of research and ideas. For instance, a colleague and I wrote a report for the dean and provost arguing in favor of lowering course caps in our department, particularly in our lower-level language and culture courses. Unbeknownst to me at the time, many of the groups I was forming were, in essence, *communities of practice* (Wenger 1999; 2002); sharing values, objectives, vision, and passion for a topic, we collaboratively deepened our understanding of the topic, and collectively developed new ideas, products, and practices. While I didn't know that I was creating what was termed communities of practice, I was, indeed, intentional in creating connections and collaborations specifically regarding my professional duties of teaching, research, and service.

By applying a scholarly model related to work responsibilities within the context of collaborative, group learning, I subsequently began to develop a core practice or method on which to base my own professional growth and development. Based on documented best practices and research in the field, a colleague and I proposed an informal, formative peer-teaching-observation group, and created forms that would guide the feedback we provided to one another. This led me to create another collaborative SoTL study investigating if and how we could intentionally improve our students' critical reading skills, and to collaborate on a grant proposal for a server that could stream movies and documentaries in the language, culture, and literature classes taught in our department. In making a concerted effort to talk one-on-one with colleagues in my department and across the university, I found common problems or needs and together we worked to address them—first researching what was published on the topic and then figuring out how to implement those documented best practices in our particular context.

During my second and third—and most hectic—years as a second-time tenure-track assistant professor, a few things happened that made me focus, once again, on mentorship: a student asked me to mentor her undergraduate honors research thesis, I was asked to participate in a discussion group to talk about mentorship, and I was on the hiring committee for a new colleague and wanted to help her transition to the job. I suddenly became responsible for mentoring other people's intellectual journeys and well-being, not just my own.

I mentored my honors student more on the basis of what I did *not* want to do: I was not going to micromanage or "correct" her ideas, she was not going to analyze a project that *I* wanted to investigate, and I was *not* going to be the "authority" on the topic or tell her how she *should* engage in the research. Our weekly mentoring appointments were very much based on the Socratic method of asking questions to clarify meaning, understanding, assumptions, and confusions, sometimes with leading questions and other times with purely process- and discovery-driven questions. I had experienced firsthand the benefits of collaborative, mutual learning with colleagues—communities focused on process and skill-building for its members—and wanted my student to benefit from the same type of experience. Therefore, I focused on helping her harness her intellectual curiosity, navigate contradictory research, deal with logical dead-ends, formulate and substantiate plausible interpretations of texts, and integrate all the ideas in coherent, effective writing, all the while managing the emotional highs and lows on the path towards discovery. It was a daunting, yet immensely rewarding and transformational, experience for both of us. In particular it sparked a mental shift in my teaching and peer relationships. Having witnessed tremendous growth as a result of a collaborative, inquiry-based discovery process, I wanted to attend to the growth and formation of the *whole* person.

At the same time, I was attending biweekly faculty lunches centering on using peer/mutual mentoring to help rediscover purpose and meaning in our professional and personal lives. This group was firmly based on nonauthoritarian mentorship—there was no expert who was going to teach us how to rejuvenate our careers or how to mentor one another. In fact, we were to mentor and be mentored by everyone in the group. What resulted was a Formation Mentoring Community (FMC) as presented in the book *Transformative Conversations* (Felten et al. 2013). FMCs help participants to reconnect with their passion for learning and discovery, to act on core values, and to align our work with those passions and values in order to combat the high stress, cynicism and isolation often felt in higher education (Felten et al. 2013).

The direct impact of my involvement in the group could be seen through a shift in the type of questions I asked my newly hired colleague. Our monthly meetings moved from "How are you holding up?" conversations to strategy sessions focused on identifying her needs and how she could fulfill them at the institution. Our monthly coffee chats were dedicated in part to tracking how those needs changed over time. As a result of these cumulative experiences I was arriving at a new definition of mentoring. I had always sought the outside mentor who would bestow knowledge on me, and yet I was slowly realizing that effective mentoring, for me, came from having a group of people collaboratively discovering and learning new things about a given topic. In short, I was tentatively starting to align my values (collective, nonauthoritarian, process-driven learning), my needs (constant intellectual and personal growth, deep reflection, positive impact on others), and my professional responsibilities (the inextricable teaching, research, and service triad).

Concomitant to my seeking out groups or communities, my perspectives and experiences in the classroom were leading me to change the way I viewed teaching and learning. Foreign language pedagogy is essentially learner-centered: students must use and create meaning in the target language to attain proficiency. Yet learning a language was only a small part of what I was asking students to do in my classes. I was constantly pushing my students to enlarge their worldviews, to challenge assumptions about other cultures, and to question everything, particularly cultural products and texts. I was asking nothing short of massive transformation, yet it was clear to me that a learner-centered model wasn't fully adequate. Students were intensely frustrated and disturbed by— sometimes openly hostile to—the questioning of their dearly held beliefs, values, and worldviews. My teaching needed to be more mentorship-based: it needed to attend to the emotional and mental aspects of transformation. Scaffolding assignments that led students step-by-step through the process of cracking open their worldviews without triggering a "fight or flight" response became the core of all my courses. I saw my faculty role shift as my definition of student learning moved well beyond my disciplinary context. Successful student learning in my classes revolved around providing opportunities for human growth and development. I favored more deep learning, more skill-building, more problem-solving, more reflection, and more meaning-making and processing as a group—all of which is precisely what I was learning and doing in my mutual mentoring communities. Each course became its own learning community as we set out on a journey of exploration and discovery—about language, about culture, about texts, about learning, about how we react to change, about the self and others.

At a critical juncture in my career, going up for promotion to associate professor, peer/mutual mentoring and a proactive, scholarly approach to work responsibilities proved essential. A trusted colleague and I read about teaching portfolios, shared information from workshops, and exchanged ideas on how to organize the sections of our tenure files. In addition, I had others read over the narrative sections of my portfolio that explained the intentionality, inter-relatedness, and cohesiveness of what I taught, researched, and contributed to the institution. I asked different colleagues to specifically look at what "products" (student works, teaching materials I generated, research articles, SoTL studies, etc.) I used to substantiate my claims. Once again my proactive, collaborative, scholarly-based approach proved to be efficacious.

Having successfully earned tenure, I then faced the "post-tenure disillusionment crisis" (Wilson 2012). Once again I turned to deep reflection, discussions with committed colleagues, and intense research to help overcome the mixed emotions and loss of focus I was experiencing. I consulted with full professors, my dean, even the Office of Leadership and Professional Development and teaching center staff, to ask what they had done, what the common struggles were, and what others did to narrow the ever-expanding paths that associate professorship seemingly laid before me. Was I going to be a professor for the next 20 years, or would I head towards administrative work—and if so, would it be with Elon's teaching and learning center or with my own department? These were just a few of the questions I pondered to help me envision my future path. I participated in reading groups and a learning community investigating contemplative pedagogies. I reflected on what values I wanted to live and work by, what needs weren't being met, and how I could meet them. I used all the books and articles I was reading to make new connections and rekindle an attention to "big" questions: What do I want students to remember five or ten years after having taken my class? What skills do I practice unconsciously in literary and cultural analysis that students need to learn and that I must explicitly teach? What core assumptions are at the heart of my discipline's way of thinking? How do I want to impact or shape the discussions happening at my institution and in my field? How do I know I have an impact on those around me? How do I reclaim a sense of control and responsibility over my own and others' learning?

The intensity of my questioning, precisely at this juncture in my career when I felt like I was supposed to have it all figured out (I was tenured faculty, after all), left me unsettled. To get myself past the post-tenure/midlife crisis I needed, first and foremost, to mentor myself: I needed to attend to the whole person and the emotional aspects of transformation. Being a parent of two young children and not wanting to miss out on their journeys of learning and growth, I realized that my pace for the past six years would simply be unsustainable unless I made a commitment to consistently and routinely "recharge my batteries." I always thought that work-life balance meant that I was supposed to give equal attention to both work and home, but this proved extremely stressful because I never carved out any time for myself. The post-tenure crisis led me to discover that balance means giving every area of your life the attention it deserves. I now feel much more confident that I can decide how to allocate my attention, because I keep present my core values and needs as I execute and shape my responsibilities. My career path doesn't just happen, I proactively construct it. Moreover, I have a core "toolbox" of successful strategies that I am confident can be applied at any career stage: participation in learning communities and communities of practice, nonhierarchical mutual mentoring, an intentional and scholarly approach to discovery and learning (especially as related to work responsibilities), deep self-reflection and awareness, an explicit set of core values to work by, an attention to the whole self, and an understanding of the importance of finding

## Guided Self-mentoring Reflection

*What gives you the most satisfaction at work?* (research, writing, planning classes, working one-on-one with students, finding solutions for problems or issues on campus, creating connections with other departments, working with student groups, etc.) *Why?*

*How often do you engage in those things that bring you satisfaction at work?* List three ways you can find to engage in them more often or more regularly.

*What do you most struggle with in regards to...?*

- teaching
- research
- service
- balancing work, family, and personal time

*Who can you talk to (inside or outside your department) for help in working through these struggles?*

*What resources on campus can help?* (Center for Teaching and Learning, Faculty Research and Development fellowships to fund research, grants office or faculty development specialist, Center for Leadership, dean, provost, etc.) [If you don't know the available resources, who can you ask to help you find them on campus?]

*What do you excel at with regards to...?*

- teaching
- research
- service
- balancing commitments

*List three ways you can practice those strengths more often.*

*What core issues or "big questions" are you passionate enough about that you want to explore them with others?* (critical thinking, problem solving, writing, literacy, identity construction, visual culture, transference, measuring student learning, disciplinary thinking, etc.)

*List two people you would like to collaborate with on a teaching, research and/or learning project.*

*How and by when will you contact them to discuss the possibility of collaborating on such?*

*What core aspirations do you need to attain to feel "successful" at work?* (Win a teaching award, be recognized by disciplinary peers as an influential thinker in your field, be invited as a keynote speaker at a conference, be a publicly recognized contributor to your institution, be in a position of power to help others, etc.)

various ways to have needs met.

I have sought out nonauthoritarian forms of mentorship because I am keenly observant of the many ways that our university cultures and structures replicate inequitable sociocultural power dynamics. Furthermore, I believe that meaning-making is done in community and that learning is dialogic—it doesn't happen in isolation. I have found value in seeking out various colleagues across campus and actively creating mentoring communities (i.e., communities of practice) centered on core ideas or values. For me, mentoring (students, colleagues, or myself) has been, and still is, intentionally and conscientiously constructed. It evolves as my needs change. It is an iterative process of inquiry, research, negotiation, integration, and decision making. Importantly, my professional learning and growth happens in concert with the research I read and publish, the colleagues with whom I exchange ideas, the way in which I teach and evaluate my teaching effectiveness, and how I contribute to the institution where I work.

Being a mentor who believes in collaboration, personal agency, and the importance of the learning and discovery process, I share my story not as a directive for behavior, but rather as a means to validate options. Context matters greatly—thus I cannot, and will not, provide a proscriptive list of things to do to be successful in academia. Instead I offer a list of guiding questions (on the facing page) to encourage your own deep reflection and discovery. The questions replicate the process of intentionality: vocalizing one's core passions and strengths, dedicating more time to them, seeking and building community, finding ways to have core needs met, and putting into place patterns, structures, and systems that support your aims. I hope the guiding questions will help you actively construct meaning and purpose in your various professional roles, as they have for me.

Discovering, distilling, and elucidating core values is a lifelong journey. Cultivating multiple communities of peer mentors helps make the journey more humane, sustainable, and fulfilling. The structure of academia—the professions, schools, and disciplines (particularly in the humanities)—encourage faculty to be wholly self-sufficient and independent, to the point of intense isolation. While I found that I could not embrace or replicate this condition, I also found that I could, working within the confines of my particular institutional cultures and contexts and with the help of intentionally cultivated mentoring communities, create a distinctive and meaningful path for myself.

**Works Cited**

Bonk, C. J., R. A. Wisher, and M. L. Nigrelli. 2004. "Learning Communities, Communities of Practice: Principles, Technologies, and Examples." In *Learning to Collaborate, Collaborating to Learn*, edited by K. Littleton et al., 199–219. Hauppauge, NY: NOVA Science.

Felten, Peter, H-Dirksen Bauman, Aaron Kheriaty, and Edward Taylor. 2013. *Transformative Conversations: A Guide to Mentoring Communities among Colleagues in Higher Education*. San Francisco: Jossey-Bass.

Knight, P., and Paul Trowler. 1999. "It Takes a Village to Raise a Child: Mentoring and the Socialisation of New Entrants to the Academic Professions." *Mentoring and Tutoring: Partnership in Learning* 7 (1): 23–34.

Wenger, Etienne. 1999. *Communities of Practice: Learning, Meaning, and Identity*. New York: Cambridge University Press.

Wenger, Etienne. 2002. *Cultivating Communities of Practice: A Guide to Managing Knowledge*. Boston: Harvard Business School Press.

Wilson, Robin. 2012. "Why Are Associate Professors So Unhappy?" *Chronicle of Higher Education*, June 3. http://chronicle.com/article/Why-Are-Associate-Professors/132071.

# My Lucky Life and Hard Times

*Leonard Cassuto*

We live in an age of memoir, but I've long felt uneasy about telling stories about myself. My favorite memoirs recount hardship. I've had a lucky professional life—and who wants to read about that? When it comes to graduate school, though, I may have a story or two worth telling, even if they're not tales of trouble and woe.

I trace the roots of everything I know to my own time in graduate school. Well, everything professional anyway. My graduate school experience inspired me, and it energized me. But not in the way you might expect.

Facts up front: I was a privileged graduate student. I went to a small, selective graduate program during the 1980s. Let's just call it Elite University. There's no doubt that an Elite PhD got me some second looks where others might have been brushed aside. But for all my good fortune, I was ignorant and anxious—and unwilling to voice my ignorance or anxiety to my own professors. That reluctance has, in its way, shaped my whole career. It certainly shaped my own approach to being a graduate advisor now.

If there is such a thing as a typical graduate student experience, mine wasn't it. I wouldn't go so far as to say I was coddled, but I certainly enjoyed freedom from want. Unlike many of the graduate students I've advised and many more I've known, I received consistently ample financial support and was able to live comfortably, if modestly. No hardscrabble student life, mine.

My Elite professors were my role models. That's to be expected. Virtually all graduate students receive their PhDs from research universities, so they spend a lot of time watching professors at research universities do their jobs. We should hardly be surprised that dissertation advisors typically become role models for graduate students at a time when they're figuring out who they are, professionally, and what they want—and that's just what happened to me.

But my professors weren't very good role models. One reason for that isn't their fault: they had jobs that didn't look like any job I might get. I could imagine myself at Elite, of course: who couldn't? Elite was all around me. But that was a fantasy. Realistically, I knew that if I got lucky and got a professor's job, it wouldn't be at a place like Elite—so my professors were modeling a life that bore little relation to my possible future.

But there was another problem with my advisors: they didn't give me much advice.

I remember that when I was considering my graduate school choices, my favorite undergraduate professor, a brilliant scholar and radiant teacher who happened to be an Elite alumna, told me that if I chose Elite, the best and worst result would be that I would be left alone.

She was right about that—in spades. Looking back, I remain surprised at just how alone I was left. Let me tell you a story to explain what I mean.

The story is about publishing. It dates from 1986 or so, when I was in the middle of writing my dissertation. "Publish or perish" had not quite trickled down to the graduate student population at Elite then. We were encouraged to publish, of course, and those who did were praised. But no one I knew carried around a sense of urgency about publishing while in graduate school. The prevailing idea was that we would write good dissertations, and we would float into good jobs and publish there.

I had written two papers during my classwork years that my professors had said were potentially publishable, but I did nothing to publish them. My reluctance to take action boiled down to inertia. I didn't know how to begin. No teacher had offered to help me revise for publication, and I was hesitant—and embarrassed, and also a little afraid—to ask for that help. So the papers just sat there, and I went on teaching (which I loved) and writing my dissertation.

The dissertation writing went smoothly for the most part. I placed myself before my two readers at one-chapter intervals before my first reader took a job at another university. I saw him more rarely after that. He would cruise through town now and then, and we would meet and talk about my ideas for a half hour or so. I found those discussions both stimulating and exhilarating. My first reader was a tremendously smart and charming guy, and when he turned his mind to my work, he would spin off ideas like a firecracker and I would try to catch the sparks. Then he would return my manuscript to me with the typos circled.

If that first reader was a fox, my second reader was a hedgehog. More imperious than charming, he maintained a severe exterior and was chary with direct compliments. He would sit at his desk as if it were a throne and conduct audiences with me. (I had feared him upon arriving at graduate school and had been prepared to steer clear of him, but that undergraduate mentor I mentioned before, a student of his from years earlier, urged me to persist. She described him as "a closed-circuit system, but with terrific voltage." She was right.) I saw a lot more of my second reader after my first reader departed, and he was my de facto advisor during the years when I wrote most of my thesis. He would always make time to receive me, but he never returned my manuscripts. With the help of some of his older students who knew his ways better, I figured out after awhile that he liked my work, and also me. It was at one of our periodic meetings that my second reader rumbled aloud about the connection between the grotesque—my thesis topic—and race. Many years later, the racial grotesque became the subject of my first book.

Neither of my committee members ever said a word to me about publishing. But one day, reading a story by Edgar Allan Poe (perhaps to teach it, I don't remember), I got an idea that I *knew* was publishable. I don't know why I felt so confident, but I was just sure of it. So I researched it, and I wrote my reading up as a sourced essay. But I still didn't know what to do next. I had a vague idea of what peer review was by then, but I had no idea how to submit myself to it. Though a fourth-year graduate student, I was an innocent lost at sea without charts or compass.

I started talking to some peers about my ignorance, and one of them suggested that I talk to an older graduate student named Curtis Fukuchi. "Curtis has published," he told me. "He'll tell you what to do."

I'd never had a real conversation with Curtis before, but when I left a note in his mailbox (this was the eighties, remember), he readily agreed to meet for coffee. He also read and commented on my essay, and sure enough, he did tell me what to do. Curtis recommended that I submit my piece to *Studies in Short Fiction*, and he told me why he was recommending that journal over others. He explained the mechanics of the submission process (including the use of such quaint artifacts as self-addressed, stamped envelopes), and he told me how long I'd probably have to wait for an answer. He described peer review and how I could expect it to work.

In short, Curtis Fukuchi taught me how to publish. My Poe essay was accepted the next year, the decision having been delayed by an editorial change at the journal. Thinking about those events for this chapter, I recently contacted Curtis after almost 30 years. He downplayed his role. "I did nothing beyond suggesting a journal and a few research articles," he said, but I know how those suggestions felt, and what a difference they made—and I thank Curtis now as I did then.

That acceptance (my first time out!) gave me plenty of confidence to poke around the machinery on my own after that. It also thickened my skin against rejections that came later. Newton's law of inertia states that objects at rest tend to remain at rest, while objects in motion tend to stay in motion. When it comes to professionalization, I'm an autodidact—but I owe that first push to Curtis Fukuchi. He set me in motion.

I don't hold it against my advisors that they didn't explain publishing to me. How could they? I'm quite certain that they didn't know much about it themselves. They had long since ascended to that pillowed plane whose residents were solicited to publish, so it had been years since either of them had published anything in a refereed journal. You might say that they were also kind of innocent.

My advisors and I were likewise innocent of the job market. Oh, I knew that prospects were bad—I had learned that before I began graduate school, and therefore knew better than to assume that I would become a professor. For one thing, I wasn't sure that I would be willing to relocate to wherever a job was. I concluded before I even started graduate school that I might wind up taking my degree, whether MA or PhD, in search of nonacademic employment.

One reason I chose Elite, in fact, was because I knew that a degree from there would help me outside the academy if I chose to head that way. I had spent a year working as a computer programmer before entering graduate school, and was confident that I could find interesting work someplace, somehow, eventually. I'm sure that confidence eased the stress that can surround dissertation-writing, because I felt very little pressure. Like I said, I'm lucky.

It helped that my advisors made it clear by their friendly treatment of me that they approved of the dissertation I was writing. They were consistently supportive that way, and I always knew that they would sign off on my work when I finished it, even if they didn't pay much attention to how to improve it. I valued that support at the time, and I've come to value it even more since, as I've seen dissertators struggle with their confidence. The approbation I received surely greased the rails leading to the finish line.

Thus benignly neglected, I happily wrote the dissertation I wanted to write, without paying attention to the prevailing critical currents that washed up in the pages of the leading journals in my field. I didn't subscribe to those journals then, and I refused to join the MLA, the professional association for my field, because I found it stuffy. I applied for my first conference near the end of my graduate school years, and was accepted (lucky again—I didn't know what I was doing)—but the conference was canceled, so I gained no experience networking with my peers.

My approach was, in retrospect, egotistical and idiotic in equal parts. I was egotistical because I thought my work valuable and worthy of attention, and idiotic in that I expected an audience to seek me out.

No one bothered me in my self-imposed professional isolation, which left me time to work. Then my dissertation was complete in draft, and I had to face the world outside. The job market suddenly loomed before me. I felt like one of the apes in Kubrick's *2001: A Space Odyssey*, warily circling the massive, inscrutable monolith, unsure how to approach it.

My department had a placement director, and I duly met with her, CV and job letter in hand. She talked to me about what sort of job I was looking for—while editing my prose at the same time. So distracted was I by this display of virtuosity that I've forgotten what I said. But I remember her summation very well: "Oh, you want to be a writer."

That assessment would motivate me ten years later, but it didn't help me much at the time. I revised my cover letter and consulted the job list, which then took the form of a booklet. I picked out some jobs to apply for. I solicited recommendations, naturally, and my advisors hit their marks in good time. They never asked me where I was applying. No one ever did. So no one ever reached out on my behalf.

I managed to secure a handful of interviews, most of them at the MLA convention in New Orleans. My department's graduate director scheduled a mock interview for each of us job candidates, which was useful.

I drove my own job search—literally. My roommate, a mathematician eager to see New Orleans, shared a road trip to the MLA convention with me. I had recently bought a car from a friend who was having trouble locating the title, so the vehicle had no paperwork. And I realized at the last minute that my driver's license was a few days expired. So I drove more than 1000 miles to my interviews without valid license or registration. I regard that as a metaphor for my entire job search.

Somehow, though, I got a job. I attribute that result to ... luck. (Though I allow that I wasn't a complete bonehead about it. When I learned that Fordham University wanted to schedule a second interview and possessed a lively adult student program, I solicited an extra recommendation from the director of the adult program at Elite where I had been moonlighting. Perhaps it made a difference. Or perhaps not.) Yes, an Elite degree helped, but plenty of other people had fancy credentials too. When you're picked out of a field of hundreds like I was, I don't see how you can regard yourself as anything but lucky.

I arrived at Fordham in 1989 with a passionate desire to teach graduate students. Of course just about every professor wants to teach graduate students. Lots of them regard it practically as their birthright, in fact—which isn't so unusual when you consider that the experience invokes their own birth as professional intellectuals. Graduate school germinates the desire to become The Professor and teach one's own graduate students in turn.

That desire became encoded in the American higher educational DNA beginning in the 1920s and 1930s. It certainly encoded itself in me. At the beginning of my career, graduate teaching looked like the pinnacle of professional existence. Looking back at that time, I realize that I was chasing something I knew little about. Although I wanted very much to teach graduate students, I had no particular ideas about how to do it, nothing special I wanted to try. Even though graduate teaching stood out as one of my major professional desires, I had no graduate pedagogical vision. I wanted to be the person with the job more than I wanted to do the job.

For someone trained as a critic, I was astonishingly uncritical. The extent to which I so thoroughly absorbed the stereotypical preferences of my workplace embarrasses me today. It also shows me the considerable power that graduate school professors possess to change minds—and lives. Moreover, *they exert that power constantly*. It can't be ignored or turned off. I'm pretty sure that my advisors weren't trying to affect my view of the world, but they did it all the same.

Fordham has two campuses, and I was hired to the one without the graduate program, so I didn't get to teach a graduate seminar for five years. That was—you guessed it—lucky for me, even though it didn't feel that way at the time. It gave me some years to plant my professional feet under me.

I needed those years to chase possible mentors and advisors wherever I could find them. I went after them directly, even aggressively, because I had come to the belated realization that I required professional advice badly. To begin with, I needed help to write a book because I had written a dissertation that was unpublishable as one. Lots of dissertations deserve the unpublishable label, but I had been led to believe that mine belonged in the "publishable" category. I lost precious pre-tenure time learning the truth through rejection and revision. I eventually rewrote my dissertation twice altogether until only a homeopathic distillation of it remained. The first rewrite landed me in the middle of a project I could not have completed in a lifetime, let alone a five-year tenure track. The second revision, centered on my advisor's question years earlier about the racial grotesque, got me a book contract—just in time to tuck it into my tenure file.

I also gained some time to mature as a teacher, and to teach many adult undergraduates, before Fordham underwent a "restructuring" that made graduate teaching available to me for the first time, right after I got tenure.

By that time, I had learned a lot about what had been missing from my own preparation. You might say that I discovered that I knew a lot of ways *not* to teach graduate school. I started planning graduate seminars that would deliver the kind of graduate education that I hadn't gotten myself.

Many of the seminars I took as a graduate student ran by what I call the beach ball method: just as a crowd at an arena bounces a beach ball at random from one person to another, the professor depends on the students to just talk—which they do, bouncing from topic to topic without design. I wanted to avoid that, so I started with structure. I learned by assessing what I was doing, and by talking to my peers and borrowing teaching techniques that I admired. Many good teachers are magpies that way.

One way that I could tell I was getting good at graduate teaching was that I started to acquire PhD students. I taught them—against my own example—how to be professional.

Fordham's English department has a diverse graduate student body. There are master's students who want PhDs and others who don't. Most of the PhD students start out with professorships in mind, but by the time they reach job market age, some decide on other careers. The ones who chase academic jobs look for a whole range of them. Fordham students consequently scatter widely on the spectrum of professorships, from research-intensive universities to community colleges.

I figured out pretty quickly that to be a credible advisor I would have to remove my head from the flowerpot I had grown up in. How else could I address the range of students before me? Gradually I evolved an advising style. Some time after that, I realized what was behind that style: I was trying to give my advisees precisely what I had not received myself.

Because I had been left alone, I was determined that my advisees should not be. So I stole an idea from Catherine Gallagher at Berkeley that I had heard about from a former student of hers. Gallagher would have her advisees over to her house for potluck suppers at which students would present their work in progress. I started doing the same thing—though at rotating locations, because my home was too far away to be the hub. Peer review focuses graduate students wonderfully, and among the other virtues of these meetings is that they lead students to impose practical deadlines on themselves—because one thing I do *not* do is enforce deadline discipline. Graduate students have to want to write their dissertations, and if they don't, that's a clue that they may be better off in another line of work. A sense of community keeps them on task.

Because I had been left to learn to publish on my own, I decided that my students would have me at their shoulder as they learned how the scholarship machine worked. So I've been active with them when they reach that stage, suggesting certain conferences, and certain possible destinations for their manuscripts and abstracts, which I also help to edit for submission. Figuring out what panel organizers and editors and peer reviewers want—and decoding their sometimes-conflicting messages—can be an inscrutable business, but it doesn't have to be a lonely one.

I suggested earlier that I didn't hold it against my advisors for not teaching me how to publish. That's not quite true. They had little business with journals because most of their writing was solicited, but so is mine these days. I don't submit very often to the venues that I direct my graduate students to approach, but I try to stay involved in their publishing lives anyway.

Because no one helped me prepare myself for the kind of job I wanted, I try to learn my students' professional goals early, so we can plan together. I'll direct the work of a student who wants to work at a community college very differently from one who wants a professorship at a school that demands a lot of publication.

Because I had to figure out the job market myself, I determined that my students shouldn't have to. I introduced the job of "Director of Placement and Professional Development" to my department, and was the first occupant of the position. For my own students I got early into the business of editing CV's and cover letters, of inspecting dossiers and helping to choose writing samples. I run a kind of open-season counseling practice for my job candidates, where we discuss not only what needs doing but also how it feels to do it. Knowing that other people—including your advisor—once had the same anxiety that you have now can make a difference.

Mostly, I want my advisees to turn their eyes outward and connect their graduate work to a job—academic or not. They should see that graduate school is as much a part of the "real world" as anyplace else. I realized that I had attended professional school only after I graduated. My students shouldn't make the same mistake. They need to realize that they're professionals right now.

As I see it, the key to my job now is to remember what it was like to be a graduate student. My advisors were committed to a certain view of the profession, and they never thought to ask what mine might be. I remember what that felt like. My graduate teaching springs from that awareness, especially the way I felt cut off from the how-to's of a professional life I was hoping to enter. I was the one who blind-folded myself in graduate school—give credit where it's due, after all—but no one paid attention.

Unable to see, I tripped and fell into the gravy. The transition from graduate student to professor knocked my blindfold off, but once I learned my new surroundings, I discovered that I liked the work as much as I had once hoped I would. Such has been my luck.

Most professors were once successful students, and I've noticed that most of them teach to an idealized version of their younger selves. I don't. My younger self was inert, willfully ignorant, and resistant to socialization into a profession that I wanted to be part of, even as I refused its conventions. I act differently now—and not only because I know that I'm a role model, like it or not. I offer my students what I didn't have, in order that they might do what I didn't do.

My public identity as "The Graduate Advisor" in *The Chronicle of Higher Education* has its roots in my early self-formation. I became an attentive teacher of graduate students partly because I didn't receive much attention while I was in graduate school myself. Years later, those blank spots led me to reflect on the question of how graduate students learn, and I discovered that it's a question too seldom considered. So now I consider it in the public square. My advisors were well-intentioned professors who were also very smart—and sometimes also very helpful. But I sit where I do because of their mistakes.

### Notes

1. Graduate seminars made their appearance in U.S. graduate school early on. Pioneered by the likes of Henry Adams, they had become widespread by the 1880s, when graduate school was still nascent in the U.S. (Veysey 1965, 153–56). The changes in scale that took hold in the 1920s gave graduate school a higher profile in the American university. Roger Geiger, a historian of higher education, describes the growth of the research university during that period, including how the admission of many more graduate students allowed for more seminars to be offered. "Productive scholars," Geiger writes, "could be favored with graduate instruction, while more-plodding colleagues handled large undergraduate lec-tures" (1986, 219). With incentives—and attitudes!—like that, the conventional teaching hierarchy, with graduate teaching at the pinnacle, took hold.

2. My student Jane Van Slembrouck offers her own description of these gatherings elsewhere in this volume.

## Works Cited

Geiger, Roger. 1986. *To Advance Knowledge: The Growth of American Research Universities, 1900–1940*. Oxford, Eng.: Oxford University Press.

Veysey, Lawrence. 1965. *The Emergence of the American University*. Chicago: University of Chicago Press.

# RESOURCES

Here follows a far-from-comprehensive selection of print and online resources for academic mentoring, with specific attention to the graduate-student-through-tenured-professor interval. Some resources will be useful to those engaged directly in the mentoring process, others to those hoping to establish, maintain, or improve mentoring initiatives in a higher ed setting.

## Print

Bland, C. J., A. L. Taylor, S. L. Shollen, A. M. Weber-Main, and P. A. Mulcahu. 2009. *Faculty Success Through Mentoring: A Guide for Mentors, Mentees, and Leaders*. Lanham, MD: Rowman and Littlefield.

This practical guide to the creation, maintenance, and evaluation of faculty development programs will be of equal value to institutions considering the implementation of such programs and those seeking to improve existing ones.

Creighton, Linda, Theodore Creighton, and David Parks. 2010. "Mentoring to Degree Completion: Expanding the Horizons of Doctoral Protégés." *Mentoring & Tutoring: Partnership in Learning* 18 (1): 39–52.

Noting the high attrition rate in doctoral programs, the authors assert the need for "mentoring pedagogy" and recommend that graduate programs transition students from an advising to a mentoring relationship earlier than is the norm.

Gottesman, Barbara L. 2009. *Peer Coaching in Higher Education*. Lanham, MD: Rowman and Littlefield.

Gottesman's "peer coaching" approach to improving faculty teaching applies a model derived from K-12 instruction to higher education. Evaluation and supervision are not covered. Chapters 4–8 provide case studies from different institutions.

Johnson, W. Brad. 2007. *On Being a Mentor: A Guide for Higher Education Faculty*. Mahwah, NJ: Lawrence Erlbaum Associates.

Arguably the single best general resource for faculty mentors, this open-eyed and pragmatic discussion defines mentoring, outlines effective mentoring practices, considers issues across the mentoring continuum, and offers advice to academic and administrative units on managing mentoring relationships.

Johnson, W. Brad, and Jennifer M. Huwe. 2003. *Getting Mentored in Graduate School*. Washington, DC: American Psychological Association.

Like Johnson's parallel publication for mentors, this how-to guide for proactive graduate student mentees covers the essential material: what mentoring is, how to find a mentor, and how to manage the mentoring relationship.

Klaw, Elena. 2009. *Mentoring and Making It in Academe: A Guide for Newcomers to the Ivory Tower*. Lanham, MD: University Press of America.

This compact (69 pp.) discussion "mentors the mentor" on the graduate student–to-tenured-professor career trajectory. Generous attention is paid to underrepresented/minority faculty.

Montgomery, Beronda L., Jualynne E. Dodson, and Sonya M. Johnson. 2014. "Guiding the Way: Mentoring Graduate Students and Junior Faculty for Sustainable Academic Careers." *SAGE Open* 4 (4): 1–11. doi: 10.1177/2158244014558043.

Focusing on graduate students and junior faculty of color, this article presents a mentoring process model that covers the continuum considered in this volume. Positing that the individualistic ethos of the dominant academic culture represents a barrier to success for minority academics, the authors advocate "critical collective communities" to assist in integrating cultural identities within the mentoring process.

Phillips, Susan L., and Susan T. Dennison. 2014. *Faculty Mentoring: A Practical Manual for Mentors, Mentees, Administrators, and Faculty Developers*. Sterling, VA: Stylus.

Both a guide to the implementation of faculty mentoring programs and a how-to manual for all parties, this publication touts the advantages of group mentoring without neglecting the traditional mentor-mentee pair (the chapters for faculty mentors and mentees are available separately as electronic downloads).

Reddick, Richard J., and Michelle D. Young. 2012. "Mentoring Graduate Students of Color." Chapter 27 in *The SAGE Handbook of Mentoring and Coaching in Education*, edited by Sarah J. Fletcher and Carol A. Mullen, pp: 412–29. London: SAGE Publications.

The authors observe a "hidden curriculum" working to the disadvantage of minority students, expose mentoring myths, advance best practices for mentoring graduate students of color, and outline important considerations for mentoring programs.

Schnaiberg, Allan. 2005. "Mentoring Graduate Students: Going Beyond the Formal Role Structure." *American Sociologist* 36 (2): 28–42.

While addressed to a sociologists, these insightful reflections by an experienced faculty mentor are relevant to all disciplines. In his attention to "generativity," Schnaiberg (without wishing to) recuperates the trusting intergenerational relationship as an ideal mentoring context.

## Online

*Graduate Mentoring Guidebook*
University of Nebraska-Lincoln
http://www.unl.edu/mentoring

Whereas many institution-based mentoring sites provide separate resources for graduate students and faculty, Nebraska-Lincoln offers a single resource addressing the continuity of the mentoring project. The virtues of this approach are exemplified in the insightful discussion of "common themes" in the mentoring relationship.

*How to Get the Mentoring You Want: A Guide for Graduate Students*
University of Michigan Rackham Graduate School
http://www.rackham.umich.edu/downloads/publications/mentoring.pdf

Perhaps the single most linked-to item on other institutions' mentoring web pages, this printer-friendly guide for graduate students long ago set the agenda for publications of its type.

### *How to Mentor Graduate Students: A Guide for Faculty*
University of Michigan Rackham Graduate School

http://www.rackham.umich.edu/downloads/publications/
Fmentoring.pdf

> Deliberately structured to align with its companion publication, "How to Get the Mentoring You Want," this classic document provides sound advice for graduate program administrators as well as faculty mentors.

### *Mentoring*
University of Washington Graduate School

http://www.grad.washington.edu/mentoring

> Parallel sections for mentors ("How to Mentor Graduate Students") and mentees ("How to Obtain the Mentoring You Need") cover all the bases in concise, often bullet-point style. Specific issues are addressed in a series of helpful two-page "Mentor Memos."

### *MentorNet*
http://www.mentornet.net/

> This high-quality resource for STEM students and professionals at all levels pairs mentees and mentors for a structured mentoring experience. It can be particularly valuable for those who lack mentoring opportunities in their immediate context. Several field-specific initiatives, such as the National Research Mentoring Network for minorities in biomedicine (www.nrmnet.net), use the MentorNet platform.

### *National Center for Faculty Development and Diversity*
http://www.facultydiversity.org

> While inspired by the needs of minority graduate students, postdocs, and faculty, this "mentoring community" offers high-quality resources (e.g., webinars, multi-week courses, a "career center" with job postings and workshops) of universal benefit, by individual or institutional subscription.

### *The Professor Is In*
http://theprofessorisin.com

> While touting creator Karen Kelsky's services as a consultant,

speaker, and advisor-for-hire, this high-quality website also hosts a peer-editing community ($5 membership) and offers an extensive archive of excellent blog posts on virtually every mentoring-related topic, organized in categories. This free advising resource is equally useful for graduate students, junior faculty, and those seeking work outside the academy.

*Research Mentoring: Cultivating Effective Relationships*
University of Wisconsin–Madison Institute for Clinical and Translational Research
https://mentoringresources.ictr.wisc.edu

This well-organized and comprehensive website contains a wealth of resources for research mentors and mentees, including curricula and assessment tools to assist in implementing mentor training programs.

*The Versatile PhD*
http://versatilephd.com

The leading website devoted to "helping graduate students and PhDs envision, prepare for, and excel in non-academic careers." Most features (e.g., sample résumés and cover letters, detailed career information and programming, online networking opportunities) require subscription; institutions may purchase STEM and humanities/social sciences content separately.

# INDEX

267